# THE FATHERS
# OF THE CHURCH

MEDIAEVAL CONTINUATION

VOLUME 13

# THE FATHERS OF THE CHURCH

## MEDIAEVAL CONTINUATION

### EDITORIAL BOARD

Gregory F. LaNave
*Pontifical Faculty of the Immaculate Conception*
*Dominican House of Studies*
*Editorial Director*

Regis J. Armstrong, O.F.M. Cap.
*The Catholic University of America*

Joseph Goering
*University of Toronto*

Peter Casarella
*DePaul University*

Frank A. C. Mantello
*The Catholic University of America*

John Cavadini
*University of Notre Dame*

Jan Ziolkowski
*Harvard University*

Trevor Lipscombe
*Director*
*The Catholic University of America Press*

Carole Monica C. Burnett
*Staff Editor*

# ROBERT GROSSETESTE

ON THE CESSATION
OF THE LAWS

*Translated by*
STEPHEN M. HILDEBRAND

THE CATHOLIC UNIVERSITY OF AMERICA PRESS
Washington, D.C.

Copyright @ 2012
THE CATHOLIC UNIVERSITY OF AMERICA PRESS
All rights reserved
Printed in the United States of America

The paper used in this publication meets the minimum requirements of the American National Standards for Information Science—Permanence of Paper for Printed Library Materials,
ANSI Z39.48-1984.
∞

LIBRARY OF CONGRESS CATALOGING-IN-PUBLICATION DATA
Grosseteste, Robert, 1175?–1253.
[De cessatione legalium. English]
On the cessation of the laws / Robert Grosseteste ; translated by Stephen M. Hildebrand.
p. cm. — (The fathers of the church, mediaeval continuation ; v. 13)
Includes bibliographical references and indexes.
ISBN 978-0-8132-1964-6 (cloth : alk. paper)
ISBN 978-0-8132-2821-1 (pbk.)
1. Law (Theology)   2. Law and gospel.   I. Title.
BT96.3.G7613 2012
241.5—dc23
2011039838

For my Mother and Father

# CONTENTS

| | |
|---|---|
| Acknowledgments | ix |
| Abbreviations | xi |
| Select Bibliography | xiii |

## INTRODUCTION

| | |
|---|---|
| Grosseteste's Life | 3 |
| Grosseteste's Works | 10 |
| *On the Cessation of the Laws* | 13 |
| Outline of *On the Cessation of the Laws* | 22 |
| A Note about the Translation | 23 |

## ON THE CESSATION OF THE LAWS

| | |
|---|---|
| Part One | 27 |
| Part Two | 109 |
| Part Three | 155 |
| Part Four | 194 |

## APPENDIX

| | |
|---|---|
| Figure 1: The cruciform figure created by Rabanus Maurus | 249 |
| Figure 2: The "circular period of human generation" | 250 |

## INDICES

| | |
|---|---|
| General Index | 251 |
| Index of Holy Scripture | 255 |

## ACKNOWLEDGMENTS

I have incurred many debts in the course of this project. I am very grateful to the St. Paul Center, its president, Scott Hahn, and its director, Rob Corzine. Without its generous grant, this translation would have taken many years to complete. The St. Paul Center, founded by Scott Hahn, promotes the study of Scripture in the Catholic tradition. I think that this translation will help in the accomplishment of that mission. I must thank Scott also for the generous use of his personal library and, finally, for his encouragement and enthusiasm for this work.

This work simply would not have taken place without the support of Alan Schreck and Max Bonilla. At a University that focuses on teaching, they carved out resources for this project, and I am very grateful to them.

When I encountered particularly difficult passages, I called on the help of a few friends. I thank Patrick Lee, Joseph T. Lienhard, S.J., Richard Smith, and Roland Teske, S.J. I am grateful too for the editorial assistance of my graduate student, Brad Gholston.

Gregory LaNave and Carole Monica Burnett at the Catholic University of America Press have been a delight to work with.

The otherwise obscure name Robert Grosseteste has become a household name in our home. I am grateful to my wife, Sara, and my children, Lucy, Peter, Elizabeth, Paul, and Anthony, for welcoming him into the common life that is so dear to me. Finally, I wish to thank my parents, Pat and Larry, to whom I dedicate this work. I owe them more than I can say.

# ABBREVIATIONS

| | |
|---|---|
| *De cess. leg.* | *De cessatione legalium* |
| *Ep.* | *Epistula.* |
| *Epp.* | *Epistulae.* |
| PL | Migne, Patrologiae cursus completus, Series Latina. Ed. J.-P. Migne. Paris. |
| PIMS | Pontifical Institute of Mediaeval Studies. Toronto. |

# SELECT BIBLIOGRAPHY

"The Electronic Grosseteste" (*www.grosseteste.com*), created and maintained by James Ginther, has a comprehensive bibliography and much else besides.

## Bibliographies

Gieben, S. "Bibliographia universa Roberti Grosseteste ab an. 1473 ad an. 1969." *Collectanea Franciscana* 39 (1969): 362–418.

———. "Robertus Grosseteste: Bibliographia 1970–1991." In *Robert Grosseteste: New Perspectives.* Pp. 415–31.

## Sources

*Decrees of the Ecumenical Councils.* Vol. 1, *From Nicaea to Lateran V.* Edited by Norman P. Tanner. Washington, DC: Georgetown University Press, 1990.

Rabanus Maurus. *De laudibus sanctae crucis libri duo.* PL 107:133–292.

Robert Grosseteste. *Commentarius in Posterium Analyticorum Libros.* Edited by P. Rossi. Florence: Leo S. Olschki, 1981.

———. *De cessatione legalium.* Edited by R. C. Dales and E. B. King. Auctores Britannici Medii Aevi 7. London: British Academy, 1986.

———. *De decem mandatis.* Edited by R. C. Dales and E. B. King. Auctores Britannici Medii Aevi 10. London: British Academy, 1987.

———. *De dotibus.* Edited by J. Goering. "The *De dotibus* of Robert Grosseteste." *Medieval Studies* 44 (1982): 83–109.

———. *De modo confitendi et paenitentias iniungendi.* Edited by Joseph Goering and F. A. C. Mantello. In "The Early Penitential Writings of Robert Grosseteste." *Recherches de théologie ancienne et médiévale* 54 (1987): 80–111.

———. *Epistulae.* Edited by Henry Richards Luard. *Roberti Grosseteste episcopi quondam Lincolniensis Epistolae.* Rerum Britannicarum Medii Aevi Scriptores, no. 25. Orig. publ. 1861; repr. Kraus, 1965.

———. *Ep.* 128. Edited by F. A. C. Mantello. "*Optima Epistola:* A Critical Edition and Translation of Letter 128 of Bishop Robert Grosseteste." In *A Distinct Voice.*

———. *Expositio in epistolam sancti Pauli ad Galatas.* Edited by James McEvoy. In *Opera inedita Roberti Grosseteste.* Corpus Christianorum Continuatio Mediaevalis 130: 3–175. Turnhout: Brepols, 1995.

———. *Hexaëmeron.* Edited by Richard C. Dales and Servus Gieben. Auctores Britannici Medii Aevi 6. London: British Academy, 1982.

———. "Robert Grosseteste at the Papal Curia, Lyons, 1250: Edition of the Documents." Edited by Servus Gieben. *Collectanea Franciscana* 41 (1971): 340–93.

———. *Roberti Grosseteste Episcopi Lincolniensis Commentarius in VIII libros Physicorum Aristotelis.* Edited by Richard Dales. Boulder, CO: University of Colorado Press, 1963.

———. *Sermo ad religiosos.* Edited by J. McEvoy. In "*Nostra conversacio in caelis est* Phil 3:20. *Sermo ad religiosos* of Robert Grosseteste." In *Robert Grosseteste and the Beginnings of a British Theological Tradition.* Pp. 125–42.

———. *Sermon 68, sermo ad religiosos.* Edited by J. Ginther. In "Monastic Ideals and Episcopal Visitations: the *Sermo ad religiosos* of Robert Grosseteste, Bishop of Lincoln 1235–1253." In *Medieval Monastic Preaching.* Edited by Carolyn A. Muessig. Leiden: Brill, 1998.

———. *Speculum confessionis.* Edited by J. Goering and F. A. C. Mantello. "The *Perambulavit Iudas* (*Speculum confessionis*) Attributed to Robert Grosseteste." *Revue Bénédictine* 96 (1986): 125–68.

———. *Statutes of Lincoln.* In *Councils and Synods with Other Documents relating to the English Church II, A.D. 1205–1313.* Edited by F. M. Powicke and C. R. Cheney, Part One, *1205–1265.* Oxford: Clarendon Press, 1964.

———. *Templum Dei.* Edited by J. Goering and F. A. C. Mantello. Toronto Medieval Latin Texts, 14. Toronto: Pontifical Institute of Mediaeval Studies, 1984.

*Literature*

Barton, J. L. "The Study of the Civil Law before 1380." In *The History of the University of Oxford.* Pp. 519–30.
Boyle, Leonard E. "Canon Law before 1380." In *The History of the University of Oxford.* Pp. 531–64.
———. "Robert Grosseteste and the Pastoral Care." *Proceedings of the Southeastern Institute of Medieval and Renaissance Studies, Summer 1976.* Edited by Dale B. J. Randall. Durham, NC: Duke University Press, 1979; repr. in Boyle, *Pastoral Care, Clerical Education and Canon Law, 1200–1400.* London: Variorum, 1981.
———. "The Fourth Lateran Council and Manuals of Popular Theology." In *The Popular Literature of Medieval England.*
Callus, D. "Robert Grosseteste as Scholar." In *Robert Grosseteste, Scholar and Bishop.* Pp. 1–69.
Catto, J. I. "Theology and Theologians 1220–1320." In *The History of the University of Oxford.* Pp. 471–517.
Cobban, A. B. *The Medieval English Universities: Oxford and Cambridge to c. 1500.* Berkeley: University of California Press, 1990.
———. *The Medieval Universities: Their Development and Organization.* London: Methuen and Co., 1975.
Cohen, Jeremy. *Living Letters of the Law: Ideas of the Jew in Medieval Christianity.* Berkeley: University of California Press, 1999.

Congar, Yves. "Ecclesia ab Abel." In *Abhandlungen über Theologie und Kirche. Festschrift für Karl Adam.* Edited by M. Reding. Düsseldorf: Patmos, 1952; repr. *Études d'ecclésiologie médiévale.* London: Variorum, 1983.

Dahan, Gilbert. *The Christian Polemic Against the Jews in the Middle Ages.* Notre Dame, IN: University of Notre Dame Press, 1991.

Dales, R. C. "Robert Grosseteste's Place in Medieval Discussions of the Eternity of the World." *Speculum* 61 (1986): 544–63.

De Jongue, Marinus. "Robert Grosseteste and the Testaments of the Twelve Patriarchs." *Journal of Theological Studies* 42 (1991): 115–25.

*A Distinct Voice: Medieval Studies in Honor of Leonard E. Boyle, O.P.* Edited by Jacqueline Brown and William P. Stoneman. Notre Dame, IN: University of Notre Dame Press, 1997.

Duffy, E. *Saints and Sinners: A History of the Popes.* 2d ed. New Haven: Yale University Press, 2002.

*Editing Robert Grosseteste: Papers Given at the Thirty-Sixth Annual Conference on Editorial Problems. University of Toronto, 3–4 November 2000.* Edited by Evelyn A. Mackie and Joseph Goering. Toronto: University of Toronto Press, 2003.

Garreau, A. *Léon IX, pape alsacien, réformateur de l'Église 1002–1054.* Paris: Tolra, 1965.

Gieben, S. "Robert Grosseteste and the Evolution of the Franciscan Order." In *Robert Grosseteste: New Perspectives.* Pp. 230–32.

———. "Robert Grosseteste and the Immaculate Conception with the Text of the Sermon *Tota Pulchra Es.*" *Collectanea Franciscana* 28 (1958): 211–27.

Ginther, J. *Master of the Sacred Page: A Study of the Theology of Robert Grosseteste, ca. 1229/30–1235.* Aldershot: Ashgate, 2004.

———. "The Super Psalterium in Context." In *Editing Robert Grosseteste.* Pp. 31–60.

———. "There is a Text in this Classroom: The Bible and Theology in the Medieval University." In *Essays in Medieval Philosophy and Theology in Memory of Walter H. Principe, CSB: Fortresses and Launching Pads.* Edited by J. Ginther and Carl N. Still. Aldershot: Ashgate, 2005. Pp. 31–51.

Goering, J. "Robert Grosseteste and the Jews of Leicester." In *Robert Grosseteste and the Beginnings of a British Theological Tradition.*

———. "Robert Grosseteste at the Papal Curia." In *A Distinct Voice.*

———. "When and Where did Grosseteste Study Theology?" In *Robert Grosseteste: New Perspectives.* Pp. 17–52.

Goering, J. and F. A. C. Mantello. "The Early Penitential Writings of Robert Grosseteste." *Recherches de théologie ancienne et médiévale* 54 (1987): 52–111.

Hackett, M. B. "The University as a Corporate Body." In *The History of the University of Oxford.* Pp. 37–95.

*The History of the University of Oxford.* Edited by T. H. Aston, vol. 1, *The Early Oxford Schools.* Edited by J. I. Catto. Oxford: Clarendon Press, 1984.

Holland, M. "Robert Grosseteste's Greek Translations and College of Arms MS Arundel 9." In *Robert Grosseteste: New Perspectives.* Pp. 121–47.

Hood, Y. B. *Aquinas and the Jews.* Philadelphia: University of Pennsylvania, 1995.

Levering, Matthew. *Christ's Fulfillment of Torah and Temple: Salvation according to*

*Thomas Aquinas*. Notre Dame, IN: University of Notre Dame Press, 2002.
Lewry, P. Osmund. "Grammar, Logic, and Rhetoric 1220–1320." In *The History of the University of Oxford*. Pp. 401–33.
Logan. F. D. *A History of the Church in the Middle Ages*. London: Routledge, 2002.
Marshall, Bruce D. "*Quasi in figura*: A Brief Reflection on Jewish Election after Thomas Aquinas." *Nova et Vetera* 7 (2009): 477–84.
McEvoy, J. "The Absolute Predestination of Christ." In *Sapientia Doctrina: Mélanges de théologie et de littérature médiévale offerts à Dom Hildebrand Bascour, O.S.B.* Pp. 212–30. Louvain: Abbaye du Mont César, 1980; repr. in McEvoy, *Robert Grosseteste: Exegete and Philosopher*.
―――――. "Language, Tongue and Thought in the Writings of Robert Grosseteste." *Miscellanea Mediaevalia* 13 (1981): 585–92; repr. in McEvoy, *Robert Grosseteste: Exegete and Philosopher*.
―――――. *The Philosophy of Robert Grosseteste*. Oxford: Clarendon, 1982.
―――――. *Robert Grosseteste*. Great Medieval Thinkers. Oxford: Oxford University Press, 2000.
―――――. *Robert Grosseteste, Exegete and Philosopher*. London: Variorum, 1994.
―――――. "Robert Grosseteste on the Ten Commandments." *Recherches de théologie ancienne et médiévale* 58 (1991): 179–80; repr. in McEvoy, *Robert Grosseteste, Exegete and Philosopher*.
―――――. "*Robertus Grossatesta Lincolniensis*. An Essay in Historiography, Medieval and Modern." In *Robert Grosseteste and the Beginnings of a British Theological Tradition*. Pp. 21–99.
O'Carroll, M. "Grosseteste, the English Friars, and Lateran IV." In *Robert Grosseteste and the Beginnings of the British Theological Tradition*. Pp. 319–69.
Pantin, W. "Grosseteste's Relations with the Papacy and the Crown." In *Robert Grosseteste, Scholar and Bishop*. Pp. 178–215.
Pegge, S. *The Life of Robert Grosseteste, the Celebrated Bishop of Lincoln*. London: John Nichols, 1793.
Perrier, Emmanuel. "The Election of Israel Today: Supersessionism, Post-Supersessionism, and Fulfillment." *Nova et Vetera* 7 (2009): 485–504.
*The Popular Literature of Medieval England*. Edited by Thomas J. Heffernan. Knoxville: The University of Tennessee Press, 1985.
Quinn, C. Taylor (Hogan). "Pseudo-Dionysius and the Ecclesiology of Robert Grosseteste: A Fruitful Symbiosis." In *Robert Grosseteste: New Perspectives*.
Rashdall, H. *The Universities of Europe in the Middle Ages*, rev. F. M. Powicke and A. B. Emden. Oxford: Oxford University Press, 1936.
*Robert Grosseteste and the Beginnings of the British Theological Tradition: Papers delivered at the Grosseteste Colloquium held at Greyfriars, Oxford, on 3d July 2002*. Edited by Maura O'Carroll. Rome: Istituto storico dei Cappuccini, 2003.
*Robert Grosseteste: New Perspectives on his Thought and Scholarship*. Edited by James McEvoy. Turnhout: Brepols, 1995.
*Robert Grosseteste, Scholar and Bishop: Essays in Commemoration of the Seventh Centenary of his Death*. Edited by Daniel Callus. Oxford: Clarendon Press, 1955.
Robson, M. "Grosseteste and the Greyfriars in the Diocese of Lincoln." In *Robert Grosseteste and the Beginnings of the British Theological Tradition*.

———. "Saint Anselm, Robert Grosseteste and the Franciscan Tradition." In *Robert Grosseteste: New Perspectives*. Pp. 233–56.
Sayers, J. *Innocent III, Leader of Europe, 1198–1216*. London: Longman, 1994.
Schenk, Richard. "Christ, Christianity, and Non-Christian Religions: Their Relationship in the Thought of Robert Kilwardby." In *Christ among the Medieval Dominicans: Representations of Christ in the Texts and Images of the Order of Preachers*. Edited by K. Emery, Jr., and J. Wawrykow. Notre Dame, IN: University of Notre Dame Press, 1988. Pp. 344–63.
———. "Covenant Initiation: Thomas Aquinas and Robert Kilwardby on the Sacrament of Circumcision." In *Ordo sapientiae et amoris. Hommage au Professeur J.-P. Torrell*. Edited by Carlos-Josaphat Pinto de Oliveira. Fribourg: Éditions Universitaires Fribourg Suisse, 1993. Pp. 555–93.
———. "Debatable Ambiguity: Paradigms of Truth as a Measure of the Differences among Christian Theologies of Religion." In *Jahrbuch für Philosophie des Forshungsinstituts für Philosophie Hannover*. Edited by R. Schenk, V. Hoesle, and P. Koslowski. Vienna: Passagen, 2000. Pp. 121–51.
———. "*Divina simulatio irae et dissimulatio pietatis:* Divine Providence and Natural Religion in Robert Kilwardby's *Quaestiones in Librum IV Sententiarum*." In *Mensch und Natur im Mittelalter*. Edited by A. Zimmermann. New York: W. de Gruyter, 1991. Pp. 431–55.
———. "The Eucharist and Ecclesial Communion." In *At the Altar of the World*. Edited by D. G. Callahan. Washington, DC: The Pope John Paul II Cultural Center, 2003. Pp. 83–87.
———. "From Providence to Grace: Thomas Aquinas and the Platonisms of the Mid-Thirteenth Century." *Nova et Vetera* 3 (2005): 307–20.
———. "Views of the Two Covenants in Medieval Theology." *Nova et Vetera* 4 (2006): 891–916.
Shaw, J. "The Influence of Canonical and Episcopal Reform on Popular Books of Instruction." In *The Popular Literature of Medieval England*.
Silver, D. J. *Maimonidean Criticism and the Maimonidean Controversy 1180–1240*. Leiden: Brill, 1965.
Smalley, B. "The Biblical Scholar." In *Robert Grosseteste, Scholar and Bishop*. Pp. 70–97.
———. "William of Auvergne, John of La Rochelle, and St. Thomas Aquinas on the Old Law." In *St. Thomas Aquinas 1274–1974: Commemorative Studies*. Edited by A. Mauer et al. Vol. 2:11–71. Toronto: PIMS, 1974.
Smith, L. "The *De decem mandatis* of Robert Grosseteste." In *Robert Grosseteste and the Beginnings of the British Theological Tradition*.
Southern, R. "From Schools to University." In *The History of the University of Oxford*. Pp. 1–36.
———. *Robert Grosseteste: The Growth of an English Mind in Medieval Europe*. 2d ed. Oxford: Clarendon, 1992.
———. *Western Society and the Church in the Middle Ages*. Penguin History of the Church, vol. 2. New York: Penguin, 1970.
Srawley, J. H. "Grosseteste's Administration of the Diocese of Lincoln." In *Robert Grosseteste, Scholar and Bishop*. Pp. 146–77.

## BIBLIOGRAPHY

Stevenson, F. *Robert Grosseteste, Bishop of Lincoln: A Contribution to the Religious, Political, and Intellectual History of the Thirteenth Century.* London: MacMillan and Co., 1899.

Thomson, S. H. *The Writings of Robert Grosseteste, Bishop of Lincoln 1235–1253.* Cambridge, 1940.

Tierney, B. "Grosseteste and the Theory of Papal Sovereignty." *Journal of Ecclesiastical History* 6 (1955): 1–17; repr. in Tierney, *Church Law and Constitutional Thought in the Middle Ages.* London: Variorum, 1979.

──────. "Limits to Obedience in the Thirteenth Century: The Case of Robert Grosseteste." In *Contraception, Authority, and Dissent.* Edited by Charles E. Curran. New York: Herder and Herder, 1969.

Tillman, H. *Pope Innocent III.* Amsterdam, 1980.

Unger, Dominic J. "Robert Grosseteste Bishop of Lincoln (1235–1253) On the Reasons for the Incarnation." *Franciscan Studies* 16 (1956): 1–36.

Wasserstein, D. "Grosseteste, the Jews and Medieval Christian Hebraism." In *Robert Grosseteste: New Perspectives.* Pp. 357–76.

Watt, J. A. "Grosseteste and the Jews: A Commentary on Letter V." In *Robert Grosseteste and the Beginnings of a British Theological Tradition.* Pp. 201–16.

Weisheipl, J. A. "Science in the Thirteenth Century." In *The History of the University of Oxford.* Pp. 435–69.

White, Carolinne. *The Correspondence (394–419) between Jerome and Augustine of Hippo.* Studies in Bible and Early Christianity 23. Lewiston: Mellen, 1990.

# INTRODUCTION

# INTRODUCTION

## GROSSETESTE'S LIFE

Robert Grosseteste was an unusual and exceptional man: from the lowest social class, but moving amid kings and popes, a scientist but also a philosopher and theologian, a talented administrator and successful teacher, a pastor devoted to the care of his flock but also a scholar dedicated to the translation of early Christian fathers and Aristotle, loyal to the Pope but fearless and bold in calling for the reform of the Curia. And what is more, he did not live a compartmentalized life and would have seen nothing odd about the various ways in which he spent himself, nothing odd in observing the stars and correcting the meteorological work of Aristotle one day and then writing a work on the sacrament of penance the next. Rather, all of these (to us) disjunctions came together as a coherent synthesis in the character of a brilliant, grave, humorous, disciplined, courageous, determined, and indefatigable man.

Grosseteste, who was born in Suffolk County around 1168 and died in 1253 in Lincoln, lived a long and fruitful life. Though historical records for the life of Grosseteste abound only after he was elected bishop, a few things can be said about the early part of his rise to prominence.[1] Before 1198 he was a Master of Arts

---

1. The story that follows and an examination of the historical documents that lie behind it are most easily found in Joseph Goering, "When and Where did Grosseteste Study Theology?" in *Robert Grosseteste: New Perspectives on his Thought and Scholarship*, ed. James McEvoy (Turnhout: Brepols, 1995), 17–52; Richard Southern, *Robert Grosseteste: The Growth of an English Mind in Medieval Europe*, 2d ed. (Oxford: Clarendon, 1992); James J. McEvoy, *The Philosophy of Robert Grosseteste* (Oxford: Clarendon, 1982), 3–48; Daniel Callus, "Robert Grosseteste as Scholar," in *Robert Grosseteste, Scholar and Bishop: Essays in Commemoration of the*

in the household of Bishop William de Vere of Hereford. There he was known not only for his excellence in the liberal arts but also for his knowledge of medicine and at least canon law.[2]

The next twenty-five years are a bit hazy for us, and there are basically three divergent scholarly judgments of what happened. The first, traditional view, advocated by Daniel Callus and James McEvoy, is that Grosseteste may have been a master teaching at Oxford in the years before 1209, a student studying theology at the University of Paris between 1209 and 1214, and chancellor of Oxford from 1214 to 1216. The second, advocated by Richard Southern, is that Grosseteste never went to the University of Paris; he was not "an Englishman fully immersed in the European tradition, reflecting all that was latest and best in the scholastic tradition of Paris and Oxford,"[3] but rather an independent and provincial English mind. By this second account, Grosseteste may have taught intermittently at Oxford before 1225, but he was not continuously associated with the school and certainly was not its chancellor before this date.[4] In 1225 Grosseteste received his first benefice and so was ordained to the priesthood and began to teach theology at Oxford and to write theological works.

Joseph Goering has offered a reconstruction of these years that combines features of the above two.[5] Like Callus and McEvoy, but unlike Southern, Goering thinks that Grosseteste could have been "chancellor" of Oxford as early as 1214. Like Southern, however, he thinks that Grosseteste was ordained around

---

*Seventh Centenary of his Death*, ed. idem (Oxford: Clarendon Press, 1955), 1–69; and Francis S. Stevenson, *Robert Grosseteste, Bishop of Lincoln: A Contribution to the Religious, Political, and Intellectual History of the Thirteenth Century* (London: MacMillan and Co., 1899). James McEvoy's *Robert Grosseteste*, Great Medieval Thinkers (Oxford: Oxford University Press, 2000), is very informative but has fewer notes to historical documents.

2. Callus mentions that natural supposition that Grosseteste would have taught in the Cathedral school at Hereford, but there is no plain evidence for it (see "Grosseteste as Scholar," 4).

3. Southern, *Robert Grosseteste*, 23.

4. For an account of the different arguments for when Grosseteste was chancellor, see McEvoy, *Robert Grosseteste*, 26–29.

5. Ginther supports Goering's view; see *Master of the Sacred Page: A Study of the Theology of Robert Grosseteste, ca. 1229/30–1235* (Aldershot: Ashgate, 2004), 3–5.

INTRODUCTION 5

1225 and began to teach theology still later. Goering, then, challenges the assumption that when Grosseteste served as head of the university he must have, therefore, been a master of theology, for only masters of theology or law could hold such a position. Goering suggests that Grosseteste was called "Master of Schools" and not "Chancellor" precisely because he was not a master of theology.[6] As Goering has it, then, Grosseteste went to Paris during the interdict of 1208 and returned to England in 1214, but he did not study theology while there.[7] Grosseteste nonetheless nurtured an interest in practical theology through reading and writing works about penance.[8] Grosseteste, Goer-

---

6. The clearest piece of evidence that we have for Grosseteste's chancellorship is from Oliver Sutton, Bishop of Lincoln (1280–99):

Bishop Robert, formerly Bishop of Lincoln, who occupied this office [i.e., the chancellorship] while he was regent in the same university, said when he was just being elevated to the episcopate that his immediate predecessor as Bishop of Lincoln did not permit the same Robert to be called Chancellor, but Master of Schools (cited in McEvoy, *The Philosophy of Robert Grosseteste*, 8; see *The Rolls and Register of Bishop Oliver Sutton, 1280–1299*, ed. R. T. M. Hill [Hereford: Lincoln Record Society, 1965], 5:60).

We do not know why Grosseteste was denied the title of chancellor; Goering discusses earlier proposals and offers his own (see "When and Where did Grosseteste Study Theology?" 47–50).

7. Cecilia Panti confirms Goering's view that Grosseteste was in Paris by drawing out some tentative implications of her work in editing some of Grosseteste's scientific works (for the editions, see *Moti, virtù e motori celesti nella cosmologia di Roberto Grossatesta. Studio ed edizione dei trattati 'De spera,' 'De cometis,' 'De motu supercelestium,'* ed. Cecilia Panti, Testi e Studi per il Corpus Philosophorum Medii Aevi, 16 [Florence: SISMEL Edizioni di Galluzzo, 2001]). Panti's work confirms a point made by Goering, that Grosseteste being in Paris helps to explain his early use of Aristotle through Averroes, whose work was known in Paris by 1225 (see Panti, "Robert Grosseteste's Early Cosmology," in *Editing Robert Grosseteste: Papers Given at the Thirty-Sixth Annual Conference on Editorial Problems. University of Toronto, 3–4 November 2000*, ed. Evelyn A. Mackie and Joseph Goering [Toronto: University of Toronto Press, 2003], 156–57). If we place Grosseteste writing *De cometis* in Paris, we solve two puzzles about this work: its Parisian (and not English) circulation, and its dependence upon and reference to Aristotle's *Meteorologica* but without any explicit mention of it. Grosseteste did not mention Aristotle by name, for mention of his natural works was forbidden at the time (see ibid., 158–59).

8. Goering draws here upon his work with F. A. C. Mantello in editing Gros-

ing suggests, used the money from his 1225 benefice to hire a vicar to care for the people of Abbotsley, and to study in Paris, where he read theological and philosophical works but did not earn a formal degree.[9] Grosseteste then returned to England and got his entry into teaching theology as lecturer to the Franciscans in 1229. Only thereafter did he teach theology at Oxford.

Each of these views is plausible, and none is altogether satisfactory. For instance, the traditional reconstruction makes Grosseteste a teacher of theology and chancellor of the University long before his ordination to the priesthood, sometime in or after 1225.[10] On the other hand, Southern's view, as McEvoy points out, must posit that Grosseteste wrote the greater part

---

seteste's penitential and confessional writings. See "When and Where did Grosseteste Study Theology?" 29–35.

9. Lesley Smith's recent article on Grosseteste's *De decem mandatis* lends some credence to Goering's (and Southern's) theory. She draws the striking contrasts between Grosseteste's and the typical scholastic treatment of the Ten Commandments, and they lead her to think that he never "studied theology himself there [at Paris] systematically." She thinks that Grosseteste wrote above all for himself. "I am sure," she writes, "that he must have listened to, spoken to, and argued with the masters in their Schools, but his theological knowledge strikes me as the knowledge of the brilliant autodidact: incisive and definite, leaning heavily on the great classical texts, but lacking structure, organization, and the sense of how to teach anyone else apart from oneself. Any other audience would be left breathless in admiration, but reaching for Thomas of Chobham or Peter Lombard" ("The *De decem mandatis* of Robert Grosseteste," in *Robert Grosseteste and the Beginnings of the British Theological Tradition: Papers Delivered at the Grosseteste Colloquium held at Greyfriars, Oxford, on 3rd July 2002*, ed. Maura O'Carroll [Rome: Istituto storico dei Cappuccini, 2003], 288).

10. Southern makes this point: "His being in deacon's orders in 1225 also suggests that he had not yet started publicly lecturing on theology. Once more, not everyone obeyed the rule that doctors in theology should be priests; but once more Grosseteste was not generally favourable to laxity." McEvoy challenges Southern's view on deacons teaching theology with the example of William of Auvergne (ca. 1190–1249): "Much in William's career is obscure, but it appears certain that he was a master in theology in 1223, was regent master by 1225, and held a canonry at Notre Dame from 1223, at the latest. Yet when Pope Gregory IX personally nominated him bishop of Paris . . . he was ordained both priest and bishop. Now, if a deacon could be a regent in theology at Paris, a deacon could lecture in theology at Oxford" (*Robert Grosseteste*, 25).

of his theological treatises in only ten years: "no human being, however gifted, could have mastered, taught, and published theology in the way that Grosseteste did, in the space of a mere decade," and all, I might add, without any formal training in theology. McEvoy continues,

Grosseteste's theological reading was little short of encyclopedic. Moreover, during the years in question he worked hard at Greek; he read Greek manuscripts (which is slow work!) of writings by Basil, Chrysostom, ... Damascene and the Pseudo-Dionysius. As one takes the measure of Grosseteste's very extensive reading in the Latin and Greek Fathers, the point comes when one is forced to perform too many mental acrobatics in order to accommodate the hypothesis of his late theological development.[11]

Goering, though, makes an observation that would support Southern's view: Grosseteste, he thinks, would have produced far more theological works if he had taught theology from 1215. His works are too few to have been written over twenty years: in fact, "the extant commentaries can be dated to the late 1220s or 1230s, and the entire corpus could easily have been produced during a teaching career of five or six" years.[12]

At various points all three of these views are persuasive, though Goering's makes the best sense of all the evidence. Even so, the evidence is so fragmentary that each must rest upon assumptions, though not outlandish ones, and conjectures, however reasonable and possible. Consider, for example, the assumptions in the traditional argument. If Grosseteste was chancellor in 1214, then he *must* have been a master of theology, and if he was a master, he *must* have studied in Paris during the interdict. At every point this argument can be both attacked and defended with circumstantial evidence.

The newer reconstructions face similar difficulties. For example, in a couple of places Southern's argument rests upon his inference that the early Grosseteste had the same thoughts on ecclesial abuses as the mature Grosseteste. He holds, for example, that Grosseteste would not have held the benefice of Ab-

11. McEvoy, *Robert Grosseteste*, 26.
12. Goering, "When and Where did Grosseteste Study Theology?" 26.

botsley without being ordained a priest because "when he was a bishop he made himself notorious for his insistence that all holders of parochial benefices should be priests."[13] Southern dismisses, perhaps rightly, the thought that Grosseteste did not live up to his own principles, for "he was not a man to be fierce in principle and lukewarm in action."[14] We know that Grosseteste had an early interest in the cure of souls, but is there evidence that he at this time had any well formed thoughts about ecclesial reform in general and benefices in particular? It may not be that Grosseteste was a hypocrite, but Southern does not consider the possibility that Grosseteste had not yet come to embrace the principles he was later famous for.

Southern invokes the same argument, viz., from Grosseteste's character, to argue that he did not lecture in theology as a deacon: "not everyone obeyed the rule that doctors in theology should be priests; but once more Grosseteste was not generally favourable to laxity."[15] Again, there is no evidence that Grosseteste as a young man displayed wanton disregard for customs or that he was inclined to abuse ecclesial policies for his own gain. But was he as scrupulous as a young man as he was as a bishop? Southern himself mentions that around 1230 Grosseteste "experienced, if not a religious conversion, at least a new commitment to Christian life and pastoral work."[16] The occasion for this renewal, we will see below, was Grosseteste's encounter with the mendicants at Oxford. Perhaps Grosseteste was not always as conscientious as when he was bishop. After all, in the 1230s Grosseteste held more than one benefice, and as a bishop he definitely frowned upon such pluralism.

More certain than the events of Grosseteste's life in these years is the suspension of studies at Oxford. At the end of 1209 a student had murdered his mistress and fled. His roommates, also students, were hanged by the secular authorities. At this the masters simply left and took their students with them. Some, in fact, went to Cambridge and so began a university there. Because of the interdict, no settlement between the town and the masters

---

13. Southern, *Robert Grosseteste*, 70.
14. Ibid.
15. Ibid.
16. Ibid., 71.

could be reached. All of the historians of Grosseteste's life agree that he would not have been one of the few masters who refused to leave with the others. Whether he was in France or in England between 1209 and 1215, he was not teaching at Oxford.

Whatever happened between 1198 and 1225, we know that in 1225 Grosseteste received a benefice at the Church of Abbotsley and ca. 1230 became Archdeacon of Leicester. These appointments are significant, of course, because of the income attached. Richard Southern sums up well the meaning of the benefice of Abbotsley: "he passed from the ever-present risk of penury and unemployment to the comfortable enjoyment of a life-long income. He was no longer dependent on patronage or pupils. He was free to exercise his talents as he wished. And, since his parish was only a day's ride from Oxford, and he might have a curate, he could spend much time in the schools without neglecting his parishioners."[17]

Around the same time that Grosseteste became archdeacon, Agnellus of Pisa asked him to be a lecturer to the Franciscans, who had only in 1224 arrived in Oxford. Under Grosseteste, says Thomas Eccleston, "within a short time they made incalculable progress both in scholastic disputations and the subtle moralities suitable for preaching."[18] Grosseteste convinced the friars that education was not only consistent with their way of life but indispensable to it. "His influence was beneficial, wide, and lasting," writes Daniel Callus, "and he founded a special tradition of learning which prevailed for several generations in the Franciscan school."[19] Grosseteste held his post as lecturer until his election as bishop in 1235.

As Grosseteste altered for the better the course of the friars' lives in Oxford, so they altered the course of his. When Grosseteste became their lecturer, he was also the Archdeacon of Leicester and held the benefice of Abbotsley and a prebend in Lincoln Cathedral. This proved too much for him, and he resigned not his lectureship but the ecclesial offices that had given him finan-

---

17. Ibid., 70.
18. Cited in Callus, "Grosseteste as Scholar," 11.
19. Ibid.

cial independence and social stature, except for the sinecure prebend in Lincoln Cathedral. Within a few years of having reached the pinnacle of his scholarly career, within a few years of acquiring prestigious positions at Oxford and in the Church, Grosseteste gave it all up to remain the lecturer of the Franciscans.

In 1235, Grosseteste was elected to the bishopric of Lincoln, perhaps as a "caretaker." The canons were divided over two candidates but ended up agreeing on the lecturer of the Franciscans, who was around 65 years old. Sometimes caretakers turn out not to be: Grosseteste died in his mid-eighties, having been bishop for 18 years.

### GROSSETESTE'S WORKS

Many of the works that we have from Grosseteste's pen owe their origin in one way or another to his teaching of the arts, philosophy, and theology. He wrote a commentary on Aristotle's *Posterior Analytics*[20] and some notes on his *Physics*.[21] Grosseteste read the Philosopher's *De Caelo* and *De generatione*, but it was, James McEvoy thinks, Aristotle's *Meteorologica* that fascinated Grosseteste and inspired him to write a number of scientific treatises: *On Comets, On the Ebb and Flow of the Tides, On Heat, On Color*, and *On the Rainbow*.[22]

Grosseteste's most famous philosophical position has been summed up by the label "metaphysics of light." "There were three things about *lux*," writes Weisheipl, "that struck him as particularly useful in understanding the universe": *lux* is productive, as God is, for *lumen* is generated from it without increase or decrease in it; *lux* produces images of itself without reference to time and space; and *lux* is stable and permanent while what it begets, *lumen*, is not.[23]

Grosseteste's theological works derive more directly from the

---

20. *Commentarius in Posterium Analyticorum Libros*, ed. P. Rossi (Florence: Leo S. Olschki, 1981).
21. *Roberti Grosseteste Episcopi Lincolniensis Commentarius in VIII libros Physicorum Aristotelis*, ed. Richard Dales (Boulder, CO: University of Colorado Press, 1963).
22. See McEvoy, *The Philosophy of Robert Grosseteste*, 16–17.
23. Weisheipl, "Science in the Thirteenth Century," 444.

INTRODUCTION 11

classroom, and we can understand these works according to the three duties of a master in theology: *legere, disputare,* and *praedicare.* Above all else, the master of theology had to lecture on the meaning of the Bible, *legere* or *lectio.* The impressive *summae* and comprehensive theological syntheses of many medieval masters have sometimes made us lose sight of just how central the Bible was to medieval theological education.[24] We cannot, however, in the case of Grosseteste (as we can, and in fact have done, in that of Thomas Aquinas, for example) make the mistake of focusing on synthetic theological works to the neglect of biblical ones, for he left us no such syntheses.

Many of Grosseteste's theological works have their origin in his biblical lectures, although we do not have the *reportationes* themselves. Close to these lectures would be his commentaries on the Psalms,[25] on Galatians,[26] and on the hexaëmeron.[27] Although it is clear that Grosseteste lectured on books of the Bible other than the Psalms, Galatians, and Genesis, these are the only commentaries that we have.[28]

Grosseteste also wrote biblical treatises that derive only indirectly from lecture notes on the Bible: *On the Cessation of the Laws* and *De decem mandatis.*[29] Both of these treatises attracted a

---

24. See James Ginther, "There is a Text in this Classroom: The Bible and Theology in the Medieval University," in *Essays in Medieval Philosophy and Theology in Memory of Walter H. Principe, CSB: Fortresses and Launching Pads,* ed. J. Ginther and Carl N. Still (Aldershot: Ashgate, 2005), 31–51.

25. On the character of these commentaries on the Psalms, see Beryl Smalley, "The Biblical Scholar," in *Robert Grosseteste, Scholar and Bishop,* 76–78; and James Ginther, "The Super Psalterium in Context," in *Editing Robert Grosseteste: Papers Given at the Thirty-Sixth Annual Conference on Editorial Problems. University of Toronto, 3–4 November 2000,* ed. Evelyn A. Mackie and Joseph Goering, 31–60 (Toronto: University of Toronto Press, 2003).

26. *Expositio in epistolam sancti Pauli ad Galatas,* ed. James McEvoy, in *Opera inedita Roberti Grosseteste,* Corpus Christianorum Continuatio Mediaevalis 130 (Turnhout: Brepols, 1995), 3–175.

27. *Hexaëmeron,* ed. Richard C. Dales and Servus Gieben, Auctores Britannici Medii Aevi 6 (London: British Academy, 1982).

28. Ginther points out that there is evidence also for lectures on the other Pauline epistles, Ecclesiasticus, Daniel, and Isaiah; see *Master of the Sacred Page,* 15–16.

29. *De cessatione legalium,* ed. R. C. Dales and E. B. King, Auctores Britannici

wider readership only after Grosseteste's death and overlap in their themes.[30] McEvoy, in fact, sees Grosseteste's commentary on Galatians together with *On the Cessation of the Laws* and *De decem mandatis* as a sort of trilogy. Of the three, *De decem mandatis* had the most pastoral orientation; it was a work of *haute vulgarization,* "on the highest shelf of popular writings," and is best understood in the context of the Lateran reform program that called for the teaching of the Ten Commandments and inspired treatises to accomplish this.[31]

While lectures on the Bible served as the spine of the course in theology, masters were also obliged to hold disputations, "in which two students debated with one another, [and] the resolution to the debate would be provided by the master, which is the main reason why these disputations should be considered as belonging to the master and not the students."[32] As he revised his biblical lectures into commentaries and worked them into treatises, so he edited his disputations, and many of his works betray their former life as a disputation: *De dotibus,* on the nuptial gifts of Christ to the Church,[33] *De veritate, De ordine emanandi causatorum a Deo,* and *De libero arbitrio.*[34] *On the Cessation of the Laws* also bears some signs of having been a disputation. It is natural, of course, that a disputation on a biblical theme would incorporate elements of a master's *lectio* as well.

Grosseteste had to preach (*praedicare, praedicatio*) on the text on which he lectured and disputed. Ginther points out that his sermons are in dire need of an editor, but that many have been preserved in Grosseteste's *Dicta,* which Ginther edited and de-

---

Medii Aevi 7 (London: British Academy, 1986); and *De decem mandatis,* ed. eidem, Auctores Britannici Medii Aevi 10 (London: British Academy, 1987).

30. Smalley notes that most of the manuscripts come from the 14th and 15th centuries; "The Biblical Scholar," 83.

31. James McEvoy, "Robert Grosseteste on the Ten Commandments," *Recherches de théologie ancienne et médiévale* 58 (1991): 179–80; repr. in McEvoy, *Robert Grosseteste, Exegete and Philosopher* (London: Variorum, 1994).

32. Ginther, "There is a Text in this Classroom," 36.

33. Ed. J. Goering, "The *De dotibus* of Robert Grosseteste," *Medieval Studies* 44 (1982): 83–109.

34. I have drawn this list from Ginther, *Master of the Sacred Page,* 17–18.

scribed as "sermons and theological *notulae,* all written while he was *in scolis.*"[35]

Grosseteste left us also a number of translations and commentaries, but these did not emerge directly from his magisterial tasks. It was his study of the Bible, however, McEvoy very reasonably claims, that led him to learn Greek and perhaps some Hebrew.[36] He became convinced that he could better understand the Scriptures as well as Greek patristic theological works if he could read them in their original languages (or, in the case of the Old Testament, at least in Greek if not also in Hebrew). Moreover, the translations that Grosseteste continued to work on throughout his episcopate were not irrelevant to his pastoral concerns: he "would have been justified in feeling," writes McEvoy, "that these writings would illuminate the origins and the beliefs of the primitive Church and so help to further that spiritual purification of the contemporary Church which was the goal of his active ministry."[37] So Grosseteste translated *On the Orthodox Faith* and other works by John Damascene, Ignatius's letters, the *Testament of the Twelve Patriarchs,* and the works of Dionysius as well as Aristotle's *Nicomachean Ethics.* Grosseteste employed a very literal style of translation which made for very awkward Latin, but his goal was to be as faithful as possible to the text; any consequent ambiguities or difficulties were taken up in glosses or an appended commentary.[38]

### ON THE CESSATION OF THE LAWS

For whom did Grosseteste write *On the Cessation of the Laws?* It had for a long time been thought that Grosseteste wrote it

---

35. Ibid., 18.
36. On Grosseteste's knowledge of Hebrew, see McEvoy, *Robert Grosseteste,* 120–21.
37. McEvoy, *The Philosophy of Robert Grosseteste,* 23.
38. On Grosseteste's method of translating, see Meribel Holland, "Robert Grosseteste's Greek Translations and College of Arms MS Arundel 9," in *Robert Grosseteste: New Perspectives,* 121–47; and McEvoy, "Language, Tongue, and Thought in the Writings of Robert Grosseteste," *Miscellanea Mediaevalia* 13 (1981): 585–92; repr. in McEvoy, *Robert Grosseteste: Exegete and Philosopher.*

against the Jews, but Beryl Smalley and King and Dales have shown this to be false. The tradition began in the late eighteenth century with Samuel Pegge, who connected *On the Cessation of the Laws* with King Henry III's establishing of a *domus conversorum* for Jewish converts to Christianity. Pegge, however, is not to be blamed because his conjecture became someone else's fact. "As this was a grand subject of contention," writes Pegge, "it may seem no improbable conjecture, that he wrote the book on this occasion."[39] Pegge's conjecture indeed becomes all the more improbable when he himself states that "this tract is entirely polemical, and is evidently written against the Jews, though he names them not; he states such arguments as might be used, or had been used, by any writers, in favour of the permanency of the law, in the fairest and most candid manner, and replies to them all with the utmost temper and moderation; insomuch that it were to be wished our modern disputants would follow the example of this great man, and would debate all points of controversy with equal coolness and equanimity."[40] Pegge describes here not a polemic with outsiders but an in-house *disputatio*.[41]

So if not for, or rather, against the Jews, for whom did Grosseteste write it? Dales and King express wonder at Pegge's assessment of *On the Cessation of the Laws* as a polemic against the Jews. The work, they say, is largely academic, and pastoral where it is not academic. "Its arguments," they write, "are altogether academic.... The work is addressed to a well-educated Christian audience, most probably clerics of the schools; the arguments

---

39. Samuel Pegge, *The Life of Robert Grosseteste, the Celebrated Bishop of Lincoln* (London: John Nichols, 1793), 31.

40. Ibid., 32.

41. On the larger question of Grosseteste and the Jews, see *Ep.* 5 (translated by Joseph Goering and F. A. C. Mantello, in Goering, "Robert Grosseteste and the Jews of Leicester," 197–200, in *Robert Grosseteste and the Beginnings of a British Theological Tradition*). See also Southern, *Robert Grosseteste*, 244–49; the more balanced treatments of Joseph Goering, "Robert Grosseteste and the Jews of Leicester," and John A. Watt, "Grosseteste and the Jews: A Commentary on Letter V," in *Robert Grosseteste and the Beginnings of a British Theological Tradition*, 201–16; and David Wasserstein, "Grosseteste, the Jews, and Medieval Christian Hebraism," in *Robert Grosseteste: New Perspectives*, 357–76.

are sophisticated; the *auctores* are numerous; the most eloquent passages, redolent with emotion and piety, deal with the Incarnation and the Atonement."[42] Richard Schenk, however, has challenged Dales and King's characterization of Grosseteste's audience. He agrees with them that *On the Cessation of the Laws* cannot be part of Henry III's alleged program of conversion but thinks that they have not reckoned with those texts wherein Grosseteste mentions his contemporaries who practice both the Jewish and Christian cult.[43] Indeed, Grosseteste seems to be writing for Christians who, he thinks, are too sympathetic with Jewish practices. This does not mean, though, that the more theological and christological parts of *On the Cessation of the Laws* are tangential to the argument; rather, what one says about the Jews (or other non-Christian religions) and about the Old Covenant has direct implications for one's view of Christ.[44] This is precisely the point: Grosseteste rejects the value of keeping the Law after the coming of Christ precisely because of what such an observance would say about Christ.

When did Grosseteste write *On the Cessation of the Laws?* The traditional date of 1231 does not hold up, at least insofar as it was tied to Henry's founding of a Jewish house of converts in that year. We are certain that he wrote it after his commentary on Galatians, for he mentions this work in 1.11.1 and 4.6.8. This fact, together with the disputational character of the work, calls for a date during or after Grosseteste's magisterial period in theology. We have seen that this dates either from 1215 or from ca. 1229, probably the latter.[45] McEvoy gives the range ca.

---

42. Richard C. Dales and Edward B. King, "Introduction," in Robert Grosseteste, *De cessatione legalium*, ed. eidem (London: Oxford University Press, 1986), xii.

43. See Richard Schenk, "Views of the Two Covenants in Medieval Theology," *Nova et Vetera* 4 (2006): 902–3. The texts of *On the Cessation of the Laws* to which he refers are as follows: 1.1.1; 1.2.17; and 4.6.3.

44. Schenk has made this point in regard to Robert Kilwardby; see "Christ, Christianity, and Non-Christian Religions: Their Interrelation in the Theology of Robert Kilwardby," in *Christ among the Medieval Dominicans: Representations of Christ in the Texts and Images of the Order of Preachers*, ed. Kent Emery and Joseph Wawrykow, 344–63 (Notre Dame, IN.: University of Notre Dame Press, 1998).

45. In the absence of other evidence for dating Grosseteste's works, scholars

1225–35,[46] but Grosseteste himself mentions that if the Jews do not recognize Jesus as the fulfillment of the prophecies, then Judah will have lacked a ruler for more than 1230 years,[47] and that it has been almost 1200 years since the destruction of the Temple (70 A.D.).[48] A date between 1230 and 1235, when Grosseteste was elected bishop, seems reasonable.[49]

What is Grosseteste's argument? The origin of *On the Cessation of the Laws* in the schools, as well as the fact that the audience consists of students some of whom may have had Jewish sympathies, goes a long way toward illuminating the overall course of the argument. To such an audience Grosseteste's long and serious treatment of the arguments for the keeping of the Law would have been meaningful. So too would have been the lengthy consideration of the various patristic authorities, especially Jerome and Augustine, and the extended and extensive theological argument that stood behind Grosseteste's own position.

Dales and King's comments on these matters are illuminating, but I would like to offer a small improvement of their estimation of the coherence of Grosseteste's argument. In their introduction they describe the structure and argument of the work. Grosseteste's arguments, they say, are not only complex in themselves, but, what is more, they are "obfuscated by the circular and tangential conventions of the author's style."[50] "Grosseteste's treatise," they say, "lacks the cogency and coherence of the formal essay, to which the modern mind is accustomed," and to their minds his arguments are complex to the point of bewilderment such that we can appreciate his achievement only at a distance.[51] I take Dales and King's words as an invitation to examine more deeply the structure and argument of *On the Ces-*

---

have turned to his knowledge of Greek as an indicator. If he displays much skill with Greek, the work is later; if not, then earlier. Applied prudently, this measure can be helpful, but it has not yet proven so in either Grosseteste's commentary on Galatians or *On the Cessation of the Laws* (see McEvoy, "Robert Grosseteste on the Ten Commandments," 171–72).

46. See ibid., 172.   47. See 2.7.13.
48. See 2.9.2.
49. See McEvoy, "Robert Grosseteste on the Ten Commandments," 172.
50. Dales and King, "Introduction," xv.
51. Ibid.

*sation of the Laws:* the argument, I think, is indeed complex but not so bewildering.

Grosseteste divided his work into four parts, the first being by far the longest, about 40 percent of the whole work. Not only the longest, Part One is also the most complex. It is divided into three sections. The first is a collection of the arguments proving the permanence of the Old Law, the second is Grosseteste's response, and the third is a set of proof-texts from the Old Testament demonstrating the end of the Law. He gives three types of arguments against his own position: first the arguments from Scripture; then the arguments from suitability; and finally an argument from the example of Christ.

Here are four examples. First consider the following argument from Gn 17.13:

> Again, the Lord says to Abraham about circumcision, "And my covenant [*pactum*] shall be in your flesh for a perpetual covenant [*foedus*]" (Gn 17.13). But how will it be an everlasting covenant if it itself is not everlasting? Again, if the Lord commands his servant to perform some service without specifying when it should end, it should not belong to the servants to decide when it should end. But the Lord has commanded Israel (in the flesh) to perform circumcision as his servant, and he did not determine when it should end. Rather, on the contrary, he removed its end when he commanded that it be an everlasting covenant and a sign of an everlasting covenant. Therefore, Israel should never stop circumcising. And it seems that the command to circumcise is not only for Israel in the flesh but for others as well, even those who are not of the seed of Abraham. For the Lord said to Abraham, "An infant of eight days old shall be circumcised among you, every manchild in your generations: he that is born in the house, as well as the bought servant, shall be circumcised, and whosoever is not of your stock" (Gn 17.12). So then, circumcision with no fixed end—or rather with the end abolished—is enjoined upon those who are not of Abraham's stock. It must, therefore, be kept by everyone.[52]

As an example of the argument from suitability, consider Grosseteste's statement that "nothing is able to be corrected, unless it is shown to be wrongly done in the first place, for what is done rightly the first time, should in no way be changed."[53]

---

52. *De cess. leg.* 1.2.5–6.
53. Ibid., 1.2.11.

Again arguing from suitability, Grosseteste points out the inappropriateness of the Lord destroying a building that he has just finished.[54] Finally, arguing from the example of Christ, Grosseteste notes that

> Christ observed the sacraments of the Old Law together with those of the Gospel; for he was circumcised and baptized, ate the paschal lamb, and handed over his own body to be eaten by his disciples. In order, therefore, to imitate him and follow his example, we also are obliged to observe the sacraments of both testaments.[55]

After giving these opposing arguments, Grosseteste writes that he will "begin a little deeper analysis" so that his opponent's position will be rendered void.[56]

Here Grosseteste's argument seems to veer off course. He begins a long treatment of the rational soul's desire for happiness and the place of obedience to positive and natural law in the achievement of the soul's desire. Grosseteste stresses that only God can give happiness and that this happiness must come from obedience not only to the natural law but to a positive law, that is, a law on an indifferent matter, like the command not to eat the fruit from a particular tree.[57] Such obedience is more perfect precisely because there is no reason to obey or disobey aside from the authority of the Law-giver. Obedience is made still more impressive when it is offered in the face of the strongest temptation to disobedience.

So, for Grosseteste, man should be given happiness only upon the conquest of temptation and perfect obedience to a positive law. When man failed the test, however, and succumbed to the Tempter, a new course of events, really, a new economy, was set in motion. The positive law that God had given to Adam now became pointless, and man had to refocus his efforts on living the natural law, which he had not yet forgotten. It was still in his heart and so need not be written. Because Noah had proven himself in the observance of the natural law, a new positive law was added so that his obedience could be perfect.[58] Man's mem-

---

54. See ibid., 1.2.13.
56. Ibid., 1.4.1.
58. See ibid., 1.7.1.

55. Ibid., 1.2.16.
57. See ibid., 1.4.5–1.5.6.

ory, however, grew worse with time, and it became necessary that the Law be written lest man have a complaint against God.[59]

It is clear, then, that man had to be given another positive law if he was to be saved, but why should this be given before the Incarnation rather than after? In order to answer the question, Grosseteste first recalls that there are four persons, as it were, in the human race: first is Adam before the fall, and all in him; second is fallen Adam, and all who fell in him; third is the Devil, and all who are damned in him; and finally is Christ, and all who are redeemed in him.[60] As we have seen, the first Adam needed no written law, either natural or positive, and it would be vain to give the written Law to the damned. The written Law is given to those fallen in Adam so that they might pass into the body of those whose head is Christ. The written Law first makes man realize that he cannot save himself, that he can be saved only by God. Second, the Law prepares man to believe in the Incarnation and Passion by alerting him to look for something that is most unexpected. It is more believable, says Grosseteste, that a person would be both man and lion than that he would be God and man.[61] To prepare man for the act of faith in the God-man, without which there is no salvation, the Law comes beforehand as a witness. One must know, though, how to read the Old Testament as a witness, and so Grosseteste offers a short lesson on how to read the Scriptures.[62]

Thus far Grosseteste's argument has taken many twists and turns, but its basic thrust is clear. One cannot adequately respond to the opponent's view of the Law except by offering a sweeping view of the economy of salvation in which one can see the place of law, positive and natural, and the place of *the* Law especially as it relates to Christ and the accomplishment of human happiness. In the course of offering the big picture, Grosseteste responded to a couple of the earlier objections as their responses became manifest. Once he had finished the "deeper analysis" with the instructions on how to read the Old Testament, he turned to the remaining objections and handled them

---

59. See ibid., 1.7.2.
61. See ibid., 1.8.18.
60. See ibid., 1.8.
62. See ibid., 1.9.

one by one,[63] and finished Part One with a demonstration from the Scriptures that the Law has ceased.[64]

From this point on, the structure of Grosseteste's argument is much clearer. In the third section of Part One, he had cited Dt 18.15 ("The Lord ... will raise up for you a prophet ... [and] him you shall hear as you would me") to prove that the Law had ceased.[65] Grosseteste recognizes at the beginning of Part Two that this proof has effect only if Jesus is the Christ promised in the Law. So, in Part Two, he says, "we will try to show, in our own way, from clear, non-allegorical texts of the Old Testament that the crucified Jesus was the savior promised in the Law."[66] Grosseteste then gives one Old Testament text after another showing that only Jesus could be the expected divine and human Messiah.

What Grosseteste proved in Part Two by Scripture can be proved by reason also, and other points besides. But in Part Three he does not wish to repeat the work of Augustine, Gregory, and Anselm, who argued for the necessity of the God-man; instead, he treats a new but related theme. He writes,

Whether God would become man even if man had not fallen, none of the sacred writers determine in the books of theirs that I have previously looked at, unless my memory fails me. But rather, they seem to imply that if man had not fallen, God would not have become man; and therefore God only became man to restore lost man. There seem, nevertheless, to be valid reasons to show simply that God would have become man even if man had never fallen. On account of this, we will omit for the moment those reasons by which the sacred writers prove that God must become man in order to restore lost man and will ask whether God would have become man even if man had not sinned.[67]

After offering arguments on this point, Grosseteste investigates what reason can show about Jesus from his birth of a Virgin at a particular time and place to his theandric deeds. I indicate these points more fully on the outline below.

Grosseteste closes *De cessatione* by answering some questions that follow upon the death of the Law: when it died;[68] whether

---

63. See ibid., 1.10.
64. See ibid., 1.11.
65. See ibid., 1.11.2.
66. Ibid., 2.1.2.
67. Ibid., 3.1.2.
68. See ibid., 4.1–2.

it can be kept after the Passion of Christ, a question that provoked a heated exchange between Jerome and Augustine;[69] whether the moral part of the Law is any different now in a time of grace than it was before;[70] and finally, how the saints in Old Testament times kept the Law when it seems, on the one hand, that they could not have kept it as salvific and, on the other, that they were obliged by God nonetheless to keep it.[71]

Grosseteste's argument, then, is both coherent and comprehensive; it is not haphazard but deliberate and purposeful, even if sometimes circuitous. His great achievement is to clarify the larger theological context in which one must view the difficult question of the relation between the Old and New Testaments. We can see that *On the Cessation of the Laws* draws out the theological, christological, and soteriological issues implicit in the question of the relationship between the Old and New Covenants. Of course, there is nothing new here, for from the beginning Christian theologians understood that the question of the relationship between the covenants is ultimately reduced to the question of who Jesus was and what he accomplished. I must leave aside the interesting question of how Grosseteste's theological positions compare with those of his predecessors, contemporaries, and successors. Suffice it to say here that he openly engages with the positions of Jerome, Augustine, and Anselm, three giants of the Western theological tradition. I hope this translation will further the study of Grossesteste's relation not only to these three, but also to the great medieval theologians of the Franciscan and Dominican traditions. Ginther intimated Grosseteste's influence here in his treatment of the question whether there would have been an incarnation had there been no sin. Grosseteste, Ginther writes, addresses the question with such intensity "that it created a new topic for scholastic theologians to examine for the rest of the century."[72] Ginther gives a list of major theologians attracted by the question: Richard Fishacre, Richard Rufus, Alexander of Hales, Guerric of St. Quentin, Albert the Great, Bonaventure, Thomas Aquinas, and John Duns Scotus.

---

69. See ibid., 4.3–4.6.
70. See ibid., 4.7–4.8, 26.
71. See ibid., 4.8, 30–38.
72. Ginther, *Master of the Sacred Page*, 128.

## OUTLINE OF *ON THE CESSATION OF THE LAWS*

I. Part One
   A. Arguments proving the opponents' position (1.1.1–3.3)
   B. Grosseteste's response: a deeper analysis (1.4.1–9.8)
      1. The big picture and the place in it of man, natural and positive law, the Laws (and the whole of Scripture), and Christ
      2. Along the way, responses to a couple of the opponents' arguments
   C. Point-by-point response to the remaining arguments of the opponents (1.10.1–33)
   D. Proof texts from the Old and New Testaments that prove the cessation of the ritual Laws (1.11.1–6)
II. Part Two: a demonstration from the Scriptures that Jesus, Son of Mary, is the expected Messiah, the God-man, foretold in the Old Testament
III. Part Three: Rational demonstrations
   A. That there would have been an incarnation had there been no sin (3.1.1–2.4)
      1. From the goodness of God
      2. From the headship of Christ and the justification of man
      3. From the marriage of Christ and the Church foretold by Adam
      4. From the beatitude of the body
      5. From the unity of the universe
      6. From the completion of the circle of generation
   B. That the God-man was fittingly born of a virgin (3.2.5)
   C. Of the place of Christ's birth (3.3.1–4)
   D. Of the timing of Christ's birth (3.4.1–8)
   E. That there could not be more than one Christ (3.5.1–13)
   F. That Jesus' deeds proclaim his divinity and humanity (3.6.1–16)
IV. Part Four: Questions arising from the death of the Law
   A. When it died (4.1.1–2.6)
   B. Whether it could be kept after the Passion of Christ? Reconciling Jerome and Augustine (4.3.1–6.8)
   C. Whether the moral part of the Law is the same before and after the Passion of Christ (4.7.1–8.26)
   D. How the saints in Old Testament times lived the Law (4.8.27–38)

## A NOTE ABOUT THE TRANSLATION

*On the Cessation of the Laws* has a modern critical edition, thanks to the efforts of Richard Dales and Edward King, and this is the text that I have used. I corrected obvious typographical errors (for example, *termini* for *temini* [1.2.6]) and occasionally decided to punctuate the text differently.[73]

I have translated myself all of Grosseteste's citations from other authors even when modern translations already exist, for his text at times differs from the modern critical texts. The exception to this is the Bible. Where Grosseteste's Latin text agrees with that of the Vulgate, I have used the translation made at Douay and Rheims, freely revised to conform to contemporary diction and usage;[74] where his text differs from the Vulgate, I have accordingly adjusted that translation. Sometimes the Latin Vulgate differed from Grosseteste's text, but it was not necessary to alter the Douay-Rheims.[75] Finally, I have followed the Vulgate's numbering of the Psalms.

It goes without saying that in this work Grosseteste uses many times the various Latin words for "law": *lex, praeceptum, mandatum,* and *legalia.* These words (perhaps with the exception of *legalia*) are for him roughly synonymous. He does not, for example, use one to refer to moral laws and another to refer to ritual laws, or one to refer to the Ten Commandments and another to refer to other moral laws. Hence, while I translated *lex* as "law," I did not always take *praeceptum* as "precept" and *mandatum* as

---

73. Here is one example from *De cess. leg.* 1.2.12. The edition (p. 12, li. 23–24) has "Nec eget lex. Necessario aliquo deferente necessario corruptibili, subiectum enim legis est humanum genus...." But I think it makes better sense this way: "Nec eget lex necessario aliquo deferente necessario corruptibili. Subiectum enim legis est humanum genus...." This way, Grosseteste is using the same expression that he did before and denying of the Law each of the three ways in which something can tend to corruption.

74. For example, Heb 2.3, "He shall not be slack," I changed to "He shall not be late." Also, I edited out "thee" and "thou," and similar words.

75. For example, for Rv 12.7, Grosseteste has: "Michael et angeli eius preliabantur cum drachone et draco pugnabat et angeli eius; et non prevaluerunt." But the Vulgate has: "Michahel et angeli eius proeliabantur cum dracone et draco pugnabat et angeli eius et non valuerunt." In either case, the translation is very well the same.

"command"; sometimes I took *praeceptum* for "command," for it would have led to some awkward redundancies otherwise.[76]

The subtitles in the text are not mine but Grosseteste's. He made these subtitles in his own hand in the margin of one of the manuscripts (*B*), and so I include them, although I have left out a few of his insignificant marginal notes. There are many marginal notes early in the work, but ever fewer as the work progresses. I have inserted a few of my own notes where commentary was necessary.

---

76. For example, Grosseteste often used the verb *praecipio* with *praeceptum* as a direct object, and I thought it infelicitous to say "commanded a command."

# ON THE CESSATION
OF THE LAWS

# PART ONE

### CHAPTER 1

HERE WERE MANY in the primitive Church who asserted that the rituals of the Old Law together with those of the New Law must be observed and that there could be no salvation without observing them. Their opinion was rejected by the decree of the Apostles written in the Acts of the same Apostles and repudiated most effectively by blessed Paul in his letters to the Romans and to the Galatians. Because, therefore, they were able to support the error of their position with authorities as well as fallacious arguments—and by these arguments and authorities even now the faith could waver in the minds of the weak—I will set out the points that seem to confirm their position as they occur to me, though my ability and memory are small and little. After these arguments are set out in my own way and refuted in their turn, I will also make the arguments that disprove this error and establish that the Law was made void by the grace of Christ.

### CHAPTER 2

*The first argument: from the covenant of Exodus 31*

1. In Exodus Moses says, "Let the children of Israel keep the Sabbath, and celebrate it in their regions. It is an everlasting covenant between me and the children of Israel, and a perpetual sign" (Ex 31.16–17). But how is the observance and celebration of the Sabbath an everlasting covenant if it is now made void? For a covenant among some persons is not everlasting unless what they agree upon among themselves remains forever. A covenant is so called either because of the act of those agree-

ing, or because of the thing brought into being by the common consent of those agreeing. But the action of the participants is not everlasting when in fact they have agreed among themselves that this kind of action cease. Therefore, if the covenant is everlasting, what the participants agree upon abides forever. But God and the sons of Israel are not said here to have made a covenant with each other except for the keeping and celebration of the Sabbath. And so there abides the everlasting observance and celebration of the Sabbath.

*Second argument: from the sign*

2. Similarly, if something is a perpetual sign, it signifies forever, and if it signifies, it exists. Therefore, if something is a perpetual sign, it exists forever. The observance and celebration of the Sabbath, then, because it is a perpetual sign, exists forever.

3. Again, if something is a sign, and it is always useful and necessary that what it signifies be signified, then the annulment of this kind of sign is never useful but always harmful. If the primary signification of the sign was useful or necessary, then in fact now and earlier it is in the same way useful and necessary that what is signified be signified. And yet if someone should say that an old sign should be made void because of the coming of a new one, this can be seen to be false by many examples. For after synonymous words are established with some sign value, they do not lose the signification that the words had before they were made synonymous with each other and given the same sign value. When light signifies fire, it does not render smoke incapable of signifying the same, although smoke precedes light and gives a previous indication of fire. And when the sign is grasped and impresses what it signifies upon the mind (although the impression in the mind is reinforced through many signs for the same thing), the impression is formed more clearly in the mind and better remembered. Clearly it is not a little advantageous for a single thing to have a multitude of signs profitably understood, chiefly when that multitude is not so great that it generates confusion nor so diverse that it hampers itself in the act of existing or in manifesting what it is to signify. But the Sabbath was given as a sign by which it is known that the

Lord himself is God. This is clear from the words of the Prophet Ezekiel, where he speaks in the voice of the Lord: "I gave them also my Sabbaths, to be a sign between me and them: and that they might know that I am the Lord that sanctify them" (Ezek 20.12). And again a little later, "And sanctify my Sabbaths, that they may be a sign between me and you: and that you may know that I am the Lord your God" (Ezek 20.20). In fact, when he said that the Sabbath is a sign, he explains immediately and adds the knowledge that the sign produces by its signification. But this knowledge is always and forever very useful and necessary, for perception is made perfect in the knowledge of God. For this reason, it is very useful and necessary for such knowledge to be signified always and clearly. Therefore, it is signified now in the time of grace. And so, whether or not there has come a new sign for the same thing, the old sign should not be abandoned if the new one is not opposed to it, either in its existence or in its signification. But there is no sacrament in the new covenant that opposes the Sabbath or that the celebration of the Sabbath opposes. There is, therefore, no reason why the celebration and sign value of the Sabbath should be destroyed. Moreover, because the signification of the Sabbath is commonly useful, because the supremely good God always does what is best in the ordering of the universe, and because there is very little reason when it comes to the supreme order that the effect be made better, it seems necessary that the sign value of the Sabbath never be made void.

*That the authors of Scripture ought to be understood to mean what they most plainly communicated*

4. But someone could explain the aforementioned authorities in another way, that is, mystically, and so he would avoid the above objections. But if someone attempts this mystical interpretation, the following argument can be brought against him. The best teacher teaches in such a way that what he wants to teach his audience by his discourse is more clearly communicated than anything else. Indeed, if something else is more clearly communicated than what he wants to teach, he is not the best teacher, but rather either an amateur or a liar. And if the best

teacher wishes to teach several truths in the same discourse, in his discourse about those many things he will communicate more clearly what he wants the audience to understand more swiftly. But the author of the stated authorities is the best teacher; therefore what is communicated more clearly in his teaching is what he wants us to understand more swiftly. What is communicated most clearly, however, through the aforementioned authorities is that the keeping and celebration of the Sabbath was commanded in such a way that it is everlasting and an everlasting sign by which it must be understood that the Lord himself is God. And this, then, is what the very author of the Law wants to teach us through these authorities.

*Third argument: from the everlasting covenant*

5. Again, the Lord says to Abraham about circumcision, "And my covenant [*pactum*] shall be in your flesh for a perpetual covenant [*foedus*]" (Gn 17.13). But how will it be an everlasting covenant if it itself is not everlasting?

*Fourth argument: from what is commanded without end*

6. Again, if the Lord commands his servant to perform some service without specifying when it should end, it should not belong to the servants to decide when it should end. But the Lord has commanded Israel (in the flesh) to perform circumcision as his servant, and he did not determine when it should end. Rather, on the contrary, he removed its end when he commanded that it be an everlasting covenant and a sign of an everlasting covenant. Therefore, Israel should never stop circumcising. And it seems that the command to circumcise is not only for Israel in the flesh but for others as well, even those who are not of the seed of Abraham. For the Lord said to Abraham, "An infant of eight days old shall be circumcised among you, every manchild in your generations: he that is born in the house, as well as the bought servant, shall be circumcised, and whosoever is not of your stock" (Gn 17.12). So then, circumcision with no fixed end—or rather, with the end abolished—is enjoined upon those who are not of Abraham's stock. It must, therefore, be kept by everyone without end.

### Fifth argument: from the curse

7. Again, when the moral Laws as well as the ceremonial Laws were recounted in Deuteronomy, Moses and the elders of Israel commanded the people, saying, "Keep every commandment that I command you this day" (Dt 27.1). And a little later, in the Septuagint, "Cursed be everyone who does not persevere in all that has been written in the book of this Law, for they have been so written that he may do them" (Dt 27.26). And again a little later, "But if you will not hear the voice of the Lord your God, to keep and to do all his commandments and ceremonies, which I command you this day, all these curses shall come upon you, and overtake you. Cursed shall you be in the city," and so on (Dt 28.15). He teaches, then, that every Law, whether ritual or moral, must be likewise observed in perpetuity; and he subjects to a curse every transgressor of even one of the Laws, exempting no one from keeping the Laws nor making any of the Laws unbinding. Every Law, therefore, must be likewise kept.

### Sixth argument: from the everlasting law

8. Again, according to Augustine, the law is twofold: namely, temporal and eternal. And the temporal law can rightly be changed at times, while the eternal must always be obeyed.[1] But in Leviticus it is said about the Sabbath, "You shall do no servile work therein. It shall be an everlasting ordinance in all your dwellings and generations" (Lv 23.21). Therefore, the Law of the Sabbath is not temporal but must be always kept by everyone everywhere; therefore, it must always be obeyed. In fact, if it were rightly able to be changed, the Law of the Sabbath should have been called a temporal law, not an everlasting one.

### Seventh argument: from the eating of blood

9. Again, before the Law,[2] and in the Law,[3] and after the Law (in the decree of the Apostles)[4] the eating of blood has been prohibited. Therefore, the eating of blood is illicit in every age,

---

1. See Augustine, *On Free Choice* 1.6.14.
2. See Gn 9.4.   3. See Lv 17.10; Dt 12.23.
4. See Acts 15.20, 29.

especially when the reason for not eating it has been expressed in the Law, namely that the life of the flesh is in the blood. But when the reason for the Law obtains, the Law should have force. It is always the case, however, that the life of the flesh is in the blood; therefore, the Law should always have force.

10. So, then, these authorities and similar ones that need not be enumerated at length command the observance of the Laws either not specifying an end or specifying everlasting observance; they seem then to prove that the Laws must be observed forever.

### Eighth argument: that what is rightly done should not be changed

11. The following sort of argument, however, can also be brought to prove the same conclusion, as is clear from the letter of Marcellinus to Augustine.[5] God, who is declared to be the God of the Old Testament, should not be pleased by new sacrifices when the old ones have been rejected. For nothing is able to be corrected, unless it is shown to be wrongly done in the first place. For what is done rightly the first time should in no way be changed, especially because such a change could charge God with inconstancy.

### Ninth argument: Plato's

12. Plato also shows in the *Timaeus* that the stars are immortal in this way, namely, because they are brought together and regulated by good order. For he says, "gods of the gods, whose maker and father I am, you are indeed my works, and although you are corruptible by nature, I want you to be incorruptible. In fact, everything joined is by nature dissoluble although it is not the will of God that what is joined and regulated with good order be destroyed. Therefore, because you are made and generated, you are in no way immortal nor wholly incorruptible. Nevertheless, you will never be destroyed or undergo the necessity of death because my will is a bond of everlasting protection, a bond stronger and more invigorating than those vital

---

5. See Augustine, *Epp.* 136.2 and 138.1.

bonds from which your life is increased and composed."[6] And so according to this argument of Plato, clearly what is joined together and regulated by good order—although it is by nature dissoluble because composed, and finite because generated and having a beginning—will nonetheless never be dissolved or brought to an end because it suits the bounty of the will of God to preserve perpetually in existence what does not lead to corruption by necessity. As it is written in the book of Wisdom, "For God made not death, neither has he pleasure in the destruction of the living. For he created all things that they might be: and he made the nations of the earth for health" (Wis 1.13–14). And the Apostle speaks similarly about the Son of God, our Lord Jesus Christ, through whom all things were made, "[Jesus Christ] was not 'It is' and 'It is not.' But, 'It is,' was in him" (2 Cor 1.19). Only being, therefore, is from God, not non-being; and only those fall into non-being that have in themselves a compulsion to corruption. And so the things that are so made that they do not have in themselves a compulsion to corruption are said by Plato to be made in good order. But they do not have in themselves a compulsion to corruption unless they are made up of contraries or have contraries or require a necessarily corruptible substance.[7] The Old Law, however, is not made up of contraries, nor does it have anything contrary, because it is the sort of thing that, if it had contraries, they would be truth and falsity, and justice and injustice. But in the Law there is no falsity or injustice, but truth and justice are everywhere in it. For the Psalmist says, "Your Law is the truth" (Ps 118.142); and the Apostle says, "Wherefore the Law indeed is holy: and the commandment holy and just and good" (Rom 7.12). And the Law does not necessarily require some necessarily corruptible substance. For the subject of the Law is mankind and the immortal soul of man. And so the Law is neither corrupted nor brought to an end, for the same reason that the celestial bodies are shown never to be corrupted.

---

6. Plato, *Timaeus* 41.

7. The Latin word that I translate here and few lines below as "substance" is not *substantia* but a substantive use of the participle *deferens*. For similar uses, see Grosseteste, *Commentary on Aristotle's Posterior Analytics* 1.7 and 1.14.

### Argument from the Lord's fulfilling and not dissolving of the Law

13. Again, if someone were to put a roof on some building and immediately demolish the finished building, he would complete the building and destroy what he has completed. But the Lord completes the Law and does not destroy it. For he himself says, "Do not think that I am come to destroy the Law or the Prophets. I am not come to destroy, but to fulfill. For amen I say unto you, till heaven and earth pass away, not one jot, or one tittle, of the Law shall pass away, till all be fulfilled" (Mt 5.17–18). Therefore, as has been said, the Lord completes the Law and does not destroy it; and if he himself does not destroy it, neither does anyone else. And so the Law has been completed but not destroyed. Therefore, the Law stands and remains.

### The witness to the permanence of the Law

The permanence of the Law is also attested by the saying "Till heaven and earth pass away, not one jot, or one tittle, of the Law shall pass away." For heaven and earth will pass away at the end of the world when "there will be a new heaven and a new earth" (Rv 21.1). And so, not the least part of the Law will fall away or pass away, until the end of the world should come, and as if foreseeing the adversaries and nullifiers of the Law—not of the whole Law but part of it—as if foreseeing the destroyers of ceremonial precepts, the Lord, in order to confirm the permanence of the whole Law until the end of the age, as if swearing an oath, said, "Amen I say unto you." And intimating that nothing of the Law's integrity will perish, he says, "Not one jot, or one tittle, of the Law shall pass away." But when the Lord said, "Not one jot, or one tittle, of the Law shall pass away," he included rituals in this precept, since they remained up to the Passion of Christ. And so the integrity of the Law was everything contained in the Lord's precept, namely, the historical ceremonial sense as well as the spiritual sense. The historical sense of the Law is much more than "one jot, or one tittle." Therefore, if "not one jot, or one tittle, of the Law shall pass away, till heaven and earth pass," all the more the historical sense will not pass away "till heaven and earth pass." For when the Lord said that nothing of the Law would be destroyed "till heaven and earth pass," part of the Law was ritual observance.

*Argument from the analogy of the building*

14. Again, what wise man would destroy a building he had just finished? For if he intended to destroy it after a brief time, why would he finish it? Because, therefore, the Son of God is the highest wisdom, he did not immediately destroy the Law which he himself made perfect.

*That I cannot use either the Apostles or catholic writers to respond to the arguments*

15. In responding to the objections here enumerated, it is not appropriate to offer assertions from apostolic writings or sacred commentators. The reason is that these objections belong to those arguing against the very Apostles and against our Catholic commentators, and against all who dissolved ritual Laws but were not able in responding to the objections to support themselves by a simple assertion or exposition of authorities from the Old Testament and the Gospel. Moreover, they did not strengthen their exposition by either irrefutable argument or plain witness of the Old Law or of the Gospel. And so, because in this disputation we take on the person of the Apostles and commentators dissolving and destroying the ceremonial Laws, we cannot for a response assert, against those wishing to prove the observance of the ritual Laws, anything that we cannot show to be true either by irrefutable argument or the obvious authority of the Old Testament or the Gospel.

*Thirteenth argument: from the example of Christ*

16. Again, he who says that he remains in Christ ought to walk just as Christ himself walked. For "he suffered leaving an example for us that we may follow in his footsteps" (1 Pt 2.21). For indeed Christ's every action is a lesson for us, that we may learn in his whole way of acting what we should do to imitate him. In addition, Gregory in his *Dialogue* says, "Everything that our Redeemer did in his mortal body furnished an example for us, that we may follow his footsteps according to the measure of

our abilities and tread upon the road of the present life without stumbling."[8] But Christ observed the sacraments of the Old Law together with that of the Gospel; for he was circumcised and baptized, ate the paschal lamb, and handed over his own body to be eaten by his disciples. In order, therefore, to imitate him and follow his example, we also are obliged to observe the sacraments of both Testaments. Truly, what is the distinction whereby we imitate him in some things but not in his observance of this?

### A distinction of the adversaries of the Scriptures

17. And so by arguments of this sort and perhaps by much more compelling ones (that are unknown to my small mind) the pseudo-apostles were able to prove their position that the Laws must be observed together with the sacraments enjoined by the Gospel. People of this sort, then, are the pseudo-adversaries of both Testaments because, although they wish to observe both at the same time, they destroy both.

## CHAPTER 3

### The knowing opponents

1. There are also other opponents of the Sacred Scripture, some knowing and some ignorant. For certain people knowingly oppose the Sacred Page, such as the Manichees and the Marcionites, who condemn the Law and the Prophets, and such as the opponent of the Law and the Prophets who said that the God of the Mosaic Law and of its Prophets is not the true God but the worst demon. Against this opponent Augustine wrote a book entitled *Against Adversaries of the Law and the Prophets*. These people try to prove that many assertions which have been written on the Sacred Page are false, cruel, unjust, obscene and foul, empty and devoid of usefulness and reasonability, of which God could not be the author because he himself is the highest truth, kindness, justice, purity, beauty, the fullness of utility, and wholly reasonable. The false accusations against the purity of the Scripture by this kind of adversary are innumerable. For there could

---

8. Gregory the Great, *Dialogues* 1.9.

scarcely be found a small part of the Scripture in which their sly and impious subtlety would not be able to fabricate a false accusation. Hence it would be laborious beyond measure and lengthy to investigate and refute the false accusations that this sort of adversary has made, is making, or has been able to make against the Scriptures. But when they impiously make these accusations, there must be a diligent and pious response, just as Augustine made in the book that I mentioned, *Against the Adversaries of the Law and the Prophets*, wherein he responded to his opponent's individual blasphemies and accusations one by one.

### The ignorant opponents

2. There are also those who ignorantly oppose the Sacred Page, some having a knowledge of the Scripture, some profoundly ignorant of it. For the ones who have knowledge of the Scripture are nonetheless ignorant of the fact that their heresy is contrary to Scripture because they have fallen into heresy on account of prideful arrogance. Not knowing their heresy is contrary to Scripture, they try to demonstrate it from the Scriptures and think that they have done so. Others, lacking a knowledge of the Scriptures, assert many positions contrary to it, such as philosophers who held that the world lacks a beginning in time and exists everlastingly, who taught reincarnation, or who said that there is a single soul of the whole world and of all living beings, and similar positions. Again to investigate their errors, or even to enumerate and disprove them, and expose their sophistry, is beyond measure lengthy and difficult. For to do this would be to argue against all heresies and impious errors of the philosophers.

### Argument that the Law ought never to have existed

3. There are or could be, moreover, still other adversaries of the Scriptures. These might say that the Old Law was never necessary, indeed, that it would have been better had it never been. For because the Incarnation of the Son of God, and the Passion of the Incarnate (and nothing else), is the liberation of the human race, and because, then, the Incarnation and Passion of the Son of God is the greatest benefit shown to the human race, it seems and could seem fitting to some that so great a benefit be

given by so great a benefactor after the fall of the human race all the more quickly. For, indeed, the longer lasting a good is, the better it is. And however much more quickly every benefit is given, and with fewer requests for it, it is that much more generous, more gracious, more agreeable, and more praiseworthy. The liberation of the human race, however, and the opening of the gates of paradise through the Passion of Christ, the more quickly it was done after the fall of humanity, the longer it has lasted and so is better. It is fitting that the benefit of the best benefactor be the best of its sort. It is appropriate, therefore, that the benefit of the redemption of the human race not have been delayed by the Son of God, the best benefactor, but all the more quickly bestowed in order that because of the timing of redemption there may be an increase in the goodness of the benefit and its value. This much can be gathered from the words of Seneca in his book *On Kindness:* very often benefits which are not very valuable in themselves become valuable because of their timing.[9] And in the Proverbs of Solomon it is written, "Say not to your friend, 'Go, and come again, and tomorrow I will give to you,' when you can give at present" (Prv 3.28). For truly the delaying of the best and hoped-for benefit afflicts the soul. For likewise it is written, "Hope that is deferred afflicts the soul" (Prv 13.12). And thus the affliction itself of the soul having to wait is a certain lessening of the expected good and a diminution in the value of the benefit. Therefore, the benefit of the liberation of the human race ought to have been given before the time of the Law, when the Son of God, the bestower of this benefit, knew and was able to bestow it before the time of the Law. And if it had been given before the Law, the Law would always have been superfluous. With these arguments and others like them, the opponents of the sacred Scripture clamor and roar.

CHAPTER 4

*A proof that the rational creature had law from the beginning*

1. So that, therefore, it may become clearer how this opponent's illusory and false accusations are to be rendered void,

---

9. Seneca, *On Kindness* 1.11.5.

and that the observance of the ceremonial precepts of the Old Law is now, in the time of grace, not only superfluous but also harmful—though their observance before the time of grace was useful and necessary for a coarse and hard people—and also that the unwritten natural law ought to have taken precedence over every written law, it seems that I ought to begin a little deeper analysis. And so I say that every rational creature naturally desires to be happy. For as Augustine asserts in the thirteenth book of *On the Trinity*, this is the common will of all from which none falls away, and it is known to all and in all.[10] The creature is able to be good from the goodness of its own creation; otherwise, it would be necessarily wretched, always seeking its end and never possessing it. For a thing would have been created in vain if the end of any natural appetite is the possession of a good that the appetite longs for, and if it should necessarily lack the possession of this good, this appetite is frustrated. Happiness, however, is to have all that one wants and to want nothing wrongly. And this is not accomplished for the rational creature unless with a pure intelligence it sees the uncreated light itself in uncreated light and sees also all creatures in their uncreated ideas, eternally expressed in uncreated light, and loves with an ordered love both the Creator, known without darkness, and creatures, individually and as a whole. The rational creature should have the firmest certitude of this loving understanding, or understanding love, that is, the firmest certitude of this enjoyment, which ought to be held without change, diminishment, or end. In addition this fullness of beatitude cannot be had by man so long as he is burdened with a corruptible and mortal body, and it cannot be had by the human soul—which has been divested of a body and naturally longs to be vested once more with its own body, made incorruptible—until it should put that body on again. This fullness of happiness, then, cannot be had by man until there comes the general resurrection of bodies. Man is not able, therefore, to acquire happiness by himself, because he cannot rise from the dead by himself. If man had remained without sin, he would have come

---

10. See Augustine, *On the Trinity* 13, *passim*.

to this full happiness without the body either dying or rising. In no other way can the rational creature acquire by itself alone such full happiness.

*Another reason (that the rational creature cannot achieve beatitude on its own)*

2. From the fact that the creature is made from nothing, it is possible for it to pass away and even to return to nothing, as is clear from the above-cited authority of Plato. Augustine also says in his letter to Dioscorus, "It stands to reason that things pass away or are able to pass away on account of nothing other than the fact that they have been made from nothing. So, then, what is in them and that they exist and remain and even by their own progress are ordained to the embrace of the whole pertains wholly to the goodness and power of God, who is the Maker of all, who is also able to make from nothing not only something but even something great."[11]

3. Again, in the twelfth book of *The City of God*, "If God should withdraw his 'constructive power,' so to speak, from things, they will no longer exist, just as before they were made, they were not. But I say 'before' not in time but in eternity."[12] Again, the same work in the fourteenth book has, "A nature could not be corrupted by a defect unless it has been made from nothing. Because a nature exists, it has been made by God; but that it falls away from God comes from the fact that it has been made from nothing."[13] Therefore, a rational creature cannot by itself alone receive the most firm certitude that the duration of its happiness would not be diminished; therefore, the rational creature cannot by its own power be happy.

*Another reason for the same position, this time from the fact that the rational creature is not an infinite reality*

4. In addition, the above-mentioned fullness of happiness is an infinite reality, for in that fullness is an understanding of in-

---

11. Augustine, *Ep.* 118.15.
12. Augustine, *The City of God* 12.26.
13. Ibid., 14.13.

finite uncreated ideas. Also in it is the understanding of infinite numbers and figures, and things that are necessarily incidental to them. The contemplation of God, as well, is not a moderate but a greater love and an ordered love for the things that are known—and it is said that they are infinite—both individually and as a whole. And this knowing love or loving knowledge cannot be finite, because it has been distributed among infinite individual objects known and loved, and it will remain without end. Every created power, however, is finite; so it is clear that it could not of itself generate anything infinite either in size or extension. Although someone could doubt whether some created power is able to be infinite in duration alone, no one, nevertheless, doubts that created power is finite and so cannot be infinite either in size or extension. Finite power, therefore, cannot do something infinite by its own power. A rational creature, then, cannot by itself acquire the above-mentioned fullness of happiness, because this fullness includes in itself infinity. Therefore, for a rational creature to become fully happy, it is necessary that it be united with an uncreated infinite power, which bestows upon it the infinite fullness of happiness. A rational creature, then, cannot have happiness unless God grant it, who alone is wholly infinite power, by which and through which and in which the creature itself of finite power receives an infinite act of happiness.

### *The happiness ought to be given to one who first obeys*

5. But because the rational creature has free will and is bound to obey its Creator freely, it would be unjust and disordered for the good of happiness to be given to a disobedient rational creature or even before it had offered a free act of obedience to its Creator. Therefore, because God is supremely just and does everything in the most orderly manner, he does not confer happiness on the rational creature until it should offer to him an obedient act of free will. Therefore, to be happy the rational creature must deserve it by its obedience, and it suits the immense divine goodness to reward the humility of obedience with the fullness of happiness.

### Explanation as to why happiness ought to be given only to someone who is obedient

6. But perhaps someone will say that it would be consistent enough with the divine goodness and generosity to give full happiness to the rational creature who has only the goodness of God's creation, that is, who has free choice but has not performed any actions from this free choice. For truly the act of free choice is of a proper power and is not a matter of the essence of the creature. Therefore, someone will say that it is fitting to bestow happiness upon someone who has the power of freedom of choice without actually using it.

### Proof from the vice of idleness

7. But this appears to be plainly false because God does not approve idleness but rather condemns it. For truly nature is never idle and does nothing idle. Idleness itself, moreover, is a vice. Indeed, not to do good when you can is a lessening of goodness, which cannot be altogether free of vice. If the rational creature, however, had existed for some time in its primordial state in such a way that it had not exercised its own free will, during that time it would have been idle, especially because it could have exercised a good act most easily, for grace was then working with it, so long as it never wanted grace to be absent. This unexercised free will, then, is idle and therefore a vice; it is not approved by the Truth but rather disapproved. For the Truth itself said that we will give an account for every idle word we utter.[14] It does not suit divine justice, I say, that happiness be given to such a creature.

### Another reason (that happiness ought to be given only to the obedient): the rational creature would not remain in what it received

8. Besides, if the rational creature did not immediately progress in goodness through a voluntary act of free will, it would not remain in what it received at creation. For whoever receives a power, in receiving it, also receives the actualization of this power

---

14. See Mt 12.36.

when he has the opportunity to act; and he who gives well a power, gives it in such a way that the recipient can act from the power when he has the opportunity to act. Whoever does not act from a power that he has received, when the opportunity to act presents itself, does not remain in what he received but rather falls from what he received. He even abuses his power when he could use it well, but nevertheless does not want to use it. Not only does he not merit a reward, but, rather, he merits a punishment, even the loss of the power that he received. The rational creature, however, at his first creation had immediately the opportunity to act well through the power of free choice that he had received. For the Creator in his bounty did not refuse the rational creature the assistance of his grace, and with this grace it was fittingly able through the power of free choice to turn an act of its own love toward the God of all, as well as toward its neighbor and itself. If, therefore, the rational creature did not immediately do this, then neither did it remain in what it had received, nor did it use well, but rather abused, the power that it had received. Consider this example. Visible color, when the light of the sun has been poured out upon it, if it were not to produce its own appearance in the air before it and in the eye beholding it, would not remain in what it received. For it received the ability to generate itself in the onlooker before it when the light of the sun has been poured out upon it. Likewise, freedom of will has received the ability when grace is present to it to burst forth in an act of ordered love.

9. Again, the dignity for which someone is praised cannot be a small good, because nothing is praiseworthy except for a good. Hence, an increase in this sort of dignity is a great good. But if happiness were given to the rational creature before it had obeyed God through an act of free choice, it would be less praiseworthy than if happiness were conferred on it through the merit of its own praiseworthy act. For truly it is more praiseworthy to have merited something by a praiseworthy act than to have received it for doing nothing. So that, therefore, the rational creature be fully praiseworthy, it was necessary that it not receive happiness except after a meritorious act. Nor did it suit the generosity of God to take away from his own creature the means to be more praiseworthy. If, however, through granting

happiness before it was merited, God had taken away from the rational creature the opportunity of meriting it, he would have taken away from it the means to become more praiseworthy. And so he would not be most generous because he would not have bestowed every gift which he could have fittingly bestowed.

### An example

10. For, in fact, a king bestows a greater benefit upon the soldier to whom he offers a greater opportunity for meriting the reward of victory. It does not, then, suit the generosity of God to take away the opportunity for meriting happiness, and it is not consonant with good order to confer happiness on someone who is not yet praiseworthy, especially because the act of happiness is to praise God without end. For, when we do this, that is, when we praise, we will be happy, just as Saint Augustine said.[15]

## CHAPTER 5

### Distinction of types of commandments

1. It is clear, therefore, that happiness should not be bestowed except upon the rational creature because of the merit of obedience. Now, obedience is the virtue by which commands are done out of love. But the commandments are twofold: indeed, certain commandments are intrinsically just, and they are known to be just of themselves or can be proved to be just immediately from truths known of themselves. This sort of commandment includes: "love God with all your strength";[16] "honor your father and mother"; and "you shall not kill" (Ex 20.12–13); and other commandments of this kind. Other commandments, however, are not intrinsically just or unjust, but in themselves indifferent. They become just and obligatory only because of the authority of the Lawgiver. This sort of command includes: "But of the tree of knowledge of good and evil, you shall not eat" (Gn 2.17); and "You shall not plough with an ox and an ass" (Dt 22.10–11); and other commandments of this sort.

---

15. See Augustine, *Ep.* 120.23; and Ps.-Augustine, *Meditations* 25.
16. See Dt 6.5.

### What the natural law is

The whole collection, however, of the first kind of commandments, that is, of actions that are intrinsically just and therefore commanded, is the natural law. In fact, the natural law is intrinsically and naturally just, and it naturally suits any rational creature to carry it out with actions that accord with the kind of thing it is.

### What the positive law (or the law of deeds) is:
### A demonstration that the natural law need not be written in the beginning or even dictated from without, and that only the positive law need be dictated from without

2. The collection of the other precepts, however, can be called a law of deeds. Indeed, every rational creature, when it is considered in the state of its first creation uncorrupted by sin—that is, by turning away from the highest good—could, by a movement of right reason uncorrupted, know the whole natural law, inscribe it immediately on its own mind by reasoning without labor or delay, and retain it inscribed on the tables of the heart without forgetfulness. Further, the rational creature could not only know the precepts of the natural law in this way, but also know that those who keep the natural law and the law of deeds are to be rewarded with happiness, but those who do not are worthy of punishment. The rational creature, therefore, considered in the uncorrupt state of its (first) creation, does not need any outwardly written law, since the natural law is unforgettably written on its mind by a movement of right reason. And if something from the law of deeds were enjoined upon the rational creature, it would be able to understand that precept without difficulty and to remember it without forgetting. Any outwardly written law would therefore be superfluous to such a creature, and that the natural law be dictated to it from the outside would also be superfluous. The law of deeds, however, ought to be dictated to the rational creature from the outside, for it could not know in matters that are indifferent what its Creator wants it to do unless he tells it; and unless the Creator expressly commands something, it would have no greater reason to be done than not to be done.

### How the natural law had been commanded from the beginning

Concerning the natural law, on the other hand, the rational creature could know by its own rational movement that the Creator wants it to be done because it is naturally and in itself just and because it is naturally just that it ought to be observed. The rational creature knows also that the very will of the Creator—that the natural law be done because it is just—is its command.

### That the positive law must be added to the natural law for full obedience

3. That obedience, however, is more perfect which spontaneously fulfills each kind of law rather than only one. And that obedience is more humble which obeys a command about an indifferent matter (which does not have a reason that it ought to be done except the authority of the commander) than that which obeys a precept that is justified in itself. In order to prove the perfect obedience of man and to crown him with the merit of consummate obedience, it befitted the wisdom and goodness of God to give man a precept in an indifferent matter, so that when he fulfills at the same time the law of deeds or the positive law together with the natural law, man may present to the Creator consummate and most humble obedience and may merit that perfect crown of happiness. Whence Augustine wrote in the eighth book of his *Literal Commentary on Genesis*, "But it was necessary that man was prohibited from something when he was placed under the Lord God, so that he might have the virtue of deserving his own Lord by obedience. I can most truly say that that obedience is the only virtue for every rational creature acting under the power of God and that it is the first and greatest vice of pride to want to use one's own power for ruin, and the name of this vice is disobedience. There would be nothing from which man would know and perceive that he possesses the Lord, unless something be commanded of him."[17]

4. Again, Augustine writes in the same work, "Man was banned from that tree, which was not evil, so that the very keeping of a

---

17. Augustine, *Literal Commentary on Genesis* 8.6.

command be good for him, and the transgression of it, evil. And how evil is disobedience alone could not be better or more diligently commended, when on account of it man was made guilty of iniquity, because against the prohibition he touched that thing which, if he had touched when he was not forbidden to, he would certainly not have sinned."[18]

5. Again he writes in the same work, "Indeed when someone touches something that would not harm him (if he or anyone else has not been forbidden to do so) whenever it is touched, why is it prohibited, unless so that intrinsic goodness of obedience itself and the intrinsic evil of disobedience itself be made manifest?"[19]

*Epilogue*

6. It is clear, therefore, how when man lived in paradise not yet corrupted by sin it was necessary that he not be given any written law, and that the natural law be dictated or commanded by no one from the outside, and that some positive law be promulgated without being written. It is clear, also, that the natural law is naturally prior to the positive law. Whence we do not read in Genesis that the Lord gave man in paradise the natural law either by a written mandate or one promulgated from the outside. We read there, nevertheless, that the Lord gave him a positive law, not in writing but by command, namely, that he not eat of the tree of the knowledge of good and evil, which was in the middle of paradise.

*It is fitting that the positive law must be added even*
*to those who always kept the natural law*

And because it is already clear that the fullest and most humble obedience consists in observing the law of deeds, or the positive law, it is manifestly appropriate that the positive law be added to the natural law both before the written Law and in the written Law. On account of this is resolved the charge of those who disparage the Mosaic Law as lacking a rationale for many

---

18. Ibid., 8.13.
19. Ibid.

of its commands. For, they say, there is no reason why someone ought not plow with an ox and an ass or wear clothes woven of wool and linen, and it did not suit, they say, the supreme wisdom of God to give the sort of commands that have no rationale. They do not understand, however, that the rationality of testing and achieving perfect obedience consists in the observance of indifferent mandates that of themselves lack rationality. And these mandates have besides this solid rationale also the mystery of a holy meaning.

7. Whether, however, there would have been immediately given to an angel at his first creation a precept of some positive law together with the natural law written within it, I have not discovered written anywhere.

*It seems fitting that a positive law would have been given even to an angel if it had remained in the natural law for some time without temptation*

It seems, however, a fitting arrangement that a positive law for the testing and achieving of perfect obedience be enjoined upon a rational creature that has endured for some time without alluring temptation in the observance of the natural law, just as has been done in the case of man, who was told, "You shall not eat of the tree of the knowledge of good and evil" after he had persevered in the observance of the natural law and had not been seduced by any temptation from the time of his creation outside of paradise to when he was afterwards established in paradise.[20] For as it has been said, the natural law is naturally prior, and there is more reason to observe it than the positive law, and in the observance of the positive law is a more perfect obedience. On account of this, an angel should have been tested first in the observance of the natural law, as in the naturally prior, and then in the observance of perfect obedience. Further, it was necessary that it be proved first whether or not it would observe a law that had more of a rationale to be

20. See Gn 2.7–8: "Then the Lord God formed man of dust from the ground, and breathed into his nostrils the breath of life; and man became a living being. And the Lord God planted a garden in Eden, in the east; and there he put the man whom he had formed."

observed; then whether or not it would observe a law that had less. For if it would not remain in the natural law, much less would it remain in a positive law. For, how would the one who does not observe what seemingly ought to be more observed, observe what seemingly ought to be less observed? Therefore, a positive law ought to be enjoined upon the creature who remains for some time in the observance of the natural law so that he may increase in perfection.

CHAPTER 6

*That the strongest victor be immediately crowned*

1. Similarly it seems to suit the order of justice that a rational creature would be immediately crowned with the reward of happiness and would be confirmed for persevering in the good, if it was at first tested and—when it was allured to sin by the strongest temptation than which none could be stronger—it resisted that temptation and conquered it. For if it conquered that temptation than which none can be stronger, it has fought rightly and has accomplished the greatest victory. And what remains after the greatest victory except the acceptance of the prize? This has been done in the case of the holy angels who conquered the strongest temptation in the beginning; for they were crowned immediately after the victory with the reward of happiness and were confirmed in the good of perseverance, just as Gregory testifies in his eighth homily on Ezekiel when he says, "because some fell, the holy angels stood fast in their beatitude and received as a reward that they would no longer be able to fall at all; their nature is solidified as if in a lump of crystal because it can no longer change."[21] In the *Morals* also Gregory says that when Lucifer fell, the holy angels merited never to lose their royal rank by falling.[22] In fact, then, a positive law was not given to the angels, because the evil angels immediately transgressed the natural law and would never again keep it; a positive law would have been enjoined upon them in vain. But the good angels, be-

21. Gregory the Great, *Homilies on the Prophet Ezekiel* 1.7.18.
22. See Gregory the Great, *Morals on Job* 34.7.13.

cause they immediately accomplished the greatest victory, were immediately confirmed in their happiness, and the burden of a law was not appropriate in such a state because to test obedience was not fitting then. It was not a time for meriting a reward but rather only for receiving a reward already merited.

### *That the angels who stood fast conquered the strongest temptation*

2. Clearly, however, the holy angels conquered the strongest temptation. In fact there are two kinds of temptation: one when something delightful attracts someone to sin, the other when something terrible impels someone to sin because of a fear that it would be present unless he sinned. In the first case, then, the strongest kind of temptation occurs when something supremely delightful presents itself, and so someone unjustly desires it, and when a great authority has made a powerful case for this desire. In the second case, the strongest kind of temptation occurs when something most terrible presents itself, and will fall upon someone if he does not sin. Here too a great authority forcefully persuades him that sinning is better than suffering the impending evil.

### *Which temptation is strongest*

The strongest kind of temptation of the first sort, however, is incomparably more powerful than the strongest kind of temptation of the second sort. For something most delightful is incomparably more delightful than something most terrible is terrible. God, indeed, is the supreme good and supremely delightful; and the punishment of Gehenna is the supreme punishment and supremely terrible.[23]

### *That the highest good is a greater good than an evil can be evil*

But the good and delight that are God are incomparably better and more delightful than that terrible punishment is bitter. In fact, no evil, either of sin or punishment, can be as evil as

---

23. See Grosseteste, *On the Ten Commandments* 1, "De primo mandato."

the highest good is good, nor as evil as the whole of creation is good. For every evil is nothing but the corruption of a good, and the corruption of a particular good is as evil as that good is good before it is corrupted. But only a created good can be corrupted; therefore, an evil cannot be a greater evil than a corruptible good is good. All other things being equal, then, in the strongest temptations of the two types of temptation, that temptation which attracts someone with something supremely delightful is incomparably stronger than that which terrifies someone with something supremely terrible. Therefore, the strongest temptation that can exist is simply that temptation which draws someone's desire with something supremely delightful when the influence of a great authority has been joined to this enticement.

### How the angels were tempted[24]

3. But the holy angels were tempted with this kind of temptation, for the apostate angel desired divinity—this must be believed by the authority of Scripture. For one cannot deduce by rational argument what were the individual, freely willed deeds of men and angels, but they can only be known either by those seeing and perceiving them as they happen or by those believing those who saw them happen. We, then, who have not seen the first sinner fall away, must trust the authority of the Scriptures dictated through the Holy Spirit on his apostasy, who knew his apostasy before it happened. Similarly it is necessary to believe the authority of the Scriptures on the sin of man. The first angel apostate, then, desired divinity as it was said, for he wanted to be similar to the Most High, not by the similarity of imitation, but by that of equality.[25] This is clear from what he said in his heart, that he would exalt his own seat above the stars of God and that he would ascend above the heights of the clouds.[26] For if he had desired only the similarity of imitation, he would have thought not about going above the clouds and stars of God but

---

24. For another account of the fall of angels, see *On the Cessation of the Laws* 3.2.3.
    25. See Is 14.14; and Grosseteste, *Hexaëmeron* 8.1.1.
    26. See Is 14.13–14.

about being equal with them. But he could not be similar to the Most High by a similarity of equality, unless he were a god equal to the Most High. And this fact could not be unknown to that apostate, because it was written about him that he was "full of wisdom, and perfect in beauty, in the pleasures of the paradise of God" (Ezek 28.12). Therefore he knowingly desired divinity, which is the supreme good, and supremely delightful. And I believe that it did not escape him that for him to be equal to God and to be a god was impossible. For often perverse minds desire inordinately and ardently what they know they cannot have.

4. So then, he knowingly desired the supreme delight, although impossible for him. But what he desired by love[27] he understood with his intellect, and what he understood with his intellect, he said in his mind. For, in fact, the rational incorporeal nature's speaking is that nature's understanding. He understood not only the good which he unjustly desired, but also his own desire and himself desiring, and he approved himself as such. Further, by the very act of desiring, in a certain way he said that what he desired ought to be desired. So says and proves Anselm in his book, *On Truth*, "By the very fact that someone does something, he says and indicates that he ought to do it."[28]

### That Lucifer was especially authoritative

Therefore, both in approving word and in deed, he said that equality with God ought to be desired. Among rational creatures he was also a most greatly authoritative person. For he was, as was said, "full of wisdom, and perfect in beauty" (Ezek 28.12), whose covering was every precious stone, who walked perfectly in his ways, just as Ezekiel says, "from the day of [his] creation, until iniquity was found in [him]" (Ezek 28.15). And likewise Job says, "He is the beginning of the ways of God" (Jb 40.14). On this verse Gregory says in the *Morals*, "God established him first whom he made more excellent than the rest of the angels."[29] And a little later, "He, then, who sinned without forgiveness was

---

27. Latin: *affectus*.
28. Anselm, *Dialogue on Truth* 9.
29. Gregory the Great, *Morals on Job* 32.23.47.

damned, because he had been made incomparably great."[30] The other angels spiritually heard—that is, they understood with their minds—the aforementioned words of that apostate.

5. Lucifer's statement about desiring divinity, expressed in his actions and in his mental word, itself persuaded others to desire to be divine. The other angels heard the most forceful persuasion because it was not only in word but also in deed asserting that divinity ought to be desired. And this was not the persuasion of just anybody but of him who held among the creatures of God a place more eminent in brilliance as well as knowledge. As Gregory says, "He had transcended the brilliance of the other angels, and therefore was called a cherub by the prophet, because there was no doubt that he had transcended all the others in knowledge." It was proposed, therefore, to the other angels to desire illicitly the highest good and the supremely delightful, and it would be desired with the addition of a most forceful persuasion. They were tempted, then, by the strongest temptation that could be.

### Epilogue

6. And so the holy angels, who were in no way swayed or moved by this temptation, but rather chose and preferred to be humbly subject to God rather than to be equal to him, conquered this most strong temptation and accomplished the greatest victory. Fittingly, therefore, as was indicated above and confirmed by authority, were they immediately rewarded with the prize of happiness and confirmed in the good after carrying out such a victory.

### That the evil angel was eternally damned because he was incomparably evil

Fittingly also was that apostate damned, because, as we remembered above, Gregory had said, "He, then, who sinned without forgiveness was damned, because he had been made incomparably great."[31]

---

30. Ibid.   31. Ibid.

*Another reason that angels cannot be redeemed as men are*

7. Furthermore, neither he nor those who sinned under his influence can be reconciled. The case with angels is just like that with men. Man could not be reconciled except through the God-man, who was able to die, and through whose justice what had been lost through man's sin was restored to God. As man, he was not only one in nature with the rest of men, but was clearly also of the same race with them. All men have been generated from the flesh of one man, who is the parent of all, and all are one in him. For just as all men are one man because of their common species, so because of their communion in the same race and in the same first parent of all, they are in a certain sense that parent himself, namely, Adam. As with men, so damned angels could not be reconciled except through a God-angel who could die, and who would be not only of one nature but also of one race with the angels who were to be reconciled. This much is most clear from Anselm's book *Why God Man*.[32]

*Epilogue*

8. It is clear, then, from what has already been said that every rational creature received at his first creation the natural law inscribed on his mind, and that the sinful angels immediately transgressed the natural law. For the natural law requires every creature who can love to love his Creator incomparably more than himself, to wish unfailingly to be subject to him, and not to turn away from this will, either because of impending terror or alluring delight. It is also contrary to nature that the creature be made equal to the Creator, and contrary to reason that the rational creature desire this equality. The sinful angels, therefore, when they desired equality with God under the leadership of the Devil, violated mainly the command to love God above all and to adore him, which is the principal command of the natural law.

*Explanation of the angels' temptation*

9. But perhaps it will seem to someone that the angels who stood fast had not been tempted by the fallen angel, because,

---

32. See Anselm, *Why God Man*, Epilogue 2.22.

as James says, "But every man is tempted by his own concupiscence, being drawn away and allured" (Jas 1.14). But the remaining angels, the argument goes, were not moved by concupiscence. For if their reason had permitted their will actually to desire something which their reason had not first judged to be desirable, they would have sinned, because they had it in their power to rule in this way by the command of reason and to restrain their will, which would not be moved to desire something without the naturally prevenient judgment of uncorrupted reason. If, therefore, they had permitted even the least movement of concupiscence against the order of reason to arise within themselves, they would have sinned. They would have abused the power of reason and free choice that they had been given, and would not be able to correct their error by themselves or return to their prior state, because they could not make themselves better. Nor should they be redeemed, and so they would have irreparably fallen with the sinful angel.

*Response*

10. It should be recognized, however, that not every temptation causes a movement of concupiscence in the one who is tempted. For we read in the Gospel that Our Lord Jesus Christ was tempted by the Devil, but he was not moved by any movement of concupiscence at the suggestions of the Devil.[33] For he did not have the tinder of sin, concupiscence, any power competing against reason, or the prevenient judgment of reason. Nevertheless, the tempter tried insofar as he was able to bring about in the Lord some appetite contrary to reason. The Devil tempted, and the Lord was tempted, but he was not tempted in such a way that the tempter brought about his intended effect. The Lord, therefore, accomplished a greater victory. For when someone is strongly urged or drawn to do something, he conquers more bravely if he yields not at all to the one urging or drawing him. What James says must be understood to refer to some effect of temptation brought about in the tempted.

33. See Mt 4.1.

*That the angels were tempted is clear
from the Apocalypse*

That the angels who stood fast were tempted is plain from what is written in the Apocalypse, "And there was a great battle in heaven; Michael and his angels fought with the dragon, and the dragon fought and his angels: And they prevailed not, neither was their place found any more in heaven" (Rv 12.7). There is no fight except where there are parties striving against each other. The dragon and his angels and Michael and his angels, therefore, opposed each other.

*Concerning the manner of their temptation*

But what was this opposition, if not the temptation made at the angels' beginning, about which we spoke earlier? The Devil did not tempt the angels who stood fast as the delights of the senses often tempt us, that is, when the delights alone are grasped but do not intend to move the will to experience them. For the Devil intended to move the angels who stood fast in such a way that they might desire something inordinately. Indeed, he was proud, and on account of this he wanted the other angels' desires, wills, and acts to be obedient and obsequious to the command of his will. Pride, in fact, always desires this, because it is the love of his own preeminence, whereby he wants to be subject to no one and to be before everyone. The Devil, therefore, wanted this to happen in the other angels, and if it happened, they would have sinned; they would have subjected themselves to the command of his perverse will.

11. In addition, because he was proud, he was jealous. For from pride, which is the love of one's own preeminence, there is immediately born jealousy, which is the love of lowering others. The Devil, therefore, wanted the other angels to be deprived of their position by the corruption of sin. Hence he wanted them to sin by desiring along with him to be divine. For, because he was jealous of them, he wanted them to desire strongly what they nevertheless could not obtain, and when they desired but did not obtain, they would be consumed by grief and sadness. Because he wretchedly wanted this, he tried to work this in them by his own influence, as we said above.

### That man was most strongly tempted

12. The first man was similarly tempted by the strongest temptation. Man could not be more strongly tempted, for it was proposed to him that he desire to be divine, and this was suggested by someone most shrewdly convincing.

### That he was most strongly tempted by pride, curiosity, and the concupiscence of the flesh[34]

In this he had been tempted most strongly by the pride of life. He had been tempted also by the strongest kind of temptation regarding the sin of curiosity, for the distinction of good from evil very much contains a love of knowing. This knowledge of what is better is also a knowledge of what is more honorable and more wonderful, for there is a power better and more honorable and more wonderful than every created nature. Man had been also tempted in the strongest way possible in his state by the temptation of the concupiscence of the flesh. For no experience could be proposed to him sweeter than what he had already experienced blamelessly by four senses, namely, sight, hearing, smell, and touch. To the healthy sense of sight, nothing is sweeter than the light of the sun, and to the ear, what could be sweeter than the harmony of the birds in paradise? He had also heard the voice of the Lord, and I do not know whether something sweeter than that could flow into the ears. Also, what could please the nostrils more than the smells of paradise? And for the sense of touch, what could be softer than human flesh of a most mild complexion? But if he were promised something sweeter than he had experienced, something that could be experienced by these four senses, I believe that he would understand the promise to be false because the experience of the sweetest sensations had taught him that the greatest sweetness for the senses was in them.

13. Furthermore, even if he could have experienced by the four aforementioned senses something more delightful than he had experienced, he would have experienced it without sinning, because his sensitive power before sin was not libidinous

---

34. See 1 Jn 2.16.

or voluptuous, and he would not have been forbidden to experience something with these senses. But perhaps he had not tasted anything up to this point.

### *The craftiness of the temptation*

On account of this he had been able to be persuaded somehow that the sweetness of tasting of the forbidden tree was the greatest, even that to taste of it was forbidden precisely so that he would not be equal in power and knowledge to the one who had forbidden him. The Devil, moreover, could not have deceived man through the mouth of another animal so cunningly as he could through the mouth of the serpent. For if the Devil had spoken by assuming human form, the cunning of his deceitful spirit could have easily been perceived, because it is true that man and woman alike would have known that there existed no men besides the two of them. But someone might object: God had earlier spoken to him under the appearance of man, and so likewise the Devil could more cunningly deceive man by speaking to him in human form just as God had earlier done, because he could, speaking thus, be believed to be God. To this it must be said that perhaps to speak so was not permitted to the Devil.

14. Furthermore, when God spoke to the ancients in human form he made known by some infallible signs that the true God was speaking to them through a created subject; and the Devil could not do this.

### *That man would have been confirmed,*
### *if he had stood fast*

15. Besides, if the Devil by speaking in the form of a man wanted to be considered God, it would not suit his particular aim in deceiving man. For he intended to persuade him to act against the precept that God had commanded, and it could not be probable that God would so quickly urge him not to do that which he had so recently and strictly commanded. Therefore, if the Devil had appeared in human form, he would have been more suspect. He would not have sounded as familiar speaking through the mouth of another animal rather than that of

a serpent, because no other animal had so great a familiarity with man. Hence, John Damascene says in his book *On the Orthodox Faith,* "But the serpent was accustomed to man, because it clung to him more than to the others and was joined to him by its pleasing movements. Through the serpent, the chief Devil made the worst suggestion to the first parents."[35]

16. Clearly man, as he was before sin, could not be drawn by a greater temptation. Therefore, as it was said above about the confirmation of the angels who stood fast, certainly man would have been confirmed in the same way if he had resisted this greatest temptation. As Anselm says in his book *Why God Man:*

> God would have confirmed the first men if they had not sinned as they did, just as he confirmed the angels who persevered. They were not yet raised, however, to the level of the angels which men were about to attain, because the number taken from them was perfect.[36] Nevertheless in their original justice, it seems that if they had conquered temptation and had not sinned, they would be confirmed with all their offspring and so not be able to sin any more. Because they were conquered and sinned, they were so weakened that, insofar as it depended on them, they could not exist without sinning. For who would dare say that injustice is more able to bind a man in servitude who consents to it at the first persuasion than justice is able to confirm him in freedom when he clings to it during the same trial? For, just as human nature was conquered and sinned (with the exception of the only man whom God knew he would make from the Virgin without the seed of a man and separate from the sin of Adam), because the whole existed in the first parents, so the whole nature would have conquered in the first parents, if it had not sinned.[37]

### *That man ought to be redeemed*

17. Man, therefore, sinned because of a persuasion from someone else and a fraudulent deception as well as from the weakness of the flesh, but not from the malice of knowledge. Since he was able to be redeemed through the Incarnation of

---

35. John Damascene, *On the Orthodox Faith* 24.3. Grosseteste has called this work the "book of Sentences" ("in libro *Sententiarum*"); see Dales and King ed., p. 32.

36. Anselm is discussing in this chapter whether the number of angels was perfect before some were lost to the fall, and whether or not man was created merely to fill up the number of the fallen angels.

37. Anselm, *Why God Man* 1.18.

the Word, it was fitting that he thus be redeemed, but the Devil not. No one ought to have the effect of redemption, however, unless he loves his Redeemer. He could not love if he did not believe. Therefore, a man who is to be saved must have a firm faith in the Incarnation of the Word of God. But he could not love him unless he kept God's commandments. As he says, "If any one love me, he will keep my word" (Jn 14.23). But those precepts which are of the natural law are everlasting. On account of this it was always necessary that they be kept by anyone at all who was to be saved.

### That there was always someone from the number of those to be saved

18. There was never a time, from the foundation of the world, in which there was not someone from the number of those to be saved. As Anselm says in the aforementioned book, "It must not be believed from the fact that man was made that there was any time when the world with its creatures (which were made for men's use) was void of someone from the human race striving after that for which man was made."[38] For it seems inappropriate that God would even for a moment permit the human race, from which the heavenly city will be perfected, and the things that he made for its use to exist in vain. For they would seem to exist in vain as long as they did not seem to exist for that for which they had been made.

### Salvation is denied to no one

19. Furthermore, no one, while he is on the way, is denied the opportunity to merit eternal life, and this cannot happen except through faith and the keeping of the commandments.

### It is concluded that from the beginning man had faith and law

Clearly, then, from the fact that man sinned, there had to be both faith that was believed, and law that was kept. But man had transgressed both the natural law and the positive law by sinning,

---

38. Ibid., 2.16.

and the positive law that he had, viz. not to eat the fruit, was no longer a law to him, because he was not in its power. In these circumstances another positive law would be given to him in vain, until he was first proven again in the keeping of the natural law.

CHAPTER 7

*That a positive law ought to have been given and was given to Noah and Abraham*

1. Therefore, man was fittingly subject to the natural law alone after his sin, until he proved himself in the obedient observance of it, and if he kept it the positive law would be added for the fullness of obedience. In this way, from sinful Adam up to Noah or Abraham there was the natural law alone. But a positive law about not eating blood seemed to be enjoined upon Noah and his successors. The positive law of circumcision was enjoined upon Abraham and his seed.

*That oblations were owed [to God] even by the natural law*

In fact, sacrifices and offerings, given to the Lord from the beginning, were not precepts of a positive law. For the natural law demands that honor and veneration be freely repaid to the benefactor for gifts that he has freely given. Hence the offering of tithes belongs to the natural law, that one could not pay less than the least part, that is, a tenth (because beyond this there is no reckoning), for gifts that have been received, because by the natural law there is owed a recompense of honor. Besides, what is commanded individually for some person and not for the many is not a law, as was the command given to Noah to build an ark and those given to Abraham to set out from his land and to make sacrifices from three-year-old cows and the like.

*That it was not yet necessary for a law to be written because of the vivacity of the memory, which is clear from [man's] longevity*

2. It would be superfluous for the natural or positive law to be written, until the memory of man was so slipshod that he could not remember the positive law given to him without the

support of the Scriptures. For there are no Scriptures except to aid a defective memory. Primeval men, however, had very strong memories, by which they could remember the law without forgetting it. The natural law is naturally easy to remember because the whole of it necessarily and logically follows from the law of charity. The positive law, though, as has been said, had not been added immediately after sin. It had been added before the writing of the Law and did not have many precepts, and it is the many precepts that make remembering difficult.

3. In primitive times, each kind of law, then, was easy to remember without writing, both because the law itself was easy to remember and because of primitive man's strong memory. Primeval men, although they had much corruption in their senses because of sin, nevertheless had, in comparison with our time, much vigor and strength in their internal and external senses; this can be manifest from their longevity and bodily toughness. They lived long lives because of their natural strength and were strong and tough because of their vitality and motive power. But the excellence of these powers cannot exist without excellence in sensitive powers. Just as, then, they lived longer than we, so they were stronger than we in the exercise of natural powers. Because of their good nature and its excellence, they did not need Scriptures, as Jerome says in his letter to the virgin Demetrias:

> It is no small argument for proving the goodness of human nature that those early men for many years were without the instruction of the Law, not at all because God at any time did not care for his own creature, but because he knew that he had made human nature in such a way that exercising justice sufficed as a law for them. For however long this newly made nature flourished and the long experience of sin did not spread like a fog over human reason, nature existed without forsaking the Law. But when human nature was clouded too much by vice and infected by the rust of ignorance, the Lord brought in the Law as a file, and so human nature was polished by the Law's frequent admonition and could return to its shine.[39]

*Again, because they had God speaking with them*

4. Furthermore the men of the primeval age, because of their clean hearts and holy conversation, had God internally speak-

---

39. Ps.-Jerome, *Ep.* 1.7; actually, Pelagius, *Ep. ad Demetriadem* 8.2.

ing to them and writing the Law on the tables of their hearts. So they did not need the external Scriptures or the visible forms of letters. Hence John Chrysostom, in his first homily on Matthew, says:

It was necessary, in fact, that we did not at all need the help of the divine Scriptures but that we exhibited a life so clean in all things that we experienced the grace of the Scriptures' spiritual life. Just as a page is written on with ink, so our hearts are written on by the Spirit. But because we closed off ourselves from this grace, come, let us seek out riches that are second-best. God has shown by words and deeds that the first way [that is, without the written Law] was truly better. For to Noah and Abraham and their descendants and to Joseph and Moses God spoke not through letters but through himself, because, plainly, he had found their hearts clean. Afterwards, however, the whole Jewish people fell into the depths of vice; then letters and tables were given to them through which they were admonished. We see that this has happened not only in the Old Testament but also in the New.

5. If, in fact, Christ did not hand over to the Apostles anything written, but promised that he would give them the grace of the Spirit instead of letters, "He," he said, "will teach you all things" (Jn 14.26). That you may know that this was much better, listen to the Lord speaking through the prophet: "I will give you," he says, "a new covenant. I will put my Laws in their minds, and I will write them in their hearts, and they will all become docile to God."[40] Paul also pointed out this superiority when he said that he had received the Law "not in tables of stone but in fleshly tables of the heart" (2 Cor 3.3). Because in the course of time, many had turned away from the path of righteousness, Paul, reversing his position, agrees that they need the written Law, as is clear from his letters of admonition. Consider therefore, how altogether mad it is that we who ought to live so perfectly that we truly do not need the written Law, but offer our hearts, as pages, to be written upon by the Spirit—how mad it is that we who have lost that first dignity and need lesser things do not take advantage even of this second remedy for our own salvation. For if it is blameworthy to need those written Laws and not to shine in the grace of the Spirit, consider how great a crime it is not to want to advance through the help of the written Law and how great a crime to despise the heavenly writings as purposeless and vain. Doubtlessly we will undergo a greater punishment.[41]

6. Man, weakened in nature by the corrupting habit of sinning, fell into ignorance and the difficulty of remembering,

---

40. See Bar 2.35; Jer 31.33; Jn 6.45; and Heb 10.16, 8.10. See also Grosseteste, *Hexaëmeron*, Prooemium 56.

41. John Chrysostom, *Homilies on Matthew* 1.1–2.

and thus could complain with the appearance of being right that he lacked something without which he could not keep the Law unless it were written for him. It was fitting, then, that the written Law be handed over to him lest a complaint of this sort have a place. As Augustine says in his commentary on Psalm 57, when he explained the verse, "If in every deed you speak justice: judge right things, ye sons of men" (Ps 57.2):

> For what wicked man is it easy to speak justly? Who, asked about justice, when he has no case, would respond easily with what is just? Since indeed truth has written on our very hearts by the hand of our Maker, "What you do not want done to you, you shall not do to another."[42] Before the Law was given, no one was allowed not to know this, and because of this those to whom the Law was not given were judged. But so that men may not complain that they lacked something, what they were not reading in their hearts was written on tablets. It is not that they did not have what was not written, but that they were unwilling to read it. What they were forced to see in their consciences was placed before their eyes. Man was compelled to turn within himself by the voice of God, as if coming from the outside. "For inquisition shall be made into the thoughts of the ungodly" (Wis 1.9). Where there is questioning, there is law. But because men sought things outside of themselves and were made to be exiles even from themselves, the written Law was given to them, not because it had not been written on their hearts. Rather, because you had fled your own heart, you are seized by that which is everywhere and are called back to within your very self. On account of this was written the Law which shouts to those who desert the law written in their hearts: "Return, ye transgressors, to the heart" (Is 46.8).[43]

### When it was necessary for the Law to be written

7. According to Augustine's authoritative text, it is clear that from the beginning man had the natural law written on the tables of his heart, and that the written Law was finally given so that man would not be able to have a complaint against God about some defect. Again, because the presumption of man about himself prevailed when he said, "He who acts is not deficient, but he who commands is," many positive precepts were fittingly given to conquer the pride of the presumptuous. But because a multitude of Laws is hard to remember, the many

---

42. See Tb 4.16 and Mt 7.12.
43. Augustine, *Homilies on the Psalms* 57.1.

commands were appropriately commended to the Scriptures to aid the faulty memory.

CHAPTER 8

*That the Incarnation of Christ ought to come after the written Law*

1. The redemption of the human race through the Passion of Christ should not have preceded in time the giving of the written Law, but the written Law should have preceded the Incarnation of the Son of God. The written Law would remain after the Incarnation in its moral precepts, which all pertain to the natural law, and at his advent would cease in its ceremonial precepts, which all pertain to the positive law or the law of deeds.

*Distinction of the persons of mankind*

And that these truths be clearly manifest, one must remember that there are, as it were, four persons in the human race, one of which is Adam along with his whole progeny naturally begotten from him. For all men were materially in Adam, and all men are Adam, in a certain way, because of the unity in which they are united in him as in a single root.[44] The second person is sinful Adam along with the whole of his progeny originally vitiated in him, and who will be born from him in original sin according to the law of concupiscence in regard to propagation. For inasmuch as they are original sinners, all men are in a certain way the one Adam, the first transgressor, in whom all have originally sinned. The third person is all the guilty and all who in the end are great sinners, with the Devil as their head. For the Devil and all those who in the end adhere to him constitute one person, who has been condemned to the fire of Gehenna forever. As Gregory says in the fourth book of the *Morals*, "For just as our Redeemer is one person with the congregation of the good—for he is the head of the body, and we the body of this head—so the ancient enemy is one person with the whole of the

---

44. On the rest of this paragraph, see John Wyclif, *On the Truth of Sacred Scripture*, ch. 28 (III, 125–26).

reprobate, because he excels them in iniquity as a head. While they are subject to his urgings, they inhere in him, as a body subject to a head."[45] The fourth person is Christ together with his body, which is the Church. As Gregory says in Book Twenty-three of the *Morals*, "It must be known that our Redeemer has shown himself to be one person with the holy Church that he assumed," and this person was granted eternal glory.[46]

2. It seems that the written Law ought to be given directly to the body of this person, for the direct end of the giving of the Law is eternal salvation. To give, however, the Law to a person who would not strive after the end of the Law (that is, to the person whose head is the devil) would be vain and pointless. But the Law is properly given to him who would strive after the end of the Law by observing it. The law of nature, which was naturally written on the tables of the heart, and in addition the positive law, which forbade the eating of the fruit from the tree placed in the middle of paradise, were properly given to the first person, Adam simply considered in his natural state together with his natural progeny. And if this person had not fallen, the written Law would never have been given. Hence, every natural son of Adam must always serve not only the natural law, but also the first positive law, until the obligation to observe that positive law will have been dismissed in the cleansing of original sin through some sacrament.

3. After this person fell in Adam and was made into a second person, namely, Adam the transgressor, he is always, as has been said, obliged by the natural law. Hence, when the whole body of the Devil, which was gathered from damned men, will have passed over from this person into that one (that is, the second into the third), clearly the whole body of the Devil is held under the obligation to observe the natural law, even though the natural law, and even more the positive law, would be given to him in vain because he would never keep any law. Clearly, therefore, the whole human race from its beginning to its end is obliged by the natural law as well as by the positive law given in paradise,

---

45. Gregory the Great, *Morals on Job* 4.11.18.
46. Ibid., 23.1.2.

CESSATION OF THE LAWS 1.8    67

except in the case of those in whom the obligation was removed by the sacrament, as we said. Clearly also the written Law was properly conferred on that person whose head is Christ. Nevertheless, out of the generosity of the Lawgiver, the written Law was publicly proposed for all wishing to keep it, so that no one could claim that he transgressed it out of ignorance. And so the written Law was given to the people of Israel, as to that person whose head is Christ; but it was not given to the Gentiles, as to that person whose head is the Devil.

4. And it should not bother anyone that many of the Gentiles have been saved and many from Israel have perished, for all the good are in the end true Israelites and belong to the person whose head is Christ. As the Apostle says to the Romans, "For all are not Israelites that are of Israel: Neither are all they that are the seed of Abraham, children [of God]; but in Isaac shall your seed be called: That is to say, not they that are the children of the flesh, are the children of God; but they that are the children of the promise, are accounted for the seed" (Rom 9.6–8). And to the Galatians, he says, "Know ye, therefore, that they who are of faith, the same are the children of Abraham" (Gal 3.7). And a little later in the same letter he says, "And if you be Christ's, then are you the seed of Abraham, heirs according to the promise" (Gal 3.29). In the end all who are evil belong to the body of the Devil, even if by chance some are now in the body of Christ according to the present justice. Redemption and liberation through the Passion of Christ was rightly given to the person whom we called Adam the transgressor, that is, fallen Adam together with the human race sinning in him in the beginning. This redemption and liberation were so given that, freed from the pit of sin, Adam may pass over into the person whose head is Christ. For although not everyone from the person of Adam the transgressor was freed through the Passion of Christ, nevertheless the Passion of Christ had proposed to rescue this person from the pit of sin. The Passion of Christ truly rescued this person, although not every part of him, because it rescued Adam, who is the root of this person together with the whole tree of those to be saved, who proceed from this root.

5. The Passion of Christ, which was rightly given to save Adam

the transgressor together with his originally unjust race, is abundant also for the absolution of every actual sin added to the original sin. As the Apostle says to the Romans, "But not as the offense, so also the gift. For if by the offense of one, many died; much more the grace of God, and the gift, by the grace of one man, Jesus Christ, has abounded unto many. And not as it was by one sin, so also is the gift. For judgment indeed was by one unto condemnation; but grace is unto justification from many offenses" (Rom 5.15–16). Some draw from Adam only the one original sin. But because of the Passion of Christ, because of its sufficient power, every actual sin is absolved along with original sin. For the Passion of Christ was not properly given to that first person, because that person would have been the same if the first man had not sinned. For this person is the whole human race considered in its natural state. But it would be impossible and useless to give redemption and liberation to the sort of man that had been established through nature, because man, inasmuch as he was this sort, was not captive, and redemption is not owed except for someone held captive under an enemy. Redemption was not conferred on that person whose head is the Devil, inasmuch as he was the sort who needed redemption, because to redeem this person inasmuch as he was this sort is to redeem also the Devil, who is this person's head. Besides, the Redeemer and the redeemed must be one in natural origin, for he who transgresses could not otherwise make satisfaction. But this person, whose head is the Devil, cannot be one in natural origin with the Redeemer. Clearly, then, this person, inasmuch as he is this sort, lacks redemption.

6. The person, therefore, to whom the Passion of Christ is appropriately given as a liberation is just like a man who had cast himself into a deep and dark pit, and from this pit he could not escape either by his own effort or by the help of another, except one alone. Let us imagine that one man has fallen into the deepest pit and let us imagine that another who alone could pull out the fallen man himself needed no outside help in pulling him out. And further let us suppose that the whole joy and good of the man pulled out was the knowledge and love of the one who pulled him out. Would not the one who could pull the

man out of the pit bestow a greater benefit upon him if he were to leave him in the pit until he would experience that he could in no way climb out of the pit by his own powers than if he were to pull him out immediately? For if he had been pulled out immediately, before he had failed in his own efforts, he could presume that somehow he might have escaped by himself. And so he would be less grateful to the one who pulled him out, and would repay him less love. And so because love was the whole good of the one pulled out, he would have received less of a benefit if he had been pulled out immediately.

7. This benefit would be increased also if, after the man who had fallen into the pit perceived that he could not rise up by his own effort, a lamp were lit for him so that he might perceive that he would not have been frustrated in his effort on account of the darkness and the absence of light. Even if a ladder were sent down to him, and if the ladder were filled with many thick rungs so that he could not complain that he could not climb the ladder because of the small number and size of the rungs on the ladder; and if some climbing ropes were also sent down to him, and some sharp spurs, and if the greatest helps for climbing were given to him, except the help of the only one who could pull him out—if all this were given to him after he fell into the pit, when he perceived that he could not escape by any help or aid except that of him alone pulling him out, he would love the one pulling him out more firmly. Hence because an increase in love would be an increase in benefit, being pulled out of the pit after the aforementioned experience would be a greater benefit than there had been from the beginning. It would increase the love of the one pulled out toward the one pulling him out, and so increase the benefit to him, if all the helps which were at first given to him (except the one who pulled him out and was alone in the position to be able to pull him out by himself) were taken away, except perhaps certain ones that would remain, which, because of their permanence, would make the one pulled more praising of his rescue and more loving toward his rescuer. For in this way it would be clear to the one pulled out that his rescuer did not need any helper, and he would thus be more lovable from his manifest and powerful kindness. For the more power-

ful kindness is, the better it is and the more worthy of love. After all the helps have been taken away with or without which the one to be pulled out of the pit could not at all proceed, it would also increase love and good-will if the one pulled out would not be pulled out like a dead tree without his own effort, but rather if his rescuer were to give him the ability to try to rise when the rescuer's hand was reaching for him. Thus his whole coming forth from the pit would be also the movement of his own effort, and the one who was pulled out would have to be praised for coming out of the pit.

8. On account of this, when all these things have been added and done, a greater benefit would be conferred than if the benefit of the rescue had been conferred from the beginning. For although the same thing was given, the benefit is greater when more is conferred upon the recipient. From this analysis of the matter, it is clear that the Son of God ought not give the benefit of redemption immediately after the fall of man, but man, fallen into the pit of sin, ought first to be left to his own effort, so that he may know by experience that he could not rise up through his free choice alone. The natural law ought also to be sent down to him, as a ladder in which the individual commands of the law are like the individual rungs for climbing on a ladder, in order that he may perceive that he could not climb up on this ladder out of the pit of sin by the effort of his own free choice. And because man was, as it were, blind because of a long time in the depths of the pit, in order that he could not complain about not having light, the benefit of a lamp ought to be given to him. This lamp is the written Law, because Solomon says in Proverbs, "The commandment is a lamp, and the Law a light" (Prv 6.23). And the Psalmist says, "Your word is a lamp to my feet" (Ps 118.105). And Peter says in his second letter, "We have the more firm prophetical word: whereunto you do well to attend, as to a light that shines in a dark place, until the day dawn, and the day star arise in your hearts" (2 Pt 1.19).

9. And man could perhaps complain about the great distance between the rungs on the ladder of the natural law, that because of the distance he, being weak, could not reach from rung to rung without the addition of intermediate rungs. Because of

this, many positive laws ought to be inserted between the mandates of the natural law. It was also necessary that a climbing rope be added, that is, the promise and bestowal of temporal goods, and the sharp spur of adversity, namely, a threat if he would not climb. But the strongest help that could be shown to man having to be pulled out of the pit of sin, with the exception of the help of redemption through the Passion of Christ, was the offering of the Christ as a victim in sign. For because the offering of Christ as a victim on the cross was the true and whole liberation of man, the help nearest to this and most like it was the offering of the same victim, not in himself but in sign.

10. It was necessary, therefore, that first the natural unwritten law come before the advent of Christ, and then the same law written, but with the addition of a manifold positive law, then the promise of temporal prosperity and the threat of adversity. In addition it was necessary that there be added the offering of Christ as victim in sacrament, and this existed in the victims of the Law that signified the victim Christ. When Christ by his Passion pulls man out of the pit of sin, to increase the benefit, to make man, pulled out of the pit, praiseworthy for his own escape, man ought to be left to his own free-will so that he use it well and himself come out of the pit by his own effort and movement with the hand of grace pulling him up. In this way, the whole act of rising out of the pit could be attributed to the rescuer, and nevertheless the whole act could be attributed to free-will striving together with grace. For grace works in us the whole of what we do well, and we work the same whole through obedient free choice. As Bernard says in his book *On Free Choice*,

> Grace works with free choice in such a way that it comes before it at first and follows it thereafter. Grace comes before free choice so that they can then work together, in such a way, nevertheless, that what was begun by grace alone is finished equally by both. They work in individual actions as mingled, not one at a time; at the same time, not one and then another. It is not part grace and part free choice, but they both work by single individual operation. Grace is responsible for the whole action, and free choice for the whole, but the whole is in grace, and from free choice.[47]

---

47. Bernard of Clairveaux, *Treatise on Grace and Free Choice* 14.47.

The whole benefit, therefore, of the aforesaid rescue belongs in this way to the rescuer, and from the fact that the entire coming out of the pit is nevertheless the proper act of the one pulled out, the benefit is much more copious.

11. And because man could not exercise the act of coming out of the pit unless he were called, supporting himself in this movement on something like a step, the ladder of the natural law must be sent down to him. Man became blind because he was in the pit for so long, and, walking in the darkness of blindness, did not know where he was going. Because of this, it was fitting that the natural law shine in the lamp of writing. For the written Law is at the same time a ladder, a way of climbing up, and a lamp. As Solomon says in Proverbs, "The commandment is a lamp, and the Law a light, and reproofs of instruction are the way of life" (Prv 6.23). But so that both the virtue of the rescuer be more manifest and the act of the one climbing out of the pit more praiseworthy—and so the bestowal of the benefit more copious—the rungs of the commands of the positive law, which had been inserted into the ladder of the natural law, ought to be taken away; likewise, the above-mentioned ropes and spurs ought to be thrown away, and the helps of the sacraments of the Law, nullified. For if these intermediary rungs were not removed, the rescuer could be thought to need their use and help; and the rescued's own action would not be as virtuous and praiseworthy with these rungs as without them.

12. Taking away these rungs, therefore, greatly increases the benefit of the rescue, because without these the rescuer would be more worthy of love, and the whole good of the rescued man is the love of his liberator. Indeed, our whole good is the love of the Son of God, who pulled us out of the pit of sin by his own Passion. Hence, because the Son of God is supremely good and powerful and wise, it is fitting that he bestow the highest benefit, and because the benefit of the liberation of man would not have been as great if the Son had freed him immediately (for man would not have been given as great an opportunity to love, and this is the whole good of man), clearly the Son of God ought not have come to liberate man except in the way outlined above.

## Response

13. Also from these points the response to the aforementioned argument is clear, the argument by which the Son of God ought to have immediately freed man because he would have thus, so it seemed, bestowed a longer-lasting good and a more gracious benefit. For the liberation of man would not be so great a benefit as it is now, if it were not bestowed in the aforementioned way; this is clear from what has been said. Indeed, the same gift, as we touched on above, is a greater benefit when it is more advantageous to the recipient. It was said, though, about a good, considered in itself, that it is better if it is longer-lasting, and similarly, about a benefit, the more quickly it is conferred and the fewer the requests for it, the more gracious it is. But when waiting, expectation, and entreaty increase the benefit itself, he who delays a gift does not bestow a small benefit simply by delaying and waiting for the entreaty of the one who will receive the gift. Indeed the father of a family bestows a great benefit on his young son by placing him under tutors and authorities until the age of adult discretion.

14. From these points it is also clear that the sacraments of the Law and the commands of the old positive law ought to have ceased with the Passion of Christ, for the powerful kindness of the liberator would be more manifest and the love of the liberated for the liberator more zealous, and so the benefit would be greater. The human race and the synagogue perceived in the Patriarchs and Prophets that they could not enter the gates of paradise, nor be snatched from the pit of sin through free choice, neither through the natural or written Law nor through the sacrifices and victims of the Law. As Jacob, who was placed under the natural law before the written Law, says, "I will go down to my son into hell, mourning" (Gn 37.35). He believed that his son Joseph, whom he knew to be innocent, had gone down to hell and that he would go down to him with tears for the loss of his son. The same Jacob, when his sons wanted to take Benjamin with them to Egypt, says, "If any mischief befall him in the land to which you go, you will bring down my gray hairs with sorrow to hell" (Gn 42.38). Jacob knew, therefore, as is clear from these texts, that he would go down to hell.

15. It seems that what Augustine wrote opposes this, when he says in the twelfth book of his *Literal Commentary on Genesis*, "We see that the mention of hell was made not in the case of the repose of the poor man, but in that of the punishment of the rich man. When Jacob said, 'You will bring down my old age to hell with sadness,' he seems to have feared more that he would be troubled by excessive sadness and go not to the rest of the blessed but to the hell of sinners." Accordingly, as he said, "I have not yet found, and am still looking, and it does not occur to me that the canonical Scriptures have anywhere used 'hell' in a good sense."[48] Nevertheless, as is clear from further on in the same book, Augustine does not so much assert this opinion but rather leaves it in doubt.

16. Other sacred writers expressly understand and write that all the saints before the coming of Christ, however many there were, had gone down to hell, although they did not go down to the place of punishment where sinners are punished. In his sixth homily, Gregory asserts that John the Baptist went to hell ahead of Christ, for he was explaining the verse, "Are you he that is to come, or should we look for another?" (Mt 11.3) Gregory says, "Coming before Christ, he had announced him to the world and by dying he went before him to hell. He says, therefore, 'Are you he that is to come, or should we look for another?' Speaking openly, he would say, 'Just as you deigned to be born for men, make known whether you also deign to die for men, so that I who am the forerunner of your birth may be also the forerunner of your death and announce in hell that you are about to come as I announced to the world that you had come.'"[49] Tobias the younger, although he was under the Law, said to an angel, "And whereas I am the only child of my parents, I should bring down their old age with sorrow to hell" (Tb 6.15). Hezekiah too says, "I said in the midst of my days I shall go to the gates of hell" (Is 38.10).[50] The Gentiles too believed that they would go down to hell; this can be clearly learned from the writings of Gentile poets.

---

48. Augustine, *Literal Commentary on Genesis* 12.33.
49. Gregory the Great, *Homilies on the Gospel* 1.6.
50. Cf. Ps 101.25.

17. Again, in early times the human race was, as it were, in a state of infancy, on account of its nearness to the condition that it had in the beginning and on account of the privilege of innocence in those things which were pleasing to God. Then it advanced, as it were, into the state of lascivious adolescence, because of a departure from its condition in the beginning and from the sanctity of the innocent life. In that state of infant innocence, law would not be written or spoken, but dispatched by the movements and direction of nature. In lascivious adolescence, however, a tutor and a law of fear is given. But when perfect age comes, then he is no more under the tutor or the law of fear, but under the law of liberty. So it happened with the human race, whose infancy was ruled by the law of nature; the next age was under the tutor, the Law of fear; the third, from the coming of the Savior, under the law of love and liberty. And it would not be fitting if man advanced to the law of liberty in some other way. Nor would it be fitting if the Liberator came before the law of liberty, or the law of liberty before the Liberator.

### Another reason for the delay of Christ's coming

18. It can be shown by many other arguments that the Law ended with the coming of Christ. Indeed, the Incarnation of the Son of God is a matter very far from the realm of the believable. For of all real possibilities, nothing is less probable than that a person be God and man. This, considered in itself, seems less able to exist than that a person be both man and lion. For these two species, man and lion, share in many things. But divinity and humanity cannot share in something because divinity is supremely simple. It is not possible that the Creator of all share in something with a creature, because if they were to share in something, what they shared in would be created. Thence the uncreated would be the creative essence in God, and the created, the essence in a creature. Therefore, humanity and divinity, which share in nothing, are more different than humanity and lioness, which share in many things. It seems less probable, therefore, that divinity and humanity, which are more different, would come together in one person, than that humanity and lioness, which are less different, would come together in one person.

*That Christ has the testimony of all*

19. Although, therefore, of all the possibilities, that one person be both God and man is the most improbable, it is, nevertheless, necessary that this be most firmly held by faith so that the human race may attain salvation. Since the just man lives only by this faith and without this faith it is impossible to please God, this most improbable of all truths, which is nevertheless very useful and necessary, must have the highest testimony of its truth so that it may be believed. And so it must be witnessed to by the nature of things, by prophecy, by willful human action, and by authoritative Scripture.

## CHAPTER 9

1. That the nature of things testifies to the Incarnation of Christ can be seen from the fact that every creature of this physical world was made on account of men. On account of this it was fitting that the world serve man with the greatest and most useful ministry that it could offer. But nothing is as useful to man as to be led to faith in his Savior. Therefore, if physical creation can signify the dispensation of the salvation of the human race, and through this signification lead man to faith in his Savior, nothing is more fitting than that the creation of the sensible world serve man by this ministry. The creature of this world can point to the incarnate Son of God; for it does not lack all likeness with this mystery, and by this likeness it can clearly point to this mystery. God, therefore, who makes all things according to the most fitting order, ordained this sensible world's creatures, which he made for man, in such a way that by their form and appearance, as if by meaningful letters, they announce to man the benefit of his salvation through the incarnate Son of God. For, because such a signification is the greatest and most useful ministry that the world can offer man, for whom the physical world was made, it cannot be that God the Father, who, for the salvation of man, "spared not even his own Son, but delivered him up for us all" (Rom 8.32), did not ordain the world to this ministry.

2. Because he who witnesses something differs from him for

whom that thing is witnessed, it was necessary that not the whole human race testify through its own voluntary actions and way of life to the mystery of the restoration of the human race. This witness, rather, had to be placed especially in some one people that would witness to this mystery for the human race by its actions and way of life. Therefore, that people from which Christ was to be born was chosen for this ministry. For this was more fitting, and on account of this the whole life and way of that people was prophetic and testified to our restoration through the Son of God. And because the voluntary acts of men cannot be known unless through the senses or through history—but history does not pass down to posterity certainties, except through writing—the life and way of that people, prophesying our salvation, had to be rendered in authoritative Scripture.

3. Likewise, because the signification of our restoration through the appearances of creatures is not clearly known to the human race, the creatures of this world that signify our restoration had to be shown through authoritative Scripture to point to the mystery of our restoration. Thus, with the help of the light of Scripture, we could know which creatures signified the mystery of our salvation, and by which of their properties, and in what manner they did so. It was also necessary that the prophetic utterance itself be entrusted to writing for the sake of posterity. Also, authoritative Scriptures had to signify the dispensation of our salvation in plain language and have no obscurity from allegory, so that the dispensation of our salvation could have the following testimonies: the testimony from authoritative Scripture made most clear by bare and manifest words announcing the dispensation; the testimony from prophetic utterance; the testimony from a human way of life; and the testimony from the creation of this world. Thus the truth of the dispensation of our salvation, which is of all truths the most unbelievable when considered in itself but which must be held most certainly by faith, would have the greatest and most evident witness of all.

4. On account of this it was made clear that the divine Scripture, which foretold the salvation of the human race, was composed in such a way that: in one of its parts it signified through words the creatures of this world and the appearances through

which it meant, in the second place, to signify the dispensation of our restoration; in its second part it signified the actions and way of life of the people of Israel, again through those actions and through their manner of life intending to signify our restoration. In these two parts, words signify things in the first place, but the meaning does not stop there, because it reaches beyond the things first signified by the words, to signify, in the second place, something which pertains to the salvation of the human race. In the third of its parts, Scripture signifies those things that pertain to our salvation in bare words that have no allegorical enigmas. In the fourth of its parts, Scripture contains prophecy, both the kind that foretells the mystery of our salvation in bare words and the kind that foretells it by means of things signified through words.

5. As Augustine says and as is clear from what has been said, Scripture was composed in such a way that whatever it signifies allegorically through things about our salvation it also signifies most plainly with bare words without allegory. The student of the Scriptures, therefore, ought to consider the fact that wherever in the Scriptures the first meaning of the words expresses either the faith of our salvation or love, there no allegory ought to be sought. But where the first meaning of the words signifies the things of creation or individual acts of a human way of life, the things signified at first through words signify secondly some mysteries of our restoration. In order to manifest most fully the meaning of the things, Scripture expresses what in the matter of our restoration a thing (of creation or of a human way of life) signifies. For example: the word "fire" indicates a certain creaturely image, and that image signifies the power of God consuming the rust that is our vices. Scripture shows this in Deuteronomy, when it says, "The Lord your God is a consuming fire" (Dt 4.24). But sometimes this image signifies God's anger, as in Jeremiah, "Lest my indignation come forth like fire" (Jer 4.4); sometimes it signifies the words of God in the mouth of a prophet, and Scripture manifests this again in Jeremiah, to whom the Lord said, "Behold, I will put my words in your mouth as fire, and this people as wood, and it shall devour them" (Jer 5.14). In this way Scripture explains what it itself signifies through the

things of creation or human action concerning our restoration.

6. The student of the Scriptures ought to fix this rule to himself as if it were a tail: where the words of Scripture signify the things of creation or the things of the way of life of the prophetic people of Israel, he should seek from another place in Scripture what each thing means, and afterwards he should investigate the meaning gathered from many symbolic things in the words that plainly describe the truth of faith or charity.[51] For example, in the Song of Songs it is said, "Your teeth as flocks of sheep, all with twin offspring" (Song 4.2). The phrase "all with twin offspring" literally means "all the sheep of the aforementioned flocks are bearing twin offspring." The student of the Scriptures ought to judge, therefore, that this phrase, understood literally, does not teach him faith or charity; so he ought to recognize that the things here signified through words themselves signify other things pertaining to faith and morals.

7. He ought, therefore, to think about, not what the name "sheep" means, but what the image "sheep" means. And the Psalmist will show him that these sheep are the people of God. For he says, "We are his people and the sheep of his pasture" (Ps 99.3). The sheep, therefore, bearing twin offspring are the men of the people of God bearing twin offspring. But this phrase does not have a fitting literal meaning; so what "offspring" signifies must be sought, and the prophet shows us, when he says, "Because of fear of you, O Lord, we have conceived and have borne a spirit of salvation" (Is 26.18).[52] This is what it means for a man to bear twin offspring: it is to bear the twin spirit of salvation. But the twin spirit of salvation is the twin love of charity, for in this twin love alone is man saved. Hence the Savior says to the lawyer who tested him and who expressed the two commands of charity, "This do, and you shall live" (Lk 10.28). Therefore, for

---

51. Cf. John Wyclif, *On the Truth of Sacred Scripture*, ch. 29 (III, 147).

52. Grosseteste's text significantly differs from that of the Vulgate, which has, "concepimus et quasi parturivimus et peperimus spiritum salutes non fecimus in terra," translated in the Douay-Rheims, "We have conceived, and been as it were in labour, and have brought forth wind: we have not wrought salvation on the earth." Grosseteste's Latin is "at timore tuo Domine concepimus at parturivimus spiritum salutis."

man to bear the twin spirit of salvation is for him to bear the twin love of charity. It is the same thing, then, to say that sheep bear twin offspring and that men bear a twin love. It is the same thing to say that sheep bear a twin offspring and that men love God and neighbor.

8. The author of Scripture, therefore, wanted through this verse in the Song of Songs to teach us that God and neighbor must be loved by every man. And this could not be communicated more clearly through the things of creation than in the combination of these words, "The sheep bear twin offspring."[53] The sheep are the people of God, the offspring is the spirit of salvific love. The author of Scripture has what belongs to the best teacher: he intended to teach through his own word that which through the same word was most clearly signified. For the allegorical text without the addition of the plain text that explains the allegory is not like the teacher's full discourse, but like his abbreviated one. But the good teacher does not aim to form the minds of his students with only the abbreviated discourse; he uses also his full discourse. And he who does not yet know how to distinguish the abbreviated discourses from the full discourses, or he who wants to comprehend clearly and plainly the meaning of the teacher from the abbreviated discourses just as from the complete and whole one, cannot be a student of any teacher or art.

CHAPTER 10

*Response*

1. By these considerations, then, is answered that earlier objection, which seemed to argue from the properties of the best teacher that the command concerning the keeping of the Sabbath and the like must be understood only in their literal sense, because the literal sense is communicated most clearly through those words. In fact, the author of the Scriptures was giving this command not as a full discourse but as an abbreviated one; he was not intending to signify things through words, but to sig-

---

53. See Song 4.2.

nify through the things themselves certain other truths, whose meaning is not clear without the addition of other words that explain the meanings of the things. When these explanatory words are added, nothing is so clearly communicated as what the author intended to teach.

2. Likewise, when the student of the Scriptures hears the command concerning the keeping of the Sabbath, because the historical keeping of the Sabbath is not a matter of the natural law and because the command, understood merely historically, does not teach faith and charity, he should understand by the aforementioned rule that the act of celebrating the Sabbath points to something pertaining to faith and morals, and he should assess its meaning from other places in Scripture. And if he should do this diligently, he would discover that Sabbath observance signifies freedom from sin. For it is said in Deuteronomy, "You shall not do any work therein" (Dt 5.14).[54] But the Truth itself shows that servile work is sin in the Gospel of John, when he says, "Whosoever commits sin, is the servant of sin" (Jn 8.34). Therefore, to do no servile work is the same thing as to commit no sin. Because corporal servile work designates sin, servile work can be considered to proceed from sin. For if man had not sinned, there would have been no servile works, which the condition of this life demands as a punishment. Just as, then, the effect points to the cause, so servile work points to sin. Sabbath observance, therefore, which is freedom from servile work through the written Law, is cessation from sin by the aforementioned rule. When, then, the student of Scripture hears that the Sabbath observance is an everlasting covenant and a perpetual sign, by his rule he immediately discerns that the author did not wish to communicate by the word "Sabbath" bodily freedom but wished to communicate by this very bodily freedom a cessation from sin. Nevertheless, because that which is nothing can signify nothing, the same hearer of Scripture could discern that the author wanted the freedom of the Sabbath to be bodily as well. The diligent student of the Scriptures, then, understands immediately two points from

---

54. On this and the following, see Grosseteste, *On the Ten Commandments* 3, "De tertio mandato."

the command to observe the Sabbath: a bodily holiday and the abstention from sin. And without a doubt he recognizes that the author intended by this precept principally to teach and to command on a matter of morality, and that the author did not wish to command about a bodily matter for its own sake, but more for the sake of the moral matter. When, therefore, something is attributed to the Sabbath observance, for example that it be perpetual or everlasting, the art of reading the Scriptures demands that the hearer discern whether that attribution applies to the historical meaning or to the spiritual meaning, or both.

3. If it be necessary, he should investigate the historical meaning using other Scriptures and the spiritual meaning using the aforementioned rule. For the Psalmist says, "Then shall I not be confounded, when I shall look into all your commandments" (Ps 118.6). For example, when Sabbath observance is said to be perpetual, he can immediately recognize from innumerable places in Scripture that this predication suits a moral meaning: for the abstention from sin ought to be perpetual. But whether or not historical Sabbath observance ought to be perpetual is not immediately clear, except from other places in Scripture. When these are seen, nevertheless, it is patently clear that historical Sabbath observance is to be abandoned. For the Lord says through Isaiah, "The new moons, and the Sabbaths, and other festivals I will not abide" (Is 1.13). And through Hosea he says, "I will cause all her mirth to cease, her solemnities, her new moons, her Sabbaths, and all her appointed feasts" (Hos 2.11).

4. It is most plainly clear, therefore, that, when these different Scriptures are taken together, the Sabbath is perpetual and, nevertheless, to be abandoned. And because it could not be perpetual and to be abandoned in the same sense, what is more evident than this? When the Sabbath is said to be perpetual, it ought to be understood to refer to the moral Sabbath, since the literal Sabbath is to be abandoned. From the collection of various Scriptural texts it is most evident that when the Sabbath is said to be a perpetual covenant, the author wanted to teach us that freedom from sin is a pleasing and perpetual covenant between God and man, and that the perpetuity of this covenant is not to be attributed to the literal Sabbath. This could not be

more clearly taught by the signs that are words and by the signs that are things.

5. But he who is not a student of the Scriptures and who is ignorant of the manner of teaching proper to the Scriptures, can receive only error from them. It is just like this: Suppose someone who does not know the manner of teaching in geometry were to hear a geometrician saying that a visibly curved line of not even a finger's length was straight and a foot in length. He would think the geometrician to be lying or insane and would take nothing from his teaching. But someone who is accustomed to the teaching style in geometry and who knows that the geometrician draws a visible line but makes proofs not about a visible line but about an intelligible line, learns and advances in the science of geometry, and he takes on its manner of teaching and honors it as it becomes most comfortable for him and suited to him.[55] In the same way, he who does not know that in the sacred Scriptures the things of nature and the actions of the Israelite people, and not just the words, are signs of our saving dispensation, and he who does not know that a passage aiming to communicate through things is in itself less than clear until it be read with another text that explains the meaning of the things, and he who thinks either that words only signify things or that a text communicating meaning through things is in itself clear, such a person can only mock the Scriptures as silly and can take from them only error.

*Response*

6. Therefore, it is clear how silly is the argument that strives to prove that the literal Sabbath is everlasting, because it is said that the covenant is everlasting. Indeed, this is no argument except to someone who is ignorant of the Scripture's own manner of teaching.

*Response*

7. Likewise, the argument proves nothing that wishes to show that the literal Sabbath is perpetual because it is called a per-

---

55. On the foregoing, see John Wyclif, *On the Truth of Sacred Scripture*, ch. 28 (III, 142).

petual sign. Indeed, this perpetual meaning is appropriate for the spiritual Sabbath, for perpetual freedom from sin is a plain and perpetual sign, because God is the Lord making us holy, just as Ezekiel says.[56]

*Response*

8. Likewise, when the student of Scripture hears what was said to Abraham about circumcision,[57] that it will be a covenant in his flesh and an everlasting pact in his seed's flesh, he immediately understands, through the above-mentioned rules, that the act of circumcision points to a matter of our salvation, and that, nevertheless, literal circumcision is in the command. He immediately investigates from other Scriptural texts what circumcision itself signifies. And Jeremiah occurs to him, when he says, "Circumcise yourselves to the Lord, remove the foreskin of your hearts" (Jer 4.4). Again, Jeremiah says, "All the house of Israel is uncircumcised in heart" (Jer 9.26). From these words, one clearly understands that circumcision in the flesh signifies the removal of waste from the heart; but the removal of waste from the heart of stone and the resulting condition of a fleshly heart without waste is an everlasting pact between man and God. About this fleshly heart it is said, "I will take out of your flesh the heart of stone and give you a heart of flesh" (Ezek 36.26).

*Response*

9. The following argument has its response from what has already been said: because the Sabbath is an everlasting law, the objection goes, the literal observance of the Sabbath ought to be everlasting. It is plain from what has been said that the moral Sabbath is an everlasting law and the literal Sabbath is a temporal law.

*Response*

10. Again, the objection—that the precept must be observed without end because God commands that the act be done with-

---

56. See Ezek 20.12.
57. See Gn 17.13.

out end—does not enjoin that the act of circumcision or anything of the sort be a precept that is performed without end. It implies only that what is signified by the historical act be done without end. For just as in other sciences predicates are not attributed to the nouns that are the subjects, but to the things signified by the nouns, so in this science in which things are signified now by one noun, now by another, the predicates themselves are attributed often not to the signs but to that which the signs signify. Further in other sciences, when the noun that is the subject is equivocal, immediately the hearer of this sort of sentence discerns whether the predicate suits the subject in all of its meanings, or in some, or only in one. It is the same with the hearer of the Scriptures: when the subject of a sentence signifies something and through the thing signified signifies, in turn, something further, he ought to investigate diligently whether the predicate of the passage suits all the meanings or some or only one.

11. It is clear also from other places of Scripture that the Laws which seem to be prescribed without end have an end fixed by the same Lawgiver. In Isaiah, in fact, the Lord shows that holocausts, victims and sacrifices, the New Moon and the Sabbath and other festivals must end; and the Lord says that he hates them.[58] But what someone hates, doubtless he wants to be ended. And in Hosea, as we touched on above, he says, "I will cause all her mirth to cease, her solemnities, her new moons, and all her appointed feasts" (Hos 2.11). But if he causes every joy of the Synagogue to cease, doubtless he causes to cease the Law and circumcision and the rest of the things in which the Synagogue especially and specifically gloried. The Lord, therefore, fixed an end to corporeal acts of this sort, but he did not fix an end to the spiritual things that they signified; rather, he takes away their end and adds to them perpetuity.

### Response

12. What is said in Deuteronomy—cursed be everyone who does not remain in all that has been written in the book of this

---

58. See Is 1.11–14.

Law by doing them—ought to be understood in the following way.[59] Whoever does not remain in the words of the Law by doing them, *so long as the words of the Law exist,* incurs a curse. But he remains in the operation of the words of the Law who does them so long as the words have the force of law. Hence, if they do not have the force of law, except for a time, he who does them only for as long as the words have the force of law can truly be said to have remained in the words of the Law, although he does not do them beyond the time in which they have force. But if he should do them beyond the time in which they have force, he would not thereby remain in the words of the Law, because the words of the Law no longer exist; rather, perhaps he acts against the Law in this case, because it has already ceased now to have the force of law. Therefore, to remain in the everlasting law is to do forever what that Law prescribes. But to remain in the temporal law is to do what the Law prescribes for as long as the Law has force.

13. Again, the Law about not eating blood is a positive law. Not to eat blood is not a matter of the natural law, because the human body could be nourished by eating blood without injury, and because all things were made for man and are subject to his power through nature. It is not against nature that something profit in its own nature from the things subjected to it; on the contrary, man can, by natural right—namely, because all the other corporeal creatures were subjected to him—licitly use them as a natural help to his nature. And this is not forbidden in any matter except by the Creator, who himself knows the reason why it was prohibited. Because, therefore, this precept is a positive law and does not express in its first meaning anything of faith and morals, and because whatever is in the Scriptures concerns faith and morals, in which our salvation, the purpose of the Scriptures, consists, it is clear to the student of the Scriptures that something that builds up faith and morals is signified by this historical precept, namely, that abstinence from the eating of blood signifies abstinence from the delight in sin. For blood signifies sin, as is clear from the words of the Psalmist when he says, "De-

---

59. See Dt 27.26.

liver me from blood guiltiness, O God, you God of my salvation" (Ps 50.16). For he did not seek to be freed from the blood of the body, nor from anything except sin. He says in another place, "One thing have I asked of the Lord, that will I seek after; that I may dwell in the house of the Lord," and so on (Ps 26.4). He, therefore, who seeks but one thing, namely, to dwell in the house of the Lord, does not seek to be free from anything except what can hinder him from dwelling there, and this is nothing but sin.

14. Therefore, as was said, abstinence from the eating of blood signifies abstinence from the delight of sin. And only this meaning is attached to the words when it is said, "The life of the flesh is in the blood" (Lv 17.11). This can be known from the fact that this phrase understood literally is silly. For if blood must not be eaten because the soul is in the blood, nor then must flesh be eaten, because the soul is in the flesh. And this is the rule of the Scriptures: that where the literal sense is inappropriate or false, one must completely withdraw from it. But the current case, simply understood, suited well a spiritual interpretation. Indeed, "the soul of the flesh" well names the soul subject to the desires of the flesh; to be truly in blood is to take delight in sin. Therefore, the soul of flesh is in blood when the soul, which is subject to the desires of the flesh, takes delight in sinning. And so one must abstain from delight in sinning, because the soul that takes delight in sin is thereby made subject to the flesh and becomes its handmaid, a captive of the flesh of which it ought to be the lord through liberty and power.

15. The precept, therefore, about not eating blood is not perpetual in the literal sense and has no literal reason for perpetual permanence, but together with other Laws, in which the Synagogue glories, ought to cease.[60] In the decree of the Apostles the eating of blood was not prohibited, but the observance of this prohibition was allowed on account of the hardness of heart of the Jews, who at that time would have been too scandalized if the observance of this prohibition had not been still allowed.[61] That all these things would come to an end because of

---

60. Cf. John Wyclif, *On the Truth of Sacred Scripture*, ch. 30 (III, 189).
61. See Acts 15.28–29.

Christ was manifest from what the Lord says through Moses in Deuteronomy: the Lord your God will raise up for you a prophet from your brothers, and you will listen to him as if to me.[62] By the precept of the Lord, therefore, that prophet must be listened to as if God. Therefore, what he teaches either by word or example, whether he speaks through himself or through another in another, must be observed as if God's command. Christ himself through the mouth of Paul put an end to this prohibition when he said, "To the pure all things are pure" (Ti 1.15) and "Nothing is unclean except for someone who believes it to be unclean" (Rom 14.14). Paul did not refuse what the council of Apostles had decreed, because, as was said, this had been permitted only because of the hardness of some hearts. That the council of the Apostles, in which Peter presided, did not prohibit the eating of blood as if it were something profane and unclean is clear from the fact that Peter had earlier learned from the Lord that nothing is profane or unclean. In fact, when the linen cloth was shown to him with reptiles, which were unclean according to the Law, and when Peter abhorred the eating of them because they were unclean, it was said to him, "What God has made clean you shall not call common" (Acts 11.9). Besides, as is known from history, Peter lived as a Gentile, not as a Jew, after he had seen the aforementioned vision. Hence, one must not in any way believe that he taught by his actions the contrary of what he himself prohibited. Therefore, in our own way, we have already dismantled the arguments which have been adduced from the literal sense of the Old Testament to show that the rituals of the Old Law must be observed with the sacraments of grace.

*That the laws ceased because they were testimonies*

16. It can be seen from what has been already said that the ceremonial actions of the people of Israel were testimonies witnessing to the Incarnation of the Son of God. But testimony—and because of this it is testimony—has in itself the absence of the manifestation and presence of the thing to which

---

62. See Dt 18.15.

it witnesses. Hence, when the manifest presence of the thing that was witnessed to has been shown, the testimony no longer has a place. Indeed, manifest presence is the opposite of testimony, just as habit is the opposite of privation, that is, the absence of the manifest presence of a thing; and this privation is essentially contained in the testimony. Just as, therefore, privation is destroyed through habit, so also testimony ceases when the thing witnessed to is presently manifest. Because, therefore, the Word of God has been presently manifested in the flesh, the testimony to this event ought to cease, and the proclamation of the thing witnessed to ought to take its place. Consider this analogy. If someone were to foretell an eclipse of the sun, for example, that would happen a year later, by his prediction he would testify about the eclipse not yet manifest. But when, at the foretold day and hour, the predicted eclipse was manifest, the whole people, seeing that the eclipse which had been foretold has now presently come, would look at the eclipse and shout that the eclipse is happening, and each would show it and announce it to the other. But this kind of announcement would not be a testimony but rather a proclamation announcing that the thing earlier attested had come.

*The reasons for the rituals*

And when those who had seen the eclipse had told it to their posterity, their posterity would have announced it again, but an announcement of this sort would not be a testimony to, as it were, a hidden thing; rather, it would be the evident and certain proclamation of a thing which manifestly came before. In this way, Christ and the dispensation of our salvation through him is now preached and proclaimed, Christ, who was earlier witnessed to by the rituals of the people of Israel.

17. In a similar way, a sign—and because of this it is a sign—manifests something hidden to him for whom the sign is made. Just as testimony has its privative opposite in the manifest presence of the thing witnessed to, so also the sign, inasmuch as it is a sign, has its privative opposite in the manifest presence of the thing signified. So, a sign, inasmuch as it is a sign, ceases when the manifest presence of the thing signified is shown. For if our

minds were manifest to each other, the signs of exterior words would be superfluous. Hence, signs would altogether cease, unless perhaps they offer some other help or have some other necessity or use, on account of which they would remain. Signs that have some other reason for being permanent (something in addition to that which makes them signs) ought to remain after the manifestation of the thing signified. Therefore, those ancient signs, insofar as they are signs, ought to have ceased in their function of signifying when Christ, whom they signified, was made manifest. But when Christ was manifest, the things of creation which signified the dispensation of our salvation through Christ began, in their own way, to preach and proclaim Christ along with us, and they stopped functioning as a sign and witness according to their property of signifying. Because, therefore, the things of creation have a manifold use and necessity other than the function of signifying and witnessing, when the function of witnessing and testifying comes to an end, they nevertheless ought to remain in existence in their own right.

18. Those rituals of the Old Law, however, end with the coming of Christ all the usefulness that they had. For, as is clear from the foregoing, the positive precepts of the Old Law had been given for these reasons: so that they might test the humble obedience of man; so that they might crush his swelling pride, which was saying that he who acted was not at fault, but rather he who commanded was at fault; so that the complaint might be taken away by which the one who had fallen into the pit of sin was able to complain that he could not climb out by the rungs of the mandates of the natural law unless the rungs of the mandates of the positive law were inserted between them; and so that, as has been said, they might be signs and testimonies of our restoration. Christ, manifested in the flesh, and his body accomplished the highest and most humble obedience when "he became obedient to the Father unto death, even death on a cross" (Phil 2.8). And the body of Christ, the Church, now in the time of grace is not swelling from presumption of its own abilities, but when it does all things well, it says that it is a useless servant. It does not now complain that, as if before its weakness, it could not climb up on the rungs of the mandates of

the natural law, unless the rungs of the mandates of the positive law were inserted between them. Rather, the Church says along with the Apostle, "I can do all things in him who strengthens me," that is, Christ (Phil 4.13). And so in all these cases, the very Laws have in themselves an imperfection opposite to a perfection, and the imperfection must be ended when the perfect comes. Therefore, the Laws end with the coming of Christ, which ended the necessity of testing obedience when swelling presumption has been replaced by true humility, by which man casts himself away and trusts by grace alone that, when confidence in the help of grace has been given, he could rise out of the pit without the help of the positive law, not by himself, but in Christ. And the rituals have no other reasons for their institution except the sort which have privation and imperfection in themselves. And therefore, when Christ came—Christ who by his presence has deprived privation through habit and perfected imperfection—"the old passed away, and behold, all things were made new" (2 Cor 5.17).[63]

*Response to Plato's argument*

19. From what has been said already, the response is clear to that argument which was taken from a similarity to the reasoning of Plato. For the ceremonial Law has in itself a necessity toward corruption and diminishment because it has in itself privation and imperfection according to all the reasons for its institution, and this privation and imperfection must be taken away by their opposites, habit and perfection, at the coming of Christ. And the Old Law does not cease because it is law, but it ought to cease because it is temporal law, because it has been given to test the fullness of obedience that has not yet been shown, because it checks the swelling of pride, because it silences distrustful complaining, because it is a sign and a testimony to a thing not yet presently manifest, and simply because it has essentially in itself defects and privations of this sort. Indeed, the fullness of obedience, the humble casting away of oneself, the hope for the help of grace, the present manifestation of a

---

63. Grosseteste's Latin differs here from the Vulgate.

thing, and other perfections of this sort put an end to the aforementioned imperfections and similar ones.

### Response to the aforementioned argument posited by Marcellinus

20. But to that argument which we gave above, taken from the letter of Marcellinus to Augustine, Augustine responds in his letter to Marcellinus. Augustine addresses Marcellinus in this way and says:

> I have taken these words from your letter and put them into mine. And if I should want to respond fully to them, time would fail me sooner than examples, in which the very nature of things and human acts change at opportune times by a certain rational order, and nonetheless, this rational order, by which they change, is not mutable. Hence let me call to mind a few things, so that my purpose, roused in a certain way by these, may hasten alertly through many similar considerations. Does not summer follow winter with the gradual addition of warmth? Does not night time turn into day time? How often the times of our lives change! Boyhood yields to adolescence, not to return. Youth follows adolescence, not to remain, and old age, putting an end to youth, is itself ended by death. All these things change, but the rational order of divine prudence, by which it happens that they change, does not change. When the farmer commands one thing in the summer, as he had commanded another thing in the winter, the rational order of agriculture does not, I think, change. And when he who was resting at night rises in the morning, he does not change his life's plan. A teacher imposed one thing on an adolescent, as he was accustomed to impose another on a boy. Teaching, therefore, stands firm and does not change when a precept changes.

> 21. That great doctor of our time, Vindician, when he was consulted by a certain man, ordered a treatment for his pain which seemed appropriate at the time; health followed the treatment. Then, after some years, the same bodily symptoms returned, and the man thought that he ought to take the same treatment, but he took a turn for the worse. Perplexed, he ran back to the doctor and told him what happened. And the doctor, as he was very sharp, said, "You, then, have taken ill, because I did not order the treatment." And so all who had heard this and who had not known the doctor well enough, thought that he did not rely on the art of medicine (I do not know which illicit power they thought he trusted in). Then, when he was questioned afterwards by some men who were astonished at what happened, it was clear that they had not understood that he would not have ordered the same treatment for that time in life. Therefore, the rational order is so strong that, although the

arts have not changed, there must be a change according to them for different times.

22. And it is not true to say that "what is rightly done once, must by no means be changed." Indeed, when the circumstances of time have changed, true reason often demands that what had been rightly done before be so changed that it cannot be rightly done unless it changes, even though they say that what is rightly done must not change; because both will then be right, if there is a different action for a different time. For it can happen at the same time in the case of different persons that one is permitted to do something with impunity, while the other is not permitted, not because the matter is different, but because he who acts is the same person acting at different times. So, for the same person, at one time it is necessary that something be done, at another time it is not necessary that it be done, not because he who acts is different from himself, but because it is when he acts that is different.

23. Whoever is able and does not neglect to consider the difference—spread, in a sense, throughout the universe of things—between the beautiful and the fitting sees perfectly how wide this question is. For the beautiful is considered in itself and praised, and the contrary of it is the ugly and deformed. The fitting, however, whose opposite is the unfitting, is judged not from itself, but from its connection to another, as if it were tied up and hung from somewhere. Certainly the proper and the improper are the same, or are considered in the same manner. Come now, and compare what we have said with the matter at hand. The sacrifice which God had commanded was fitting in early times, but now is not. For he commanded another sacrifice that was fitting for this time, and he knows, much more than man does, what is suitably employed and when it is suitably employed. He, as the immutable Creator and moderator of mutable things, knows better what he ought to bestow, add, take away, increase, or decrease until the beauty of the whole world, parts of which are the things that are suited to their own times, issues forth like a great song from an unspeakable director, and until those who rightly worship God pass from here into the eternal contemplation of vision, even when it is a time for faith.

24. They are deceived who think that God commands these things for his own use or pleasure. And they are rightly disturbed when God changes things, as if by a mutable desire, and commands that one thing be offered to him at an early time and another at a later time. But it is not so. God commands nothing for his own benefit, but for the benefit of him whom he commands. Therefore, he is the true Lord who does not need a slave, but whom the slave needs. In the Old Testament Scriptures, at that time when those sacrifices were still offered (which now are not offered), it was said, "I have said to the Lord: You are my God, for you have no need of my goods" (Ps 15.2). God, therefore, did not need those sacrifices, and never needs anything. Rather, they are signs of heavenly gifts, either the imbuing of the soul with virtues or the

obtaining of eternal salvation, by whose celebration and function the beneficial ministries of piety are exercised not for God but for us.

25. It would take too long, however, to consider appropriately the variety of signs, which are called sacraments when they concern the things of God. Just as God is not mutable because he commands one sacrifice to be offered in the morning, and another in the evening, one in one month, another in another month, one in one year but not in another, so God is not mutable because he commanded one sacrifice to be offered in an earlier age, and another in a later age with the purpose of suitably arranging, throughout changing times without any change of himself, the signs that pertain to the most saving teaching of religion. In fact, these things were in the divine plan, and, when the new were established, the earlier rituals were not suddenly displeasing as if to a changing will; rather, this was fixed and established in the very wisdom of God, to whom the Scripture speaks concerning the changes in things even in ancient times, "you shall change them, and they shall be changed. But you are always the selfsame."[64] In order that they may know this, who are moved by these objections, it must be mentioned to them that the change in the sacraments of the Old and New Testament had been foretold by the voices of the Prophets. So, they will see, if they can, that what is new in time is not new with him who made all times and who timelessly has all the things that he has arranged in each of the times because of their variety. In that Psalm that I recalled to demonstrate that God does not need our sacrifices ("I have said to the Lord: You are my God, for you have no need of my goods" [Ps 15.2]), a little later it says, in the person of Christ, "I will not gather together their meetings for blood offerings" (Ps 15.4), that is, by victims that are animals, by which victims the assembly of the Jews was previously gathered. And in another place he says, "I will not take calves out of your house, nor he-goats out of your flocks" (Ps 49.9). And another prophet says, "Behold the days will come, says the Lord, and I will establish over the house of Jacob a new covenant, which I arranged with their fathers when I led them out of the land of Egypt."[65] And there are many other testimonies to this matter, by which it was foretold that God would do this, but it would take too long to call them to mind now.

26. If it is now sufficiently established that what is rightly decided upon at one time could be rightly changed at another time—by an act of the one changing things, not because of a change in his plan, which the rational order contains and where there exist together the things which cannot happen at the same time in time because different times do not unfold at the same time—someone perhaps would expect to receive from us an account of this change. You yourself know how long

---

64. Ps 101.27–28; Heb 1.12.

65. Grosseteste's text deviates here from both the Vulgate and the LXX. See Jer 31.31–32; LXX Jer 38.31–32; and Heb 8.8–9.

an affair this would be. Nevertheless, what would perhaps suffice for a sharp man can briefly be said: it was necessary that when Christ was about to come, he be announced beforehand by some sacraments, but when he had come, that he be announced by others. It is just as the difference in the events compelled us, just now speaking about it, to change the verbs, since "to be announced beforehand" is one thing, and "to be announced" is another, and since "when he was about to come" is one thing, and "when he had come" is another.[66]

This is Augustine's response to the argument posited in the letter of Marcellinus.

*Response to the argument that the Lord came
not to destroy the Law but to fulfill it*

27. In order to respond to the argument that the Lord came not to destroy the Law but to fulfill it, two kinds of things must be distinguished. One kind of existence is permanent existence, another is transient existence. For example: the substance of the body of heaven has permanent existence, and the substance of the body of the sun and the like. But a year and a month and a day, and the like, which consist of motion and succession, have transient existence. To fulfill but not to destroy a thing whose existence is permanent is to perfect it, and to preserve it perfect in its existence permanently and without end. In this way God fulfills and does not destroy the body of heaven, because he has perfected it and preserves it stably and permanently in perfect existence. In this way he fulfills and does not destroy the rational souls that he daily creates. In this way he will fulfill and will not destroy our bodies at the general resurrection. To fulfill, however, and not to destroy a thing whose existence is transient is to lead it through its natural progression continually unto its end, which is naturally suited to the consummation of its passing away. To fulfill a thing and not to abrogate it is not to abolish it before it reaches its suitable end and not to extend it beyond its end. In this way God fulfills and does not destroy the year, when he leads the sun on the course and way natural to it, from and back to the same point of the Zodiac. But if he were to abrogate the motion of the sun before it returned to the same point or,

---

66. Augustine, *Ep.* 138.1.2–8.

in the space of the same year, to extend the motion of the sun beyond the point from which the sun began the year, or if he were to lessen the length of the year by increasing the speed of the sun, or to extend the year by making the sun unnaturally slower—if he were to do this, he would destroy and not fulfill the year. The existence of a seed is similar in that through germination it passes into something naturally produced from the seed. Hence, he truly fulfills and does not destroy the seed who brings it about that the seed germinate at the opportune time and that it pass into another more perfect form. For example: to fulfill and not to destroy the seed of a tree or a seed of grain is to cause it to die by decaying in soil and through germination to pass into a tree or an ear of grain, and so to cease to have the form and existence of a seed. Therefore, he fulfills and does not destroy a seed who in the aforementioned way brings the seed to non-existence, because the true existence of the seed is to pass in this manner into non-existence. But he who hides a seed in a storeroom and keeps it for many years and does not allow it to germinate by dying and does not allow something more imperfect to pass away by dying and germinating—he who does this truly destroys the seed and ruins it.

*Response to the argument that the Law is everlasting*

28. The twofold kind of law is similar, as is clear from what has been said. One kind is everlasting and permanent, as in "You shall love the Lord your God with your whole heart, and your neighbor as yourself" (Mt 22.37–39). The other kind, however, is temporal and transient, such as the Law of circumcision and Sabbath, and the other rituals. To fulfill and not destroy the everlasting law is to keep it perpetually in existence in Christ, and to infuse those who do the Law with the virtue of charity. Through this infusion the works of the Law live in those who do it, and without this infusion the works of the Law are dead. In this way Christ fulfills and does not destroy the enduring and everlasting law of charity. And he came into the flesh to fulfill the Law in this way and destroyed nothing of this fulfillment by destroying the law of charity or imposing a temporal end to it. Those who keep this kind of law fulfill it and do not

destroy it when they perform its works perseveringly and out of love. In this way, Christ the man, too, fulfilled and did not destroy the Law. Christ fulfilled and did not destroy the temporal and transient Law because he led it from its beginning through its proper progress to its end in time, an appropriate end suitable for its passing away. Christ did not cut off the Law before it reached its suitable end, and did not extend the Law beyond its suitable end; rather, he ended it at its proper time and, as if it were a seed, he made it live by dying according to its carnal sense and operation and caused it to germinate and produce a spiritual sense and operation. And nothing of this kind of Law dies, so long as everything that concerns it be done and if it is fully kept during the time when its passing is appropriate. Something of this kind of Law would die, however—and in fact it would be a transgression of this kind of Law—if it were kept as if it had the force of law after the suitable and fixed time of its passing away, just as it would be a transgression if it were not kept and instead omitted (as if it did not have the force of law) at the time when it was properly in force. Therefore, Christ fulfilled each law, the everlasting and the temporal, by giving to the former permanence and the life of charity, and by giving to the latter an end by killing to an extent the literal sense and by generating a spiritual sense and work.

*Response to the argument that every action of Christ . . .*

29. We must respond also to the objection that the sacraments of the Old Law ought to be observed along with the sacraments of the New Law because Christ performed both kinds of sacraments and his every action is a lesson for us, offered that we may imitate it in action. In response it must be said that the faithful imitate every action of Christ in their own way and truly do what Christ did. They—Christ and the faithful—are not, nevertheless, circumcised and baptized together; nor do they offer together the figurative lamb and Eucharist. Indeed, Christ observed the sacraments of the Old Law in order to show that they were his true witnesses. For, as was said above, the very sacraments of the Old Law witnessed to the dispensation of our restoration through Christ, but it pertains to him concerning

whom the testimony was furnished, to confirm, when he himself appeared, that the testimony spoken about him was true. Thus it happens also in secular court—and those concerning whom testimony is offered strive with great effort for this—that they prove to be true the testimonies offered about themselves. That the sacraments of the Old Law were true testimonies could not be proved in a better way than that Truth itself completed these sacraments even in deed.

### Why Christ kept the Laws

30. Besides, because Christ himself, supremely just, fulfills all justice of every law, whether natural and everlasting or temporal and positive, he completed the sacraments of the Old Law even in deed. Those temporal and ceremonial Laws had the force of law right up to the point of his Passion. Again, he kept the ceremonial Laws, although he was the Lord of the Law and the Sabbath, in order to give to us the example and form of humility. And so also we would not refuse to be under those subject to us and less than we for their own benefit. The greater we are, the more we humble ourselves. For this is perfect humility: to subject oneself to one's subjects for their benefit and out of love. As the Scripture has, "He that is the greater, let him become as the younger; and he that is the leader, as he that serves" (Lk 22.26).

31. Christ performed the sacraments of each Testament so that he might unite in himself, the cornerstone, the two walls of the building that is the worship of God. For one building, as it were, is the whole rite of worshiping God from the beginning of the human race to the consummation of the world. This building, nevertheless, is something passing, and hence its parts ought to follow each other in turn. It belongs to Christ, the true architect and corner foundation, to unite the wall of the worship of God according to the rite of the Law of love with the wall of the worship of God according to the ceremonial rites. Because, therefore, everyone does what he intends in the end by his deed, Christ did this by observing the old sacraments along with the new. That is, he confirmed his testimonies, he fulfilled the fullness of justice, he humbled himself before and obeyed those under him, he finished what had to be finished by

his own end, he joined what had to be joined, and he made new what had to be made new. All of this we ought to do in imitation of him, although it is now not appropriate that we do the same things by the same instruments. And, if an action that ought to be imitated is set before us, it is not necessary that we do it by means of the same instruments and with the same matter. For I can work by one instrument with lead what another works by another instrument with gold.

### That the Old Covenant, which had to be observed of old, now ceases

32. In our own way, then, we have responded to those arguments adduced to prove the permanence of the ceremonial precepts together with the sacraments of grace. The observance of the Laws with the sacraments of grace not only lacks benefit, but also very much harms. For the very Laws, as was shown above, are now useless because the time of action, on account of which they had been established, is passed. But to do something useless and not for the right purpose is not lacking in vice and fault. Besides, those Laws are now dead, because they now lack a life of pious signification.

33. Again, if they were now kept, they would be significant impediments to greater goods, for man's labor and diligence could not fulfill at the same time the mandates of both Laws. The ceremonial mandates, just as Peter says, are a yoke which neither Peter himself nor the fathers of old were able to carry. Furthermore, if those Laws were observed, they would lead to dangerous error, for they would be believed to be necessary for salvation, and so the sincerity of faith in our salvation through Christ would be corrupted, and without this sincerity of faith it is impossible to please God.

## CHAPTER 11

1. Many other effective arguments could be adduced to show that the Laws have ceased because of Christ. We have written some of these, as we were able, in a commentary on Galatians, and so we stop writing them now.

*That the Old Covenant, which had to be observed of old, now ceases: proof-texts from the Old Testament that prove the cessation of the ritual Laws*

2. What has been already proved through reason concerning the abolition of the Old Law can be confirmed through the authority of the same Old Law, with which the authority of the New Law and the harmonious and uniform truth of the sacred writers agree. For it is written in Deuteronomy, "The Lord ... will raise up to you a Prophet of your nation and of your brethren ... him you shall hear [as if he were I]" (Dt 18.15). No one can doubt that that prophet is Christ, who must be heard as the author of the Law by the authority of the Law. If, therefore, he himself by example and in his teaching taught that the ceremonial rituals ended, he agrees that they now end. But by fasting and afflicting himself with hunger for forty days he abolished the Sabbath on which, according to the Law, one who is subject to the Law ought not afflict himself. When the disciples wanted ears of grain on the Sabbath and rubbed them in their hands, he made himself their advocate against the Pharisees, and thus confirmed already the end of the Sabbath. It was fitting, as shown above, that he keep the Laws; and it is also fitting that he himself imposed an end and limit on the Laws, that he showed himself to be the Lord of the Law, and that he taught this not only by speech and word but also by deed and example. In Jeremiah also, it is written, "I spoke not to your fathers, and I commanded them not, in the day that I brought them out of the land of Egypt, concerning the matter of burnt offerings and sacrifices. But this word I commanded them, saying: Hearken to my voice, and I will be your God, and you shall be my people" (Jer 7.22–23). Again in Jeremiah it is written, "I will make a new covenant with the house of Israel" (Jer 31.31).[67] And in Baruch it is written, "I will make with them another covenant that shall be everlasting, to be their God, and they shall be my people" (Bar 2.35). And in Ezekiel it is written, "I gave them statutes that were not good, and judgments, in which they shall not live" (Ezek 20.25). Again in Jeremiah it is written, "To what purpose

---

67. See Heb 8.8–9.

do you bring me frankincense from Saba, and the sweet-smelling cane from a far country? Your holocausts are not acceptable, nor are your sacrifices pleasing to me" (Jer 6.20). In Isaiah also it is written, "To what purpose do you offer me the multitude of your victims, says the Lord? I am full. I desire not holocausts of rams, and fat of fatlings, and blood of calves and lambs and he-goats. When you came to appear before me, who required these things at your hands, that you should walk in my courts? Offer sacrifice no more in vain; incense is an abomination to me. The new moons and the Sabbaths, and other festivals, I will not abide; your assemblies are wicked. My soul hates your new moons and your solemnities; they are become troublesome to me, I am weary of bearing them" (Is 1.11–14). In the Lamentations of Jeremiah it is written, "The Lord has caused feasts and Sabbaths to be forgotten in Zion: and has delivered up king and priest to reproach, and to the indignation of his wrath" (Lam 2.6). In Hosea the Lord says, "And I will cause all her mirth to cease, her solemnities, her new moons, her Sabbaths, and all her appointed feasts" (Hos 2.11). And further on in the same book, "The children of Israel shall sit many days without king, without prince, and without sacrifice, and without altar, and without ephod, and without theraphim. And after this the children of Israel shall return, and shall seek the Lord their God, and David their king: and they shall fear the Lord, and his goodness in the last days" (Hos 3.4). Again in Micah, it is written:

What shall I offer to the Lord that is worthy? Wherewith shall I kneel before the high God? Shall I offer holocausts unto him, and calves of a year old? May the Lord be appeased with thousands of rams, or with many thousands of fat he-goats? Shall I give my firstborn for my wickedness, the fruit of my body for the sin of my soul? I will show you, O man, what is good, and what the Lord requires of you: verily, to do judgment, and to love mercy, and to walk solicitous with your God (Mi 6.6–8).

And through Malachi the Lord says, "I have no pleasure in you, says the Lord of hosts, and I will not receive a gift of your hand. For from the rising of the sun even to the going down, my name is great among the Gentiles, and in every place there is sacrifice, and there is offered to my name a clean oblation" (Mal 1.10–11). In the Psalms the Lord says, "Sacrifice and oblation you did not desire: but you have filled my ears. Burnt offering and sin offering you did not require. Then said I: Behold, I come" (Ps 39.7–8). Again, in another Psalm, "I will not reprove you for your sacrifices," and so on, down to, "Offer to God the sacrifice of praise: and pay your vows to the Most High" (Ps 49.8–14). And again in another Psalm, "I will not gather together their meetings for blood offerings," that is, by the animal-victims by which the assemblies of the Jews were previously gathered (Ps 15.4). Again, another prophet says, "Behold, the days are coming, says the Lord, and I will perfect the house of Jacob over a new covenant which I made with their fathers when I led them out of the land of Egypt."[68] Daniel says, "And he shall confirm the covenant with many, in one week: and in the half of the week the victim and the sacrifice shall fail" (Dn 9.27). In Jeremiah it is written, "Behold the days are coming, says the Lord, and I will make a new covenant with the house of Israel, and with the house of Judah: Not according to the covenant which I made with your fathers, when I took them by the hand to bring them out of the land of Egypt: the covenant which they made void, and I had dominion over them, says the Lord. But this shall be the covenant that I will make with the house of Israel, after those days, says the Lord: I will give my Law in their bowels, and I will write it in their heart: and I will be their God, and they shall be my people. And they shall teach no more every man his neighbor, and every man his brother, saying: Know the Lord: for all shall know me from the least of them even to the greatest, says the Lord: for I will forgive their iniquities, and I will remember their sin no more" (Jer 31.31–34).

*Testimonies from the New Testament,*
*that the Laws have ceased*

3. These texts and many similar ones are the testimonies of the Old Testament which show that ceremonial rituals were going to end, and we know through Christ that they already have ended. In the New Testament also there are many testimonies to the same thing, for, as was said above, Christ destroyed the Laws by his example and by his word. The Apostle says to the Romans,

---

68. The Vulgate is badly misquoted here. See Heb 8.8–9 and Jer 31.31–34.

"You are not under the Law, but under grace" (Rom 6.14). Again, he says, "But now you are loosed from the law of death, wherein we were detained; so that we should serve in newness of spirit, not in the oldness of the letter" (Rom 7.6). And again, "For the end of the Law is Christ, unto justice to everyone who believes" (Rom 10.4). The Apostle says to the Galatians, "For I, through the Law, am dead to the Law" (Gal 2.19). And a little later, "For as many as are of the works of the Law, are under a curse" (Gal 3.10). After a few verses he adds, "But Christ has redeemed us from the curse of the Law, being made a curse for us" (Gal 3.13). Again he says, "You are made void of Christ, you who are justified in the Law: you are fallen from grace. But we in spirit, by faith, wait for the hope of justice. For in Christ Jesus neither circumcision avails anything, nor uncircumcision: but faith that works by charity" (Gal 5.4–6). And a little later, "But if you are led by the Spirit, you are not under the Law" (Gal 5.18). But at the end of the same letter the Apostle says, "For in Christ Jesus neither circumcision avails anything, nor uncircumcision, but a new creature" (Gal 6.15).

4. These few testimonies from these two letters we have added in the middle as if they were more evident at first hearing, although, as we said above, a large part of the letter to the Romans and the whole letter to the Galatians aim to show that the Laws have ended. In the letter to the Ephesians the Apostle says about Christ, "For he is our peace, who has made both one, and breaking down the middle wall of partition, the enmities in his flesh: Making void the Law of commandments contained in decrees; that he might make the two in himself into one new man" (Eph 2.14–15). And in the second letter to the Corinthians, comparing the Old Testament with the New, he says, "For even that which was glorious in this part was not glorified, by reason of the glory that excels. For if that which is done away was glorious, much more that which remains is in glory" (2 Cor 3.10–11). And after a few verses he says, about the veil over Moses' face, "The selfsame veil, in the reading of the Old Testament, remains not taken away (because in Christ it is made void)" (2 Cor 3.14). Again, to the Hebrews the same Apostle says, "If then perfection was by the Levitical priesthood (for under it the people re-

ceived the Law), what further need was there that another priest should rise according to the order of Melchisedech, and not be called according to the order of Aaron? For the priesthood being translated, it is necessary that a translation also be made of the Law," and so on, down to, "For the Law brought nothing to perfection" (Heb 7.11–19). There are many other testimonies about the end of the Law in the same letter, which the diligent reader can easily consider by himself.

*Testimonies from sacred writers on the cessation of the Laws*

5. A chorus of sacred writers agrees with these texts. For Augustine says in the third book of *On Christian Doctrine:*

> At the time after the resurrection of the Lord the clear indication of our liberty came to light, and we were not burdened with the onerous performance of those signs which we now understand; rather, the Lord himself and the apostolic discipline handed on a few things for the many, which are most easy to do, most august to understand, and most pure to observe, like the sacrament of baptism and the celebration of the Body and Blood of the Lord.[69]

Again in his book *On True Religion* he says:

> Now whereas piety begins with fear, it is perfected by charity: the people, restrained by fear, were burdened with many sacraments during the time of slavery under the Old Law. For this Law was beneficial for such people, so that they may desire the grace of God which was about to come, as the Prophets sang. And when he came, we were called to liberty by the very wisdom of God when a man was assumed. A few most salutary sacraments were established, which united the society of the Christian people, a free multitude under the one God. Many things, however, which had been imposed on the Hebrew people (an enslaved multitude under the same God), were removed in fact, but remain in faith and spiritual interpretation. And so they do not bind the mind in slavery but exercise it in freedom.[70]

Jerome, in a certain letter to Augustine, says, "Paul the Apostle was not ignorant of the fact that Peter was the leader of the decree that after the Gospel, the Law did not have to be kept."[71] A

---

69. Augustine, *On Christian Doctrine* 3.9.13.
70. Augustine, *On True Religion* 17.33.
71. Jerome, *Ep.* 112.8.

little later in the same letter he says, "I proclaim that the ceremonies of the Jews are dangerous and deadly for Christians, and whoever observes them, whether he be a Jew or a Gentile, falls headlong into the Lower World of the Devil."[72] Again, Jerome says in another letter, "The whole of Jewish worship has been destroyed, and whatever victims they offer, they offer not to God, but to renegade angels and unclean spirits."[73] Again, Jerome says in the first book of his *Commentary on the Letter to the Galatians:*

> There is, in fact, no discourse of the Apostle, whether given in a letter in his absence or given by him being present, in which he does not labor to teach that the burdens of the ancient Law have been put away, and that all that went before in types and images—that is, the idleness of the Sabbath, the injury of circumcision, the cycle of first days of the month and that of three feasts per year, the scrupulosity with food, the cleansing and defilement on individual days—that all of this suddenly ended because of the grace of the Gospel, which the faith of the believing soul fulfills, not the blood of victims.[74]

Again, in the second book of the same commentary he says, "Before the Gospel of Christ shined in the whole world, the legal precepts had their own brightness. But after the greater light of evangelical grace shined and the Sun of Justice[75] appeared in the world, the light of the stars was hidden, and their rays became dark. As the Apostle says in another place: 'For even that which was glorious in this part was not glorified, by reason of the glory that excels' (2 Cor 3.10)."[76] Again, Augustine says about Psalm 67, "Indeed, all those things happened to them in figure, until the day should break and the shadows be removed."[77] Again, he says about Psalm 73:

> The sacraments of the New Testament give salvation; the sacraments of the Old Testament promised a savior. When, therefore, we already possess what was promised, why do you seek things that promise, since you already have the Savior? I say this, "you possess what was promised," not because we have already received eternal life, but because Christ has

---

72. Ibid., 112.14.
73. Jerome, *Ep.* 121.10.
74. Jerome, *Commentary on the Letter to the Galatians,* prologue.
75. See Mal 4.2.
76. Jerome, *Commentary on the Letter to the Galatians* 2.4.
77. Augustine, *Homilies on the Psalms* 67.8.

already come, who was foretold by the Prophets. The sacraments have changed; they were made easier, fewer, salutary. Why are not the things promised the same? Because then the Land of Canaan was promised, a land copious, fruitful, and flowing with milk and honey; a temporal kingdom was promised; temporal happiness was promised; an abundance of children was promised; and the subjection of enemies was promised. All these things pertain to earthly happiness. But why was it necessary that this be promised first? Because what is spiritual is not first; what is bodily, is; afterwards comes what is spiritual.[78]

Again, Augustine says about Psalm 77, "Those who receive the covenant of God in such a way that they do not divest themselves of the old vanity, are like the enemies of his people, who put the captured Ark of the Covenant next to their idols. And indeed those old idols fall against the will of their worshipers because 'all flesh is grass, and all the glory thereof as the flower of the field' (Is 40.6)." Again, Augustine says to Jerome, "I say, therefore, that circumcision of the foreskin and things of this sort were divinely given to an earlier people by a covenant, which is called old, so that they signify future events. And such things had to be fulfilled by Christ. I say that when these events came to pass, those signs remained for Christians, but only to be read for the understanding of promised prophecy, and not necessarily to be done, as if the revelation of faith were still awaited."[79] And a little later he says, "For because faith had already come, which was observed prior to those observances and revealed after the death and resurrection of the Lord, they lost, as it were, the life of their function."[80] Again, Augustine, when he explained this verse of the Apostle's letter to the Colossians ("Let no man seduce you, willing in humility and the religion of angels" [Col 2.18]), says to the bishop Paulinus:

The Apostle feared that they, to whom he writes these words, would be seduced by the shadows of things, by the sweet name of knowledge, and that they would be turned from the light of truth which is in Christ Jesus our Lord. The shadows of future things must be removed because their light, Christ, had come. Paul determined that in these circumstances one must guard against this concern, under the name of wisdom and knowledge, for various and superfluous observances, both

78. Augustine, ibid., 73.1.
80. Ibid., 82.16.

79. Augustine, *Ep.* 82.15.

## CESSATION OF THE LAWS 1.11     107

from the superstition of the Gentiles (especially from those who are called philosophers) and from Judaism.[81]

Again, he says to Maximianus about circumcision, "This sacrament held back the river Jordan and led it back to its source.[82] Although the Lord himself made void this sacrament by his crucifixion, nevertheless he received it when he was born. For those signs have not been condemned; rather, they yield to their more fitting successors."[83] In his book *On the Usefulness of Belief*, Augustine says, "In the precepts and mandates of the Law, which it is not right for Christians to use—such as the Sabbath, circumcision, sacrifices, and the like—there are such great mysteries that every pious person understands that nothing is more dangerous than to accept one of these precepts according to the letter, that is, according to the word. But he also understands that nothing is more salutary than what is revealed by the Spirit. Hence the verse, 'The letter kills, but the spirit quickens' (2 Cor 3.6)."[84] Again, about the old sacrifices he says in *Against the Opponents of the Law and the Prophets*, "The people of God does not offer such sacrifices to God since the unique sacrifice has come. All of the old sacrifices were the shadows of the unique sacrifice; they do not condemn it but signify it. For just as one thing can be signified by many sayings and many words, so one true and singular sacrifice is signified beforehand by many figurative sacrifices."[85] John Damascene says, "Those who keep the Law of Christ have been made the superior to the Mosaic Law. 'For when what is perfect came, that which was in part has been made void.'[86] The letter has been made void by the veil of the Law, that is, the veil cut by the crucifixion of the Savior, and by the Spirit, flashing with tongues of fire. Bodily things remained quiet, and the Law of slavery was fulfilled, and

---

81. Augustine, *Ep.* 149.24.
82. See Ps 113.3, 5, which reads: "The sea saw and fled: The Jordan was turned back.... What ailed you, O you sea, that you did flee: and you, O Jordan, that you were turned back?"
83. Augustine, *Ep.* 23.4.
84. Augustine, *On the Usefulness of Belief* 3.9.
85. Augustine, *Against the Opponents of the Law and the Prophets* 1.18.37.
86. See 1 Cor 13.10.

the Law of liberty was given to us."[87] Again John says, "When the truth is made manifest, the type and shadow are useless. On account of this, it is superfluous now to be circumcised, and it is contrary to holy baptism. 'For he who is circumcised is obliged to observe the whole Law.'[88] The Lord was circumcised to fulfill the Law, but he observed the whole Law and the Sabbath to fulfill and secure the Law."[89] In Book Fifteen of *The City of God*, Augustine, speaking about the Laws, says, "And because the shadows were about to pass away with the coming light, the free Sara, who signified the free city, says, 'Cast out the bondwoman and her son' (Gn 21.10)." Again, he shows in the same book that the transition from the Old Testament to the New, and likewise from the old priesthood and kingdom to the new priest and king, Christ, had been prefigured in the fact that "when Eli was a reprobate priest, Samuel replaced him in the service of God and performed the office both of priest and of judge, and when Saul was rejected, King David was established in the kingdom."[90]

6. There are many assertions of this kind from sacred writers, and they harmoniously affirm the abolition of Old Testament rituals after Christ. Indeed, if they were collected in one place, they would become a great mass of words. We, then, are content with the compendium of assertions already mentioned, which have been brought into agreement with what has been said so far. Here, then, we end this part of our treatment.

---

87. John Damascene, *On the Orthodox Faith* 96.3.
88. See Gal 5.3.
89. John Damascene, *On the Orthodox Faith* 98.2.
90. Augustine, *The City of God* 15.2, 17.4.

# PART TWO

### CHAPTER 1

HE FIRST TEXTUAL authority from the Old Testament that we offered in the first part, as a testimony to the end of the Law—namely, from Deuteronomy, "The Lord ... will raise up to you a prophet ... of your brethren ... him you shall hear [as you would me]"(Dt 18.15)—does not have the force of testimony unless it is shown that the man who was called Jesus is the Christ promised in the Law. Because of this, it will not be useless to show this from Old Testament texts.

*Christ*

In order to make firm our faith, we must, beginning with Moses and the Prophets, know how to proclaim Jesus. We must do as Jesus himself, Peter, and Paul did: Jesus, when, beginning with Moses and all the Prophets, he explained to the two disciples going to Emmaus all the Scriptures which were about him;[1]

*Peter*

Peter, when he says in the Acts of the Apostles, "Those things which God beforehand showed by the mouth of all the Prophets, that his Christ should suffer, he has so fulfilled" them through the Passion of Jesus, whom the Jews crucified (Acts 3.18); and the Apostle Paul, when he confounded the Jews by affirming that he, Jesus, is the Christ promised in the Law.[2]

2. In order to corroborate our faith and to confirm the end of the Laws through the aforementioned proof-text from Deu-

---

1. See Lk 24.27.
2. See Acts 17.3.

teronomy, we will try to show, in our own way, from clear, non-allegorical texts of the Old Testament that the crucified Jesus was the Savior promised in the Law. The Lord says to Abraham in Genesis, "In you shall all the kindred of the earth be blessed" (Gn 12.3). And again, in the same book the Lord says, "Can I hide from Abraham what I am about to do: Seeing he shall become a great and mighty nation, and in him all the nations of the earth shall be blessed?"(Gn 18.17–18) And further on in the same book he says again to Abraham, "In your seed shall all the nations of the earth be blessed" (Gn 18.18; 22.18). Therefore, what was said above, that all peoples must be blessed in Abraham, must be understood in the light of the saying that they must be blessed in his seed. For it cannot be understood to mean that the promise was fulfilled in Abraham, because if it had meant this, it would not have been added that all peoples must be blessed in his seed. Indeed, what is proper to the root is not attributed to the branch; on the contrary, what is fitting for the branch can be wholly attributed to the root. And he did not say "in seeds," as if in many, but he said "in your seed," as if in one.

### *That he is the promised one, God and man*

3. Therefore, there would be one man of the offspring of Abraham, in whom all peoples would be blessed. Because he is the seed of Abraham, he is true man; but because all peoples will be blessed in him, he is true God. Indeed, although at one time or another a mere man blesses other men—just as we read that Isaac blessed his son Jacob, and Jacob, his twelve sons, the Patriarchs, and innumerable other examples—nevertheless, we have not ever read that all peoples will be blessed in some mere man however excellent and virtuous he may be.

### *In whom there is blessing*

4. For no one is blessed unless he is freed from guilt and foreordained to eternal glory; for, otherwise, he is under a curse. Therefore, to be blessed in someone is to be freed from blame and foreordained to eternal life in him. But no one, except God alone, frees from blame and foreordains to eternal

life. The seed of Abraham, then, in whom all peoples were foretold to be blessed, must be man and God.

### An opposing argument

5. Perhaps someone might say that we can receive the effect of blessing *in someone,* without receiving that effect *from him;* rather, we receive it from God on account of his merit or love. But the statement that the peoples will be blessed much more familiarly communicates that they themselves will receive from him the effect of blessing, as for instance we say that air is illuminated and becomes light in the sun, because the sun illuminates the air by its light and makes the air to shine with light in itself.

### On mirrors

And if the light of the sun falls upon a mirror and is reflected toward dark air and illuminates it, we do not say that the air is light in the mirror but that it is light in the sun. Thus, therefore, he who is blessed by God only through the merit of another or on account of the love of another, is not called light or blessed in the other, but rather in God, who illuminates through grace and cleanses the darkness of guilt. He, therefore, in whom all peoples are blessed gives the effect of blessing; he, then, is God himself.

6. Isaiah shows that this blessing is freedom from guilt and that the promised one, in whom all peoples are blessed, will truly free from guilt, when he says, "There shall come out of Zion he that shall deliver, and shall turn away ungodliness from Jacob. And this is to them the covenant: when I shall take away their sins" (Rom 11.26–27).[3] This text also shows that he is one God with the Father, for, because God alone takes away sin, these words clearly indicate that both, he who promises here the one to come from Zion and he who is promised to come, take away sin by one indivisible operation. This agrees with what the Psalmist says in the person of the promised one, "But I am appointed king by him over Zion, his holy mountain, preaching

---

3. See Is 59.20–21.

his commandment. The Lord has said to me: You are my son; this day have I begotten you" (Ps 2.6–7). What follows shows that this cannot apply to David himself, for he did not reign to the ends of the earth, but his reign was confined to a narrow piece of land.

CHAPTER 2

1. However bold someone may be, he could not deny that in some man from the offspring of Abraham all peoples are blessed and that they receive in him, if they wish, the effect of blessing, that is, cleansing from guilt and the conferral of grace and glory. And it will not be able to be denied that this man, in whom all peoples receive the effect of blessing, is the best of men and most acceptable to God, whether he gives the said effect or whether God gives it on account of his merit and love. Because this sort of man is unique, it is necessary that no other be similar to him in excellence. For if all are blessed in one, why would there be another in whom all would be blessed again? Psalm 71 says about this one man, "Give to the king your judgment, O God: and to the king's son your justice" (Ps 71.2). About the king's son the following verse is added at the end of the same Psalm, "And in him shall all the tribes of the earth be blessed: all nations shall magnify him" (Ps 71.17). One man, therefore, is promised to be from the seed of Abraham, in whom all peoples will be blessed, and about whom David speaks in the aforementioned Psalm. But in the verse of the Psalm just before the one mentioned, he is shown to be eternal, and so God. For it says about him, "Let his name be blessed for evermore: his name continues before the sun" (Ps 71.17). But that which is not begun before the sun, but continues, is eternal. The angels can be said to be created and established before the sun by a priority of nature, but not by a priority of time, because, "He that lives forever created all things together" (Eccl 18.1). But the angels could not be said to continue or to have continued before the sun. Therefore, the only thing that continues before the sun is God. And his name is not said to continue before the sun in the same way as all created things are said to have existed

from eternity in the mind of God in their eternal ideas. For if it were so, the prophet would have attributed nothing more to him than what belongs to a creature, by saying that his name continues before the sun. But it is established that the prophet wanted to demonstrate his spiritual excellence when he said that his name continued before the sun.

2. Isaiah expressed the simultaneously divine and human nature of the one in whom all peoples are blessed, when he said, "Behold a virgin shall conceive, and bear a son, and his name shall be called Emmanuel" (Is 7.14). Because he was conceived and born of a woman he is shown to be true man, and in the name Emmanuel, which means "God with us," he is shown to be God and man. For everyone is what he is truly called. Therefore, if he is truly called "God with us," he himself truly is God with us. The prophet could ascribe so excellent a dignity (namely, to be conceived and born of a virgin) to none other than him in whom all peoples receive blessing. And he should not be called God derivatively and commonly, as many are said to be gods, but by a proper name. For he does not say, "He will be called Emmanuel," but "His name shall be called," as is proper to him, "Emmanuel" (Is 7.14).

3. Again, Isaiah expresses his twin nature when he says, "For a child is born to us, and a son is given to us, and the government is upon his shoulder: and his name shall be called, Wonderful, Counselor, God, Mighty, the Father of the world to come, the Prince of Peace" (Is 9.6). Indeed, the words "a child is born and a son given to us" show him to be true man. The name that follows, however, has a sixfold expression and can suit no one except God, who in the book of Judges speaks in an angel, saying, "Why do you ask my name, which is wonderful?" (Jgs 13.18) And again, speaking in the angel with whom Jacob wrestled, he says, "Why do you ask my name," which is Wonderful? (Gn 32.29) No one could say that it was not God who spoke here in the angel who wrestled with Jacob, because the same angel (or man, as he is called in another place) says to Jacob, "Your name shall not be called Jacob, but Israel: for if you have been strong against God, how much more shall you prevail against men?" (Gn 32.28) Eternal Wisdom, which is God, says in Proverbs, "I,

wisdom, dwell in counsel, and am present in learned thoughts" (Prv 8.12). And a little later, "Counsel and equity are mine, prudence is mine, strength is mine. By me kings reign, and lawgivers decree just things. By me princes rule, and the mighty decree justice" (Prv 8.14–16). He, therefore, who is this wisdom, is named by the proper name "Counselor."

4. Again, it is fittingly said only about God that his name be called God; and the name of God alone, who is fortitude in himself, is this name: "Strong." For those who are strong by a participation in strength do not have the proper name "Strong"; rather, they have the name by a common derivation. And so the Psalmist says, "The Lord, who is strong and mighty: the Lord, mighty in battle" (Ps 23.8). Who else is the "Father of the age to come" than he who says through the prophet Malachi, "If, then, I be a father, where is my honor? And if I be a master, where is my fear?" (Mal 1.6); or who says through Jeremiah, "Therefore at least at this time call to me: You are my father, the guide of my virginity" (Jer 3.4)? Again in the same prophet, "You shall call me father and shall not cease to walk after me" (Jer 3.19). Who else is the prince of peace, except him who is peace in his substance? He says through Isaiah, "I created the fruit of the lips, peace, peace to him that is far off, and to him that is near" (Is 57.19). And again in the same prophet, "I will make your visitation peace, and your overseers justice" (Is 60.17).

5. And these six names would not be called one name for anyone except God, in whom there is no multiplicity, but wholly unity. For when a creature is called by many names, it is said to have many names, and the names are not said to be one name. It would not be fitting to say, "The name, Cicero, will be called Marcus Tullius," or "The name, Peter, will be called Simon Cephas." No one can say that the prophet spoke these names about someone other than him in whom all peoples are blessed. This is clear from the fact that so great an excellence in name could not be suitable for another, as well as from what the prophet says before and after this passage. For the prophet had said that "the people [of the Gentiles] that walked in darkness have seen a great light," and that "to them that dwelt in the region of the shadow of death, light is risen" (Is 9.1–2). A little later he adds,

as it were, the reason for this, when he says, "For a child is born to us" (Is 9.6) and so on. It is as if he said, "The child who was born will illuminate the peoples walking in darkness and living in the shadow of death." But by what light if not the light of truth and grace, which introduces the effect of the blessing to those peoples? What immediately follows about the child who was born testifies to this: "He shall sit upon the throne of David, and upon his kingdom; to establish it and strengthen it with judgment and with justice, from henceforth and for ever" (Is 9.7). For this cannot be understood about any earthly king who rules the earthly kingdom of David, but about him alone in whom all the peoples are justified and blessed forever.

6. The words of Baruch expressly manifest the God-man, when he says about the author of wisdom, the provider of the earth with flocks, the sender and the summoner of light and the stars, "This is our God, and there shall be no other accounted of in comparison to him. He found out all the way of prudence, and gave it to Jacob his servant, and to Israel his beloved. Afterwards he was seen upon earth, and conversed with men" (Bar 3.36–38). But how was God otherwise seen and how did he otherwise converse with men, if not in the form of a man, just as John says, "The Word was made flesh, and dwelt among us, and we have seen his glory, the glory as it were of the Only-begotten of the Father" (Jn 1.14)? And again in his canonical letter he says, "That which was from the beginning, which we have heard, which we have seen with our eyes, which we have looked upon, and our hands have handled, of the word of life: For the life was manifested; and we have seen and do bear witness, and declare unto you the life eternal, which was with the Father, and has appeared to us" (1 Jn 1.1–2).

CHAPTER 3

1. Also, it cannot be denied that he who was promised from the seed of Abraham, in whom all peoples are blessed, is the same person about whom Jacob says, "And he shall be the expectation of nations" (Gn 49.10). For whom else could the peoples expect, if not him in whom they will be blessed? And

it cannot be said that the same person is not the expectation of the Prophets. But he whom the Prophets have expected is God. As Isaiah says, "Bind up the testimony, seal the Law among my disciples. And I will wait for the Lord, who has hid his face from the house of Jacob, and I will look for him" (Is 8.16–17). And again, Isaiah says, "And the Lord of hosts shall make unto all the peoples in this mountain a feast of fat things, a feast of wine, of fat things full of marrow, of wine purified from the lees. And he shall destroy in this mountain the face of the bond with which all the peoples were tied, and the web that he began over all nations. He shall cast death down headlong for ever: and the Lord God shall wipe away every tear from every face, and the reproach of his people he shall take away from the whole earth: for the Lord has spoken it. And they shall say in that day: Behold, this is our Lord God, we have waited for him, and he will save us: this is the Lord, we have patiently waited for him; we shall be joyful in his salvation" (Is 25.6–9).

2. How will death be cast down headlong for ever and tears and disgrace carried away, if not by that blessing which will destroy the chains of sin and confer the grace and glory which were promised in the seed of Abraham, and if not in him who is the expectation of the peoples, about whom Jacob says, "I will look for your salvation, O Lord" (Gn 49.18)? About him who was awaited Isaiah says this: "Behold, this is our Lord God, we have waited for him, and he will save us: this is the Lord, we have patiently waited for him, we shall be joyful in his salvation" (Is 25.9). Isaiah clearly makes known here that he who is the expectation and salvation of the peoples is the Lord God. And the prophet has not passed over here his humanity. For how could he say, "Behold, this is our Lord God" (Is 25.9) unless he were talking about what is visible and demonstrable to the eye of the flesh? Jeremiah in Lamentations also says, "The Lord is my portion, said my soul: therefore will I wait for him" (Lam 3.24). David also says, "And now what is my hope? Is it not the Lord?" (Ps 38.8) And again, "With expectation I have waited for the Lord" (Ps 39.2). Consider that the expectation of the peoples and of the Prophets is the Lord. And again, their expectation is a man from the seed of Abraham, who will lead the race. Ha-

bakkuk witnesses to his humanity when he says, "And he shall appear at the end, and shall not lie: if he makes any delay, wait for him: for he shall surely come, and he shall not be late" (Hab 2.3).

3. For how will he appear in the end, if he is not made visible through the assumption of the flesh at the end of time? In case, therefore, someone would be so bold as to say that one person is the expectation of the peoples and another person that of the Prophets, these testimonies clearly show that he, who is their expectation, is at the same time man and God. Again, in Psalm 44 it is said about him that he is "beautiful in form above the sons of men" (Ps 44.3), whom God has blessed forever. To him then it is said, "Your throne, O God, is for ever and ever: the scepter of your kingdom is a scepter of uprightness. You have loved justice, and hated iniquity: therefore God, your God, has anointed you with the oil of gladness above your fellows" (Ps 44.7–8). He is, therefore, one and the same God. To him it is said, "Your throne, O God, is for ever and ever" (Ps 44.7–8), and this is because he is beautiful in form above the sons, on his lips grace has been poured out, and he has been blessed by God forever and anointed with the oil of happiness above his fellows.

4. Again, in Psalm 86 a man is said to be born in a certain city, who being the same as the Most High founded the city. It is necessary that this man exist after the city, because he was born in it; and it is necessary that he exist before it, because as Most High he founded it. This cannot be fitting for some mere man, but only for him who is in his person God and man, who as man exists in time after the city in which he was born, and who as divine (and in his divinity he exists from eternity as the Most High and has founded all things) exists in time before that city. But however bold someone may be, he cannot deny that he who is the expectation of the peoples, in whom all the peoples are blessed, is, as we said above, the best of men, most acceptable to God, and even without sin. For how could there be the forgiveness of all sin in him, if he himself were stained by some sin? How could all things be forgiven on account of him, if he needs to be forgiven in someone else?

### Proof that he is clean from sin

Therefore, it is necessary that he be clean from all sin, and so be immune from every lie, because every lie is a sin. Habakkuk expresses this immunity from lying in the verse that I quoted above, "and he shall appear at the end and shall not lie" (Hab 2.3). Again, Isaiah expresses his immunity from sin and from lying when he says, "Because he has done no iniquity, neither was there deceit in his mouth" (Is 53.9).

5. Because it has been shown that the promised one was not a liar but in all things truthful, if we show that he asserts that he is God, it is sufficiently proven that he truly is God. Let us, therefore, leave aside this argument for the moment, so that we can arrive at a clearer proof of him and turn to other things. Let us suppose that the promised seed of Abraham is God and man, and let us show through what succession of generations he will descend from Abraham. It occurs to us first that he would not descend except through Isaac, for the Lord said to Abraham, "Sarai your wife you shall not call Sarai, but Sara. And I will bless her, and of her I will give you a son, whom I will bless, and he shall become nations, and kings of people shall spring from him" (Gn 17.15–16). And a little later, "Sara your wife shall bear you a son, and you shall call his name Isaac, and I will establish my covenant with him for a perpetual covenant, and with his seed after him. And as for Ishmael I have also heard you" (Gn 17.19–20). And a little later he adds, "But my covenant I will establish with Isaac" (Gn 17.21). And what is the covenant of the Lord for a perpetual covenant if not that in which man is justified and reconciled forever with God? But he is blessed in that in which he is justified. Therefore, the Lord has this firm good will and decree for Isaac, that through him there would descend from Abraham he in whom all peoples will be blessed. Again, the Lord says to Abraham in Genesis, "In all that Sara has said to you, hearken to her voice: for in Isaac shall your seed be called" (Gn 21.12). Therefore, either Isaac himself is the seed, in whom all peoples will be blessed, or it would descend from Abraham through Isaac. But this seed is not Isaac himself, because it is promised also to those who are begotten from Isaac, like Jacob, Judah, Jesse, and David, as will be clear below.

6. In the prophecy of Balaam the one to be born from Jacob is shown to be the same as the one awaited by the peoples and desired by them. The prophecy says, "A star shall rise out of Jacob and a scepter shall spring up from Israel: and shall strike the chiefs of Moab, and shall waste all the children of Seth. And he shall possess Idumea: the inheritance of Seir shall come to their enemies, but Israel shall act manfully. Out of Jacob shall he come that shall rule, and shall destroy the remains of the city" (Nm 24.17–19). In this prophecy he who is to be born from Jacob is foretold to dominate, and he is called a star and a scepter. And because we do not see these things fulfilled in the letter, they must be more appropriately understood concerning no one except the promised one in whom all peoples will be blessed, whom David in Psalm 109 calls the Lord and a scepter and one shining with the splendor of the stars. For whom else did David call his Lord besides the promised one, when he says, "The Lord said to my Lord: Sit you at my right hand" (Ps 109.1)? Or to whom would God the Father speak these words if not to the greatest man who is most acceptable to him, in whom all the peoples will receive blessing? Again, the words that follow—"The Lord will send forth the scepter of your power out of Zion: rule you in the midst of your enemies" (Ps 109.2)—cannot be directed to anyone except to him to whom it was foretold, "Sit you at my right hand" (Ps 109.1). These words express his dominion and his being named a scepter. The splendor of the star is also expressed in the Psalm when the verse is added, "With you is the principality in the day of your strength: in the brightness of the saints" (Ps 109.3). Therefore, David is clear about the one who Balaam prophesied would rise from the seed of Jacob. In this Psalm David also expresses the eternal divinity of the one to come when he says, "With you is the principality" (Ps 109.3), and when he says, "Before the day star I begot you" (Ps 109.3).

### From Judah

7. The one to be born of Judah is sufficiently expressed because in the blessing of Judah the one to come, who is the expectation of the peoples, is prophesied. And, although the same

one is prophesied in the blessings of some of the other sons of Jacob, he is not prophesied as plainly nor with so many and so great prophetic proclamations of the one to come.

### From Jesse

Isaiah shows that the same one will be born of Jesse, when he says, "there shall come forth a rod[4] out of the root of Jesse, and a flower shall rise up out of his root" (Is 11.1). For the following words cannot be appropriate for any corporeal rod or flower, nor for any man except him in whom all peoples will be blessed. And the sevenfold Holy Spirit would be said to rest on him and to fill him, for no one else in this life is clean from all sin. As Job says, "Can man be justified compared with God, or he that is born of a woman appear clean?" (Jb 25.4) But he who has sin makes himself now worse, now better; and when he is better he participates more in the Holy Spirit, and when he is worse, he participates less. The Holy Spirit is more *moved* in him, or *over* him, than *rests* on him. And he is not filled with the Holy Spirit in any parts that have sin. Although, therefore, we find it written that the Holy Spirit rests upon the humble and that certain men had been filled with the Holy Spirit (such as John the Baptist), nevertheless what Isaiah says about the rest and repletion of the sevenfold Spirit could not be so truly and excellently appropriate for anyone as it is for him about whom the same prophet says that iniquity was not in him, "neither was guile found in his mouth" (1 Pt 2.22).[5] It is agreed, however, that the prophet attributed rest and repletion, through the excellence of the sevenfold Spirit, to the rod and flower that were about to come forth from the root of Jesse.

8. Moreover, that excellence of justice which follows could not be fitting for anyone except him in whom all are blessed and justified. It could be said about him that "he shall not judge according to the sight of the eyes," because God attributes to him what is his own, when he says to Samuel in the first book of Kings, "Not according to the look of man do I judge: for man sees those

---

4. Latin: *virga*, the same noun translated here as "scepter."
5. See Is 53.9.

things that appear, but God beholds the heart" (1 Sm 16.7). Again, what human judge judges apart from what he hears from the litigants? But he in whom all the peoples will be blessed shall not "reprove according to the hearing of the ears. But he shall judge the poor with justice, and shall reprove with equity for the meek of the earth; and he shall strike the earth with the rod of his mouth, and with the breath of his lips he shall slay the wicked. And justice shall be the girdle of his loins: and faith the girdle of his reins" (Is 11.3–5). To what man or earthly king, however just he may be, could such things be attributed? On the contrary, taken together, these attributes can be fitting only for a person who is man and God. For he must be a man who comes forth from the root of a man and whom the sevenfold Spirit fills, but he must be true God who judges not according to the vision of the eyes and argues not according to the hearing of the ears. For only he who "beholds the heart" can do this.

9. What follows cannot be literally and historically true, namely, that "the wolf shall dwell with the lamb: and the leopard shall lie down with the kid" (Is 11.6), and the rest of the things that are listed there about the peaceful cohabitation of beasts. And the reason that Isaiah gives for this peaceful cohabitation would not fit the historical sense, even if it were true. For it is said that this sort of peaceful cohabitation of beasts will exist, "for the earth is filled with the knowledge of the Lord, as the covering waters of the sea" (Is 11.9). An abundance of knowledge, however, makes only those who can receive knowledge to dwell in peace. Those who can receive knowledge, though, are not irrational beasts, but only men. Therefore, that prophecy about the peaceful cohabitation of beasts can signify only that men, who were like beasts in their affections and in their various and contradictory ways, will live together in a peaceful, united way of life, as they will be filled abundantly with the knowledge of the Lord through him who comes forth from the root of Jesse. This prophecy of Isaiah, therefore, shows that the promised one, in whom all peoples are blessed, will come forth as God and man from the offspring of Jesse, and he will unite the various ways of life of moribund peoples into a single harmony through the knowledge of the Lord. For he in whom all peoples are blessed

and justified must unite all men in a unified way of life, and even in a unified knowledge of how to live. Therefore, God the Father addresses him through the Psalmist, when he says, "Ask of me, and I will give you the Gentiles for your inheritance, and the utmost parts of the earth for your possession. You shall rule them with a rod of iron, and shall break them in pieces like a potter's vessel" (Ps 2.8–9). The prophecies of Isaiah and the Psalmist also show that the promised one is the scepter about which Balaam prophesied.

10. It is also shown that the promised one will be born from the offspring of David. For the Lord says to David through the prophet Nathan in 2 Samuel, "And when your days shall be fulfilled, and you shall sleep with your fathers, I will raise up your seed after you, which shall proceed out of your bowels, and I will establish his kingdom. He shall build a house to my name, and I will establish the throne of his kingdom for ever. I will be to him a father, and he shall be to me a son," and so on (2 Sm 7.12–14). Augustine shows most plainly, in Book Seventeen of *The City of God*, that this prophecy is not fulfilled in Solomon, nor in any other offspring of David except our Lord Jesus Christ. I do not wish to insert this demonstration here because it is lengthy, and the reader will be able to find it easily in the aforementioned book. The prophecy of Jeremiah also shows that the promised one will be born from the seed of David: "Behold, the days come, says the Lord, and I will raise up to David a just branch: and a king shall reign, and shall be wise, and shall execute judgment and justice in the earth. In those days shall Judah be saved, and Israel shall dwell confidently: and this is the name that they shall call him: the Lord our just one" (Jer 23.5–6).

12. Clearly this prophecy was not fulfilled in any of the kings who were descended from David up to Jesus Christ. For it is written in Sirach, "Except David, and Hezekiah, and Josiah, all committed sin. For the kings of Judah forsook the Law of the Most High, and despised the fear of God" (Sir 49.5–6); and it goes on to show that all the kings of Judah, apart from the three mentioned, ruled in foolishness and injustice. And what Jeremiah says here cannot be understood about any of those three mentioned, because Jeremiah himself foretold that the promised one would

come, and when he was saying this, David, Hezekiah, and Josiah were already dead. For the Word of the Lord came to Jeremiah in the days of Josiah, the son of Amon and the king of Judah, in the thirteenth year of his reign. And the Word of the Lord came to him in the days of Jehoiakim, son of the king of Judah, up to the end of the eleventh year of Zedekiah, son of Josiah, king of Judah, up to the deportation from Jerusalem. These words were spoken under Jehoiakim or Jeconiah, and it is not written that one of these three had been called by the people, "the Lord our just one" (Jer 23.6). Again, Jeremiah says, "In those days, and at that time, I will make the bud of justice to spring forth unto David, and I shall do judgment and justice in the earth. In those days shall Judah be saved, and Israel shall dwell securely: and this is the name that they shall call him: The Lord our just one. For thus says the Lord: There shall not be cut off from David a man to sit upon the throne of the house of Israel" (Jer 33.15–17). But did not the same prophet prophesy the end of the earthly reign of David himself? And did not the same kingdom come to an end in his time? For he says, "Say to the king, and to the queen: Humble yourselves, sit down: for the crown of your glory will come down from your head. The cities of the south are shut up, and there is none to open them: all Judah is carried away captive with an entire captivity" (Jer 13.18–19).

13. We hold, then, as is evident from what has been said, that the one promised from Abraham, in whom all peoples are blessed, is God as well as man descending from Abraham through Isaac, Jacob, Judah, Jesse, and David.

*On a good king*

He calls back all nations to a harmonious and unified way of life, and so will rule all (for true dominion and a true kingdom corrects a perverse way of life and leads those who quarrel on account of vices back to the unity of virtue), and he is free from all sin.

*That the birth of the Messiah is from a virgin*

That he was conceived as a man and born of the Virgin the above-quoted prophecy of Isaiah makes clear, "Behold a virgin shall conceive, and bear a son, and his name shall be called Emmanuel" (Is 7.14). For if he were conceived through the carnal union of a man and a woman, he would have drawn the stain of original sin, which, as said above, is not possible. Jeremiah introduces his perfection in wisdom and virtue when he was in the womb of his mother: "For the Lord has created a new thing upon the earth: and a woman shall compass a man" (Jer 31.22). For it is nothing new if a woman should have a baby in her womb, or if she should in some other way compass a man, but it is wonderfully new that a child, because of his greatness in the womb, be a man perfect in the gift of wisdom.

### The place of his birth

14. The prophet Micah shows the place of his birth, when he says, "And you, Bethlehem Ephrata, are a little one among the thousands of Judah: out of you shall come forth unto me he that is to be the ruler in Israel: and his going forth is from the beginning, from the days of eternity" (Mi 5.2). These words, though, as is clear from the text that follows, could suit only the one who is God and man, promised to come from the stock of Abraham. The place of his birth here, then, evidently expresses what the Jews openly confessed when Herod asked them.

### CHAPTER 4

### The manner of life and the death of the Messiah

1. Isaiah prophesied that he who, as God and man, exalted over other men, would come to save the peoples, would suffer insult, injury, contempt, and voluntary death, through which he would free the peoples from the death of sin and punishment. He prophesied very clearly even the manner of the Passion when he said:

> Behold, my servant shall understand, he shall be exalted, and extolled, and shall be exceeding high. As many have been astonished at you, so shall his visage be inglorious among men, and his form among the sons of men. He shall sprinkle many nations, kings shall shut their mouth at him: for they to whom it was not told of him, shall see: and they that heard not, have beheld. Who has believed our report? And to whom is the arm of the Lord revealed? And he shall grow up as a tender

plant before him, and as a root out of a thirsty ground. There is no beauty in him, nor comeliness, and we have seen him, and there was no sightliness, that we should be desirous of him. Despised, and the most abject of men, a man of sorrows, and acquainted with infirmity, and his look was, as it were, hidden and despised, whereupon we esteemed him not. Surely he has borne our infirmities and carried our sorrows, and we have thought him, as it were, a leper, as one struck by God and afflicted. But he was wounded for our iniquities, he was bruised for our sins. The chastisement of our peace was upon him, and by his bruises we are healed. All we like sheep have gone astray, every one has turned aside into his own way, and the Lord has laid on him the iniquity of us all. He was offered because it was his own will, and he opened not his mouth. He is led as a sheep to the slaughter, and shall be dumb as a lamb before his shearer, and he shall not open his mouth. He was taken away from distress, and from judgment. Who shall declare his generation? Because he is cut off out of the land of the living; for the wickedness of my people have I struck him. And he shall give the ungodly for his burial, and the rich for his death, because he has done no iniquity, neither was there deceit in his mouth. And the Lord was pleased to bruise him in infirmity, but he shall lay down his life for sin, he shall see a long-lived seed, and the will of the Lord shall be prosperous in his hand. Because his soul has labored, he shall see and be filled: by his knowledge has the just one himself justified my many servants, and he shall bear their iniquities. Therefore will I distribute to him very many, and he shall divide the spoils of the strong, because he has delivered his soul unto death, and was reputed with the wicked: he has borne the sins of many, and has prayed for the transgressors (Is 52.13–53.12)

that they not perish.

2. The story of the Gospel, which narrates his Passion in a manner similar to this prophecy, clearly declares that this prophecy was fulfilled in the man who is called Jesus. For he was truly the servant of the Lord who did not come to be served but to serve,[6] who even deigned to wash the feet of his disciples when he truly knew,[7] as John says, "Jesus, knowing that his hour was come, that he should pass out of this world to the Father" (Jn 13.1). And again John says, "Jesus therefore, knowing all things that should come upon him" (Jn 18.4). And in another place, "And Jesus knowing their thoughts," was himself lifted up on the cross (Mt 12.25). Hence he said, "If I be lifted up from the earth,

---

6. See Mk 10.45.
7. See Jn 13.2–11.

I will draw all things to myself" (Jn 12.32). And again he says, "As Moses lifted up the serpent in the desert, so must the Son of man be lifted up" (Jn 3.14).[8] He himself was lifted into heaven at the Ascension. In fact, he was lifted up before those looking on, as the Acts of the Apostles says, "And a cloud received him out of their sight. And while they were beholding him going up to heaven," and so on (Acts 1.9–10). Luke also says, "And it came to pass, whilst he blessed them, he departed from them, and was carried up to heaven" (Lk 24.51). Mark says, "And the Lord Jesus, after he had spoken to them, was taken up into heaven, and sits on the right hand of God" (Mk 16.19). And what could be more exalted than to sit at the right hand of God, or more exalted than a servant of God, knowing that he was perfect in wisdom, age, and grace, being made obedient to the Father unto death: "For which cause God the Father also has exalted him, and has given him a name which is above all names, that in the name of Jesus every knee should bow, of those that are in heaven, on earth, and under the earth, and that every tongue should confess that the Lord Jesus Christ is in the glory of God the Father" (Phil 2.9–11). All of these things have now been clearly fulfilled in the Lord Jesus, son of Mary, who is called God by all peoples and at whose name every knee bends, because "angels came and ministered to him" (Mt 4.11). The demons obeyed his command, even unwillingly, and all the nations serve him and confess him.

3. Many were astonished at him when he healed every illness, cast out demons, "commanded the winds and the sea" (Mt 8.26), gave light to the man blind from birth, raised from the dead the man who was stinking for four days, and fed so many thousand men with so little bread and fish. As Matthew says, "And after the devil was cast out, the dumb man spoke, and the multitudes wondered, saying, 'Never was the like seen in Israel'" (Mt 9.33). Clearly the deeds of the Lord Jesus caused (and cause) amazement and wonder, more than the deeds of any other man about whom anything has ever been related in any book of history. And just as his deeds were exceedingly

---

8. See Nm 21.8–9.

amazing, so the sight of his Passion was exceedingly shameful. Hence, especially among all men, he was inglorious in his reproachful Passion; and nevertheless, his Passion was very truly a most glorious thing. But what was seen with human eyes, in the form of the servant that he had assumed, was an exceedingly shameful punishment and disgrace. On account of this, Isaiah speaks of his visage and form among the sons of men, for among the sons of God, who saw with the eye of faith the truth of the Word of God in addition to the form of the slave, the sight of him was not inglorious. Nevertheless, to the eyes of carnal men thinking carnally, as was said, his Passion was inglorious, because he was counted among criminals and sinners, sentenced to the kind of death to which the most wicked men were condemned at a place and during a time open to the public; the hour of the day was made known, a multitude of people were gathered for the festal day, those who knew him were standing nearby and looking on, and his crucifiers did not pity him but insulted and jeered at him. How great were the wonder and amazement at him of so many when he sat upon an ass and came to Jerusalem, and, "A very great multitude spread their garments in the way: and others cut boughs from the trees, and strewed them in the way: And the multitudes that went before and that followed, cried, saying: 'Hosanna to the son of David: Blessed is he that comes in the name of the Lord: Hosanna in the highest.' And when he was come into Jerusalem, the whole city was moved, saying: 'Who is this?'" (Mt 21.8–10) But, as was said, in proportion to the greatness of this amazement at him was his disgrace on the day of his Passion.

CHAPTER 5

1. The same Lord Jesus sprinkled many nations; that is to say, he sprinkled all the baptized with the waters of baptism and with the sprinkling of his own blood, for whoever is baptized in Christ Jesus is baptized into his death and his blood.[9] Baptism, indeed, is the sacrament of the blood of the Lord Jesus.

---

9. See Rom 6.3–4.

As Peter says, "Unto obedience and sprinkling of the blood of the Lord Jesus Christ." The sprinkling written about in Exodus signified the one of which Peter spoke: "Dip a bunch of hyssop in the blood that is at the door, and sprinkle the transom of the door therewith, and both the door lintels" (Ex 12.22). Again, in the same book it is written about Moses, "And he took the blood and sprinkled it upon the people, and he said, 'This is the blood of the covenant which the Lord has made with you concerning all these words'" (Ex 24.8).

2. This sprinkling was also signified in the book of Numbers by the sprinkling of the water of expiation mixed with the ashes of a burnt red heifer.[10] It was unheard-of in any history until the present time that anybody but the Lord Jesus in any way sprinkled many peoples. Because of the Lord Jesus, kings shut their mouths.[11] For kings are philosophers, who seemed to be leaders of the world because of their philosophical wisdom, and their mouths—that is, the wisdom that they taught and wrote—have been silenced by the folly of the preaching of the cross of Christ.[12] Because of Christ, the kings also opened their mouths, when they commanded that those who confess the Christian name be killed. But now they shut their mouths on account of him, because out of reverence and fear of him, they restrain their mouths not only from every cruel and malicious word but even more from an idle word. How many kings have we heard restrain their mouths out of reverence for the Lord Jesus from uttering cruel commands that they would have commanded if their fear and honor of him had not shut their mouths? When, therefore, a powerful man reveres Christ in another person, and on account of that restrains his mouth from a cruel command, he shuts his mouth for Christ, whom he reveres in another. In all the matters in which today the kings of the earth defer to Churchmen, do they not defer on account of Christ and shut their mouths for Christ, lest they command the possessions of the Church to be plundered?

3. And this is because the nations and their kings saw Christ

---

10. See Nm 19.1–10.
11. See Is 52.15.
12. See 1 Cor 1.18, 23.

already with the eyes of faith; they were not told about him as the Jews were through the Law, the Psalms, and the Prophets. And did those who did not hear through the Law and the Prophets consider what they believed with understanding? Perhaps the many to whom nothing was told about Christ, and who heard nothing about him, received faith in him when they questioned his disciples, as Cornelius, to whom Christ had not been preached, summoned Peter and was baptized by him.[13] And something similar happened with Philip and the eunuch.[14]

4. How many have been purified by the sprinkling of the blood of Jesus Christ before the years of discretion, and, when dying in this state of purification, see and contemplate the glory of Christ? And to these, nevertheless, nothing had been told about Christ, and they had heard nothing about him. Thus far are the words of the Lord, to which those with whom he was talking respond in the following words: they say, "Lord, who has believed our report? And to whom is the arm of the Lord . . . revealed?" (Jn 12.38)[15] The Septuagint has, "O Lord, who has believed," and so on, although our codices do not have, "O Lord." Who are these hearers and answerers if not the Prophets? For the Lord, the Father, spoke chiefly to them and in them. It is, then, as if they said, "We heard what you said above about your servant, and just as we heard and saw, so we have said to others." But "who has believed our report" (Is 53.1), that is, who has believed what we heard from you and what others have heard us say, as if the believer is rare in comparison with the unbelievers? And is he worthy of admiration who is the sort that believed our report? "And to whom is the arm of the Lord revealed?" (Is 53.1)—the arm of the Lord, that is, the strength of the Lord, manifest in what was foretold about the servant of the Lord.

5. The chorus of prophets further described the properties of the aforementioned servant, when it said that "he will rise" before the face of the Lord "just like a bush" (Is 53.2). In fact, a bush rises from the earth without the corruption of the earth, without plowing, and often without the scattering of seeds. Thus

---

13. See Acts 10.1–8.   14. See Acts 8.38.
15. See Is 53.1.

from the earth, that is, the flesh of the Blessed Virgin, Jesus Christ arises: he was born without the corruption of his mother, without the plowing of a carnal father, without the reception of the seed of man. Symmachus has "branch" instead of "bush."[16] And the Septuagint has "we announced, as it were, a child before his face." When we bring these two texts together, the aforementioned servant is understood to be the child who is born, not by the law of procreation from a woman by the seed of a man, but by the law governing the production of a branch from a tree. This following verse has the same sense, "and as a root out of a thirsty ground" (Is 53.2).

6. Nevertheless this last verse introduces perhaps more explicitly the fact that his rising was supernatural, for a root tends to rise not from dry land but from irrigated land. Aquila has "impassable" instead of "dry," and in this reading one can bring in the integrity of virginity.[17] For a root that rises up from impassable land rises without sowing or planting. This was prophesied above when it was said, "There shall come forth a rod out of the root of Jesse" (Is 11.1). The angel expresses this manner of Jesus Christ's rising, as if a bush from the land of virginal flesh, when he appeared to Mary, who asked: "How shall this be done, because I know not man?" He says, "The Holy Spirit shall come upon you, and the power of the Most High shall overshadow you. And therefore also the Holy which shall be born of you shall be called the Son of God" (Lk 1.34–35). And an angel said to Joseph, Mary's husband, that what was conceived in her is of the Holy Spirit.[18] Behold, he was conceived supernaturally in the Virgin by the working of the Holy Spirit, and he was conceived from a Virgin without the seed of man, just as a bush, branch, and root in dry and impassable land rises up without plowing, sowing, planting, and watering. And it happened wonderfully by the providence of the Holy Spirit that one translator said "dry" and another "impassable." And so that dry land was understood to be un-irrigated. For if it is impassable, who would irrigate it?

---

16. See Jerome, *Commentary on Isaiah* 14.53.
17. See ibid.
18. See Mt 1.20.

## CHAPTER 6

1. After this, the infirmity of the Lord Jesus' Passion is plainly described. For what he suffered in his Passion was to human and carnal eyes, as was said above, not beautiful, decorous, or glorious. In fact, the Septuagint has, "He did not have beauty, nor glory." For what did he suffer in his Passion to the human eyes of the flesh, except the cross, the nail, the lance, the crown of thorns, nakedness, wounds, the flowing of blood, the gall, the vinegar, the tears of those nearby, the twisting of his hands, the shedding of his hair, the hatred and mockery of his enemies? Some lack a beautiful appearance in death, because the killing itself disfigures their bodies. This kind of death nevertheless is not necessarily shameful, but often is glorious. But death on a cross at that time was not glorious, but shameful. Similarly, some soldiers are disfigured in fighting, but because they conquered bravely, the disfigurement from the fight is itself decorous and glorious. In this way the disfigurement of Christ was truly most decorous and glorious, although in the sight of the carnal, who did not understand, it was most shameful.

2. The next verse is spoken in the person of the crucifiers, "And we have seen him, and there was no sightliness" (Is 53.2). Things that are seen are said to have sightliness when they can delightfully engage the eyes of onlookers because of something beautiful in them. But things are without sightliness when they have no beauty that can engage the sight of the eyes. Because, then, there was nothing in Christ's suffering that could delightfully engage the carnal eyes of those who saw it, it is well said that "there was no sightliness" (Is 53.2). The translation of the Septuagint agrees with this; it has, "And we saw him, and he had no beauty nor comeliness." Why, then, were you looking, O crucifiers? It was not to delight in his sightliness and appearance, but in his shameful disfigurement. You envied his glory and on account of your envy you handed him over. For the evangelist says about Pilate, "For he knew that for envy they had delivered him" (Mt 27.18).

3. The next verse is, "We have been desirous of him, despised, and the most abject of men, a man of sorrows, and acquainted

with infirmity" (Is 53.2–3). For all desired the Messiah who was promised in the Law, but when he appeared to all the peoples, the Jews were blinded by envy and did not recognize the one who was desired; rather, they despised him and condemned him to a most foul death. Was he not despised by those who spat upon him, covered his face with blows, struck his head with a reed, and saluted him genuflecting in mockery? Moving their heads, they said, "Aha! You that destroy the temple of God" (Mt 27.40); and, "If he be the Son of God, let him come down from the cross, and we will believe him" (Mk 15.29). Herod also, and his army, spurned him and made sport with him. With the crucifiers he was "the most abject of men" because they preferred to him a man who was a brigand and a murderer.

4. For how could he be placed among men in a lower or humbler place than behind a man who was a brigand and a murderer? He was a man of sorrows, because he suffered sorrows of punishment and death more bitterly than all other men. Nevertheless, in this suffering of the greatest sorrows he was most patient. In patience, he was acquainted with infirmity, for what we accept we are acquainted with; but patience that accepts infirmity is acquainted with it.

5. The prophet introduces the idea of patience when he adds "acquainted with infirmity" (Is 53.3), but the Septuagint said this more explicitly: "a man in suffering and acquainted with the bearing of infirmity." And what is more manifest than this patience, when he prayed for his crucifiers, saying, "Father, forgive them, for they know not what they do" (Lk 23.34)? The face of divinity had been hidden under the cloak of infirmity, and God himself was despised in man, because there was one person, God and man. And because the face of divinity was hidden, the man himself was not thought well of; that is, he was not considered great. For if they had recognized the Lord, they would never have crucified him. We carry our weaknesses—that is, the punishment of our infirmity, the punishment with which we are born—and our sorrows, the punishment that we bring upon ourselves. We carry our own weakness, I say, and not another's, because we have them willy-nilly from the condition of our birth. But he carried not his own weaknesses, by the condi-

tion of his birth, but he took on ours by a free act of will. Or we can take the text this way: "weaknesses" could be understood to be "guilt"; and "sorrows," "punishments." Hence the Septuagint has, "he has borne our sins, and suffers for us" (Is 53.4). For he carried our sins in his own suffering and took them away from us in the satisfaction that he offered for us.

6. And although by the punishments that he paid for us, he carried our sins and not his own, nevertheless the prophet says in the person of the crucifiers, "And we have thought him as it were a leper" (Is 53.4), that is, as unclean because of sin, as another translation has it. For leprosy was considered unclean in the Law. He was thought to be similar to a leper, because leprosy is an infectious uncleanness, and he was thought to infect others.

7. For some said that he was good, others that he was not, that he led the crowds astray. And again: "We have remembered that that seducer said," and so on (Mt 27.63). Again, lepers by Law were thrown out of the camp, and the Jews conspired against Christ in order to separate from the Synagogue any who confessed him. Because, therefore, a leper was thought to be guilty by uncleanness, he was also considered a sinner and deserving to be whipped; he was thought to be stricken by God with pestilence as a punishment and humbled beneath the enemy who oppresses him to the point of hanging him along with the brigand. But, although he had been thus reckoned a sinner and struck and humiliated as if for his own sin, nevertheless he was wounded with the nails and lance not on account of his own but on account of our iniquities; and he was worn down by whipping, blows, the crown of thorns, and the reed with which they struck his head, not for his own, but for our wicked deeds. He himself witnesses to this at the Supper, when he says, "This is my body, which is handed over for you, and this is my blood, which is poured out for many for the remission of sins."[19]

8. And because he was wounded and worn down not on account of his own sins but on account of ours,[20] the discipline of

---

19. *Canon of the Mass;* see Lk 22.19 and Mt 26.26–28.
20. See Is 53.5.

our peace is because of him, the discipline, namely, of the rod by which we can be corrected, and it is because of him that we can be reconciled with God the Father, whom we offended. For because without deserving it in his own body, he took on for us the discipline of the rod, which we deserved for our transgression, he satisfied God the Father on our behalf and reconciled us, being "our peace, who has made both one" (Eph 2.14). But he brought us peace not only by taking on the rod for us, but he also cleansed us by offering for us the sacrifice of his own blood and by consecrating the sacrament of baptism in his blood. "For he that believes and is baptized shall be saved" (Mk 16.16).

9. And, as we have already said, "This is my blood . . . which was shed for many unto remission of sins" (Mt 26.28). And there was a great need for this cleansing, because "all we like sheep have gone astray" because we left the path of justice and of truth (Is 53.6), which is Christ. And each, going his own way, has turned away from what is right, and so he follows not the righteousness of the divine will but the fluctuation of his own will. In order for us to return to the way of righteousness, Righteousness itself was made the way for us, becoming one with us in the punishments that we deserve for our injustice so that we may become one with him in his justice. Therefore, the Lord put on him the punishments of all our iniquities, so that he may, as it were, hold us by the fleece of our punishments and carry us on his shoulders to the place from which we went astray.[21]

10. And so that he not be thought to have shared in our punishments unwillingly, Isaiah added, "He was offered because it was his own will" (Is 53.7). For he did not suffer unwillingly, who had foretold his death and the manner and time of his death, who had rebuked Peter so harshly when he discouraged him from suffering, who could throw all his adversaries to the ground with a single word, as was evident when he said to those who sought to apprehend him, "'I am he'; they went backward, and fell to the ground" (Jn 18.6). Isaiah adds, "And he opened not his mouth" (Is 53.7) because when Pilate said, "Do you not speak to me?" (Jn 19.10), he did not want to respond. Or as the Septuagint has it: "Afflicted, he did not open his mouth." And so

---

21. See Is 53.6.

that it not be thought that his mouth did not open before Pilate because of fear, indignation, or some other sort of emotion, the prophetic word shows that he did it from patience, gentleness, and simplicity. For a sheep and even more a lamb, when it is led to the slaughter and when it is shorn, does not rebel or cry out, but bears all things in innate simplicity and gentleness.[22] The prophet introduces the idea that he, who is signified by the paschal lamb, must be immolated. And because he bore everything with patience, by the Resurrection and the Ascension he was removed from distress and from judgment, that is, from the distress of punishment and death, the judgment that Pilate unjustly decreed at the insistence of the Jews for the Judge of all.[23] Or as the Septuagint has it, "his judgment was removed in humility"; that is, because he appeared in humility, the truth in judgment was removed from him, for he was judged unjustly.

11. And, although he suffered so humbly such humiliations, he is not nevertheless shameful. On the contrary, the excellence of his divine and human generation are so great that no one, or almost no one, can tell of it.[24] And it is not a strange thing that his generation be unspeakable and unusual, because his death must also be wondered at. For some through death are cut off from the land of the dying; he, through death, was cut off from the land of the living. For he himself in this life was the fullest possessor and inhabitant of the heavenly homeland. Or as the Septuagint has it, "His life was taken from the earth." And the difficulty of speaking about his generation could be explained by the fact that the humility of his death hides the greatness of his generation from the minds of the proud. Isaiah adds the reason for his death when he says, "For the wickedness of my people have I struck him" (Is 53.8). Or in the Septuagint, "He was led to death by the iniquities of my people." Jeremiah agrees with this in the fourth chapter of Lamentations, when he says, "The breath of our mouth, Christ the Lord, is taken in our sins" (Lam 4.20). Isaiah adds to this what Christ brings about by his death, when he says, "And he shall give the ungodly for his burial, and the rich for his death" (Is 53.9). By "ungodly" the Gentiles must be un-

22. See Is 53.7.   23. See Acts 8.33 and Is 53.8.
24. See Is 53.8.

derstood, who were ignorant of the worship of God, for piety is the worship of God; and by "rich," the Jews must be understood, who had the covenant, the Law, and the Prophets. From these two groups, Christ gathered the Church through his death and burial.

12. He gave to God the Father those he had gathered into the unity of the Church in exchange for his death, to which the Father handed him over. Certainly it is known about the impious Jews who killed Christ that, for killing him, Christ, after his Passion, handed the Jews and their scribes, Pharisees, and their too-affluent priests over to the Romans, and subjected them to servitude. And he could do this justly, "because he has done no iniquity, neither was guile found in his mouth" (Is 53.9, 1 Pt 2.22). This cannot wholly apply to a mere man who has not sinned in word or deed, because the Scripture says, "No one is pure from uncleanness, even if his life is a single day" (Jb 14.4–5, LXX), but only to him who carried our sin and was wounded for our iniquities, by whose bruise we were healed, and in whom, according to the promise made to Abraham, all nations will be blessed.

13. But if he was clean of all sin, why was he thus wounded? Not by necessity, but by the will of the Father and his own will. For he says to the Father, "That I should do your will: O God, I have desired it" (Ps 39.9). And again, "Not what I will, but what you will" (Mk 14.36). And we read above, "He was offered because it was his own will" (Is 53.7). The prophet adds at this point some words about the effect of his death, when he said, "If he shall lay down his life for sin" (Is 53.10), which ought rather to be understood affirmatively and causally, as if because he laid down his life for the sin of the human race, "he shall see a long-lived seed" (Is 53.10). And consider what he says, "He laid down his own life" (Jn 10.17). For the Lord Jesus himself says, "I have power to lay my life down, and I have power to take it up again. No man takes it away from me but I lay it down of myself" (Jn 10.17). But the long-lived seed is that which grows from the seed that fell into good earth, and bore fruit thirty-fold, sixty-fold, and a hundred-fold, "and the will of the Lord shall be prosperous in his hand" (Is 53.10), so that whatever the

Father wants is fulfilled by his power.[25] The will of the Father was the completion of the heavenly city with men and angels. Sinful man twisted this will insofar as there was sin in him, but in the hand of Christ, who restored lost man by his death, this will is set straight again.

14. This verse follows: "Because his soul has labored, he shall see and be filled" (Is 53.11). His soul labored, seeking rest among the Jews but not finding it. Hence he says, "The foxes have holes, and the birds of the air nests: but the Son of man has nowhere to lay his head" (Mt 8.20). And we read earlier in that prophet, "I am weary of bearing them" (Is 1.14).[26] For the labor of the teacher is lack of discipline in the students. Nevertheless, this labor sees that churches are rising up in the whole world, and he is satisfied with their faith. For his food is for us to do the will of the Father,[27] and we do this by faith working through love.[28] "By his knowledge"—that is, in his teaching—"shall the just one himself justify my many servants"—that is, the believers in the whole world—"and he shall bear their iniquities," as was explained above (Is 53.11–12). "Therefore"—that is, on account of the aforementioned—"will I distribute to him very many"—namely, those coming from the east and the west and those reclining with Abraham, Isaac, and Jacob in the various houses in the kingdom of heaven (Is 53.12). About these the Psalmist says, "Ask of me, and I will give you the Gentiles for your inheritance, and the utmost parts of the earth for your possession" (Ps 2.8). "And he shall divide the spoils of the strong," namely, of the Devil and his attendants (Is 53.12).

15. For their spoils were all the unfaithful whom Christ, who is stronger, snatched from the strong Devil, and he divided them among the leaders of the Church: those of the circumcision to Peter, and the Gentiles to Paul. As the Psalmist has it, "The king of powers is of the beloved, of the beloved; and the beauty of your house shall divide spoils" (Ps 67.13). This, then, was handed over to him by the Father, because he "has delivered his soul unto death" (Is 53.12), as was said above, "and with the wicked he was

25. See Mt 13.23.
27. See Jn 4.34.
26. See also Jer 6.11.
28. See Gal 5.6.

reputed," that is, among brigands according to Mark (Mk 15.28). Or as the Psalmist says, "I was counted among them that go down to the pit," that is, into hell (Ps 87.5). And when "he has borne the sins of many" on the cross, "he has prayed for the transgressors" (Is 53.12), that they not perish; that is, he said to the Father about his crucifiers, "Father, forgive them, for they know not what they do" (Lk 23.34).

16. In a way, the Psalmist depicted even the mode and circumstances of the Passion, when he said, "They have dug my hands and feet. They have numbered all my bones. And they have looked and stared upon me. They parted my garments amongst them; and upon my vesture they cast lots" (Ps 21.17–19). What could be clearer than this prophecy? The hands and feet of the man who was called Jesus were fixed by the driving of nails; his body was stretched on the cross, as it were making all of his bones countable; the soldiers divided his garments among themselves; and they cast lots for his tunic, to see who would take it.[29]

CHAPTER 7

*On the time of the Messiah's coming*

1. Jacob in his blessing for Judah expressed the time of the arrival of him in whom all nations will be blessed, and who alone is the holy of holies.[30] He said, "The scepter shall not be taken away from Judah, nor a ruler from his thighs, till he come that is to be sent, and he shall be the expectation of nations" (Gn 49.10). Therefore, Jacob indicated that the time when the scepter would be taken from Judah and the reign from his offspring would be the time of the arrival of him who is the expectation of the nations. But it is known from history that the Jews always had rulers or princes from their own nation up to the time of Herod, who was foreign-born and under whom Jesus was born. This Herod, as history reports, was the son of a certain Antipater, who on his father's side was descended from

---

29. See Mt 27.35.

30. On this paragraph, see Roger Marston, *Quodlibetal Questions* II, q. III, 1, 1 (ed. Etzkorn and Brady, 105).

the Idumeans, and on his mother's side, from the Arabs. He received the power to rule over the Jews from the Romans and from Augustus, after their priest, Hyrcanus, was captured and carried off by the Persians. In the fifteenth book of *The City of God*, Augustine explicitly reports from the ancient histories the lineage of the kingdom of the Jews from the Prophets to this Hyrcanus, the defection in Hyrcanus of the ruling power from the Jews, and the transfer of it to Herod, the foreigner.[31]

2. Daniel implied the same time when Gabriel spoke to him and said:

Seventy weeks are shortened upon your people, and upon your holy city, that transgression may be finished, and sin may have an end, and iniquity may be abolished; and everlasting justice may be brought; and vision and prophecy may be fulfilled; and the saint of saints may be anointed. Know you therefore, and take notice: that from the going forth of the word, to build up Jerusalem again, unto Christ the prince, there shall be seven weeks, and sixty-two weeks: and the street shall be built again, and the walls in straitness of times. And after sixty-two weeks Christ shall be slain: and the people that shall deny him shall not be his. And a people with their leader that shall come, shall destroy the city and the sanctuary: and the end thereof shall be waste, and after the end of the war the appointed desolation. And he shall confirm the covenant with many, in one week: and in the middle of the week the victim and the sacrifice shall fall: and there shall be in the temple the abomination of desolation: and the desolation shall continue even to the consummation, and to the end. (Dn 9.24–27)

3. This computation of seventy abbreviated weeks, when it is diligently considered, runs up to the time of the Lord Jesus, and it can neither be extended beyond nor compressed before this time. Bede, in his *On the Times*, makes clear and explains this computation; he distinguishes eight kinds of weeks.[32] This word, week (*hebdomas* or *hebdomada*), was taken from the Greeks. For they say *ebdomos* (ἔβδομος), which is derived from *epta*, which means seven. That gives us as it were *eptamos*; with *a* changing to *o*, we get *eptomos*; and with *p* changing to *b*, and *t* to *d*, we get *ebdomos*.[33]

---

31. See Augustine, *The City of God* 18.45.
32. See Bede, *De temporum ratione* 8 (ed. Jones, 195–98).
33. See Grosseteste, *Hexaëmeron*, prooem., 51.

### Distinction of "weeks"

So then, the first week was in the creation of the world, when God, after all his work was finished in six days, rested on the seventh. The second week is the now-recurring cycle of that first week. The third week is the one that consists of seven sets of seven days, and this kind of week is observed in the celebration of Pentecost, which lasts for seven whole sets of seven days, that is, for forty-nine days, with one day added so that their number may be filled out to fifty. The fourth kind of week consists of seven months, and just as the seventh day in the cycle of days was honored, so the seventh month was honored under the Old Law, on which happened the day of expiation, when the high priest only once a year left the people outside and entered the holy of holies. The fifth kind of week consists of seven years, and in this whole seventh year of this "week" the people were exempt by command of the Law from farm-work, just as they are on the seventh day and the Sabbath. The Lord said, "For six years you shall sow your field; on the seventh you shall rest" (Lv 25.3). The sixth kind of week consists of seven weeks of years, that is, of forty-nine years, and when they were completed, the fiftieth year was the jubilee. But sometimes this kind of year consists of weeks of solar years, and sometimes of weeks of lunar years; and when it consists of lunar years, it is called the seventh kind of week. The eighth kind of week consists of the six ages of the world and the seventh of those who rest, which exists without the running of a cycle.

4. And note that every kind of week ends with some solemn feast according to the precept of the Law: the first and second kinds end with the Sabbath; the third, with Pentecost; the fourth, with the feast of expiation; the fifth, with the seventh year, in which they abstain from farm-work and free seven Hebrew slaves; and the sixth, in the Jubilee year. The eighth ends with that unending feast which will happen without end with the glorious resurrection. In addition, because there were not more feasts in the Law, like the Sabbath and the seven ways in which the "weeks" ended, there were not more kinds of weeks, except that the "week" that consists of years can be subdivided, just as the year is, into solar and lunar. And that week which

consists of lunar years is not simply called a "week," but an "abbreviated week," just as the lunar year is an abbreviated year. This is, as we said, the seventh kind of week.

5. So then, Bede explains the aforementioned prophecy of Daniel about Christ, when he says:

The seventh kind of week is the one Daniel uses, and, by the custom of the Law, he understands each individual "week" as seven years. He shortens, however, those years by a new calculation, namely, figuring each of them as twelve lunar months, and he does not add individual intercalary months to the second or third year, as is ancestral Law; rather, when the intercalary months, which are accustomed to increase with eleven years of epacts,[34] increased to the number twelve, he inserted them all at once as a whole year. But he did this not because he was envious of those seeking an understanding of the truth, but because, by prophetic custom, he was training the minds of those seeking understanding. He doubtlessly preferred that his pearls be concealed and investigated by his sons with a fruitful toil, than that they be disclosed and trampled by swine with haughty disdain. Now, so that these truths may shine more clearly, let us see what the angel said to the prophet: "Seventy weeks," he says, "are shortened upon your people, and upon your holy city, that transgression may be finished, and sin may have an end, and iniquity may be abolished; and everlasting justice may be brought; and vision and prophecy may be fulfilled; and the saint of saints may be anointed" (Dn 9.24). No one doubts that these words refer to the Incarnation of Christ, who bore the sins of the world and fulfilled the Law and the Prophets. He was anointed "with the oil of gladness above his fellows" (Ps 44.8). And no one doubts that "seventy weeks" at seven years per week clearly implies four hundred and ninety years. But one must note that the weeks were not simply added or computed; rather, he asserts that they were abbreviated, obliquely reminding the reader to recognize that the text customarily indicates shorter years. "Know you therefore," he said, "and take notice: that from the going forth of the word, to build up Jerusalem again, unto Christ the prince, there shall be seven weeks, and sixty-two weeks: and the street shall be built again, and the walls in straitness of times" (Dn 9.25).

6. When Ezra was speaking, we learned that Nehemiah, when he was the cup-bearer of King Artaxerxes in the twentieth year of his reign, obtained from him in the month of Nisan the restoration of the walls of Jerusalem, as Cyrus much earlier allowed the Temple to be rebuilt.[35] He accomplished this work, as has been said, in a difficult time, for he was being attacked by the neighboring peoples so much that the

---

34. The difference in days between a solar year and a lunar year.
35. See Neh 1.11–2.1.

individual builders were said to have swords girded about their waists and to fight with one hand while they repaired the wall with the other.[36] So then, from this time down to Christ the Leader there were seventy weeks, that is, 490 years of twelve lunar months, which is 475 solar years. The Persians reigned for 116 years, from the aforementioned twentieth year of King Artaxerxes to the death of Darius. From this point the Macedonians ruled for 300 years until the death of Cleopatra. Then the Romans held power for 59 years until the seventeenth year of Tiberius Caesar. These years, taken together, make 475, as we said, and they consist of twenty-five 19-year cycles. For nineteen times twenty-five is 475. And because seven intercalary months are added to each 19-year cycle, twenty-five multiplied by seven is 175, which are the intercalary months of 475 years.

7. If, then, you want to know how many lunar years they make, divide 175 by 12, and it will result in 14. For 12 times 14 is 168. So then, 175 months make 14 years, and seven months are left over. Add these to the aforementioned 475, and together they are 489. Add also the seven leftover months and part of the 18th year of the reign of Tiberius, when the Lord suffered, and you will find that there are seventy shortened weeks from the aforementioned time up to his Passion, that is, 490 lunar years. At the time of his baptism, when he was anointed as the holy of holies, and the Holy Spirit descended upon him as a dove, you will find not only that the seven and the 69 weeks had been completed, but also part of the seventieth had already begun.[37] "And after sixty-two weeks," he says, "Christ shall be slain: and the people that shall deny him shall not be his" (Dn 9.26). Not immediately after the 62 weeks, but at the end of the 70th week Christ was killed. And this week, as far as we can guess, he [the angel] separated this week from the others because he was about to say more about it. For Christ was crucified in that "week" and was denied by a faithless people, not only at the time of his Passion but continuously, from the time when he began to be preached by John. This verse comes next, "And a people with their leader that shall come, shall destroy the city and the sanctuary: and the end thereof shall be waste, and after the end of the war the appointed desolation" (Dn 9.26). It does not pertain to the 70 weeks, for it had been foretold that those weeks extended up to the time of Christ's leadership. But Scripture shows, after the prediction of his coming and Passion, what would happen to this people who did not wish to receive him. For it says that a leader, Titus, would come, who in the fortieth year after the Passion, with the Roman people, would destroy the city and the sanctuary, and there would not remain a stone upon a stone. But after these first-fruits as an anticipation, to explain

36. See Neh 4.17–18.
37. See Mt 3.16; Lk 3.22; Jn 1.32; and Mk 1.10.

the week that he had omitted, he returns to the event: "And he shall confirm the covenant with many, in one week" (Dn 9.27). "In one week," that is, the last one, in which John the Baptist, the Lord, and the Apostles converted many to the faith by their preaching. "And in the middle of the week the victim and the sacrifice shall fall" (Dn 9.27). The middle of this week was the 15th year of Tiberius Caesar when the baptism of Christ began, and the purification by sacrifices began to be gradually disdained by the faithful. Again, what follows applies to later times: "There shall be in the temple the abomination of desolation: and the desolation shall continue even to the consummation, and to the end" (Dn 9.27). And both the history of the ancients and the events of our time today witness to the truth of this prophecy. We have explained the whole testimony of the prophecy, inasmuch as our ability supported us, because we know that it is unknown to many readers that a special kind of week is demanded. For they are deceived who think that the Hebrews used such years. Otherwise, the whole sequence of events of the Old Testament wavers. Nor would the age of anything be understood to be as great as it has been written to be; rather, it would be reduced to the course of the moon. Indeed, we read that the ancient Greeks thought that the lunar year consisted of 354 days, and that they intercalated 90 days at once (which are generated if one fourth of a day together with the eleven days of epacts are multiplied by eight) always to the eighth year, the 90 days being distributed in three months of 30 days. But the Jews customarily added the thirteenth lunar month, which we call an intercalary month, only to the second or third year, as the well known example of the 14th paschal moon clearly proves. One ought well to know that Africanus thinks the course of "weeks" to be finished in the fifteenth year of Tiberius Caesar, when, he believes, Christ suffered. Even though Africanus calculates from the same starting point as we, we draw out the course of "weeks" to the 18th year of the reign of Tiberius Caesar and believe that Christ suffered in this year, as the *Chronicle* of Eusebius has it. Africanus, then, has the reign of the Persians at 115 years, that of the Macedonians at 300, and that of the Romans at 60. But the diligent reader should choose which calculation he thinks ought more to be followed.[38]

8. Bede's reckoning of the seventy weeks up to the Lord Jesus' Passion is clear enough; it cannot be understood otherwise, nor the truth be discovered as conveniently in another way, first of all because an abbreviated week can be understood only as a reckoning of lunar years. For a week consisting of seven days cannot be distinguished into shortened and unshortened. The same is

---

38. Bede, *De temporum ratione* 9.

true with a week consisting of seven weeks, or a week consisting of seven months, although some months number 30 days, and some, 29 days. For we do not say that two months have been finished when 58 days have passed. When, however, a lunar year is called a shorter year; and a solar year, a longer one; and when some reckon time by solar years, as we do, and others reckon it by lunar years, as the Arabs do, a shortened week can only be understood as what has been reckoned from some number of lunar years. Therefore, a shortened week is either seven lunar years, and so seventy shortened weeks are 70 times seven lunar years, that is, 490 lunar years; or a shortened week is seven times seven lunar years, that is, with one set of seven lunar years being as a day. And seven of this sort of day is reckoned a week, that is, forty-nine years. And according to his way of calculating, seventy weeks are seventy times 49, that is, 3430 lunar years, which amounts to 3327 solar years plus ten lunar months and seven or eight days. This number is calculated thus: 3430 multiplied by twelve is 41160, which is the number of lunar months in 3430 lunar years; 41160 divided by 235, which is the number of new moons in a 19-year cycle, is 175, which is the number of 19-year cycles in 3430 lunar years, with two lunar years and eleven months remaining. Again, 175 times 19 is 3325, that is, the number of solar years in 175 nineteen-(lunar) year cycles. Then, the two lunar years and eleven months which were left over, converted into solar years, are two solar years, ten lunar months, and seven or eight days. This, added to 3325, is 3327 solar years, ten months, and seven or eight days. Therefore, as was said, 70 shortened weeks are either 475 solar years, according to Bede's reckoning, or almost 3328, as just mentioned.

9. The starting point for the reckoning of these years must be taken either from the time when the angel Gabriel said to Daniel, "Seventy weeks," and so on (Dn 9.24); or from the other time that the angel expressed in the following verse, when he said, "Know you therefore, and take notice," and so on (Dn 9.25). For the way in which he said what he said does not permit any interpretation except that that number begins from the time when he is speaking or when he determines or expresses by saying so. No one can say that Daniel did not intend to fix the time for the

CESSATION OF THE LAWS 2.7 145

fulfillment of his prophecy. For Josephus says about him in Book Ten of the *Antiquities:*

> From this we believe that God was speaking to Daniel not only about events in the future, as he has spoken to other prophets, but we also believe that he established the time when these events must be fulfilled. Indeed, although earlier prophets foretold evils, and on account of this were not well received by the kings and the people, Daniel was a prophet of good things for them, and because of the glory of what he foretold, he seemed to have the favor of all. And because what he foretold came to pass, he acquired among the people the trust that what he foretold was true, and he is held in divine esteem. For what he left behind from that which he had written for us was a proof of the authenticity of his prophecy, and no difference [between what he predicted and what happened] could be recognized.[39]

10. From these words of Josephus it is clear that Daniel intended to indicate the time of his prophecy's fulfillment. If, therefore, 70 shortened weeks begin from the time when the angel Gabriel spoke to him, and if the 70 shortened weeks are understood as 490 lunar years, it is clear according to the abovementioned reckoning of Bede that the end of these years had arrived before the year of the Passion of the Lord Jesus, which was in the eighteenth year of the reign of Tiberius Caesar; it is clear how long the kingdom of the Persians preceded the twentieth year of King Artaxerxes, when Nehemiah obtained permission to rebuild the walls of Jerusalem. For around the time of the beginning of the Persians' reign under Darius, son of Artaxerxes, who destroyed the rule of the Babylonians, these words were spoken by the angel to Daniel. From the beginning of the Persians' reign down to the 20th year of Artaxerxes, according to the chronicles of the historians, 115 years passed.[40] By this reckoning the seventy weeks must be finished more than a century before the Passion of the Lord Jesus.

11. But according to the words of the prophecy, at the end of these "weeks," "he was anointed as the holy of holies" (Dn 10.2). Therefore, the messiah came when more than a hundred years had passed before the Passion of the Lord Jesus. But the Jews at

---

39. Josephus, *Antiquities of the Jews* 10.7.267.
40. See Ezr 7.4.

this point could show us no other messiah than the Lord Jesus, no one who had come before the Lord Jesus, had reigned on the throne of David, and had done all that was foretold must be done by the messiah when he came. Again, if the seventy weeks begin from the time that the angel indicated, when he mentioned the rebuilding of Jerusalem, this rebuilding is understood in one of two ways: either as that which was begun under Cyrus, in the first year of his reign, and finished under Darius, son of Idapsis or Astipastis, in the forty-sixth year since it had begun; or as that which was done under Nehemiah in a difficult time, about which Bede spoke above. If one understands the rebuilding to be the one done under Nehemiah, the seventy weeks extend, as shown above, to the Lord Jesus. But if the rebuilding applies to the foundation of the Temple under Cyrus or to the finishing of it under Darius, it will be necessary, in the manner indicated, that the messiah come before the Lord Jesus by the length of time by which the foundation of the Temple under Cyrus, or the finishing of it under Darius, preceded the rebuilding accomplished through Nehemiah. Therefore, unless the reckoning of the aforementioned seventy weeks, which are fulfilled in the coming of Christ, starts from Nehemiah, the Jews and all who accept this prophecy must find another christ, who lived long before the Lord Jesus, and who is the holy of holies, putting an end to sin, destroying iniquity, bringing everlasting justice, in whom the whole prophetic vision is fulfilled.

12. But if they could not find another christ besides the Lord Jesus, and if the prophecy of Daniel is not a lie, then the aforementioned seventy weeks must begin as indicated with the building of the walls of Jerusalem through Nehemiah, and they must finish in the Lord Jesus, in whom all the other prophecies about the Christ of all the Prophets and Psalms were harmoniously fulfilled. Or someone might wish to understand the seventy weeks as 3430 lunar years, which amounts to, as was said, 3327 solar years, 10 months, and seven or eight days. But according to this view, whatever is taken as the starting point for reckoning the seventy weeks, even if it be the building of the Temple by Solomon (which no one would say, because the angel says that Jerusalem is built *again*), the christ would still be far in the future.

13. But if anyone should say that the christ is still to come, the prophecy of Jacob would refute him. It says that the prince and leader would not be lacking for Judah, until he should come, who must be sent and who is the expectation of the nations.[41] For it has lacked one for already more than 1230 years. Besides, when all the other predictions of the Prophets about Christ have been clearly fulfilled in the Lord Jesus, and when this prophecy could more familiarly and plainly be understood about Jesus than otherwise, how stupid is it that this prophecy, only by its own estimation, not be applied to him without any reason or authority to apply it to another? Again, let us suppose that there are two men in whom all the predictions about the christ are filled according to reasonable and evident interpretations. Would not the prophetic prediction cause more error and ambiguity than certitude, more schism than unity, and more ignorance of the Savior than knowledge of him? And because this is not possible, let all the predictions, according to a reasonable and evident interpretation, be fulfilled in the Lord Jesus. Just as no other has yet appeared in whom the prophecies were fulfilled, so no one will appear later in whom the prophecy about the christ will be able to be interpreted as fulfilled.

## CHAPTER 8

1. Those who understand the seventy weeks as solar years do not care or consider that it says "shortened," which the prophet by all means said with purpose. Moreover, those who understand the text in this way do not arrive precisely at the time of the Passion of Christ. But some extend their reckoning of the "weeks" up to the destruction of the Temple by the Romans. To show more clearly how much more appropriate is the explanation that notes that the text says "shortened," and to make it clear that the seventy weeks in this prophecy cannot be understood to be 3327 solar years, it would not be vain for us to return to the very words of the prophecy and explain them more fully. So, then, it says, "Seventy weeks are shortened upon your people,

---

41. See Gn 49.10.

and upon your holy city, that transgression may be finished" and so on, down to, "and let the holy of holies be anointed" (Dn 9.24). Or as another translation has it, "upon the city of your sanctuary."

2. In this verse it is plainly expressed that the seventy shortened weeks, from whichever point they begin, must be fulfilled in the coming of the holy of holies and in the anointing of him when he comes, because he is the one in whom all nations are blessed.[42] Transgression, sin, and iniquity will be finished; and everlasting justice may be brought,[43] because he is the effect of blessing, the removal of guilt, and the introduction of enduring justice. And because the whole prophetic vision announces beforehand the holy of holies, who is the expectation of the nations, in whom all nations are blessed, no one doubts that the manifest presence of this man is the fulfillment of the prophetic vision.

3. Because the extension of this time, that is, the seventy shortened weeks, is said to be "upon the people," "upon the city," and "upon the sanctuary," it necessarily follows that the people, the city, and the sanctuary endure and last with the extension of this time upon them. For if something is upon another, the other is under the rest. On account of this it is necessary that the people, the city, and the sanctuary have permanence under the length of time comprised by the seventy weeks. When, therefore, the people, city, and sanctuary (which is nothing other than the Temple) were captured by the Romans and were so ruined that not a stone remained upon a stone, it is manifestly clear that the seventy weeks can in no way be extended beyond the aforementioned capture by the Romans. It is also, then, clear that the end of the seventy weeks and the anointing of the holies must not be expected at some later time, but have been fulfilled in the aforementioned capture or earlier.

4. The period of time of these seventy shortened weeks must not exceed 490 lunar years, and because this period did not begin from the time when the angel spoke to Daniel, the angel

---

42. See Gn 22.18; 26.4.
43. See Dn 9.24.

determines the beginning of the period when he says, "Know you therefore, and take notice: that from the going forth of the word, to build up Jerusalem again, unto Christ the prince, there shall be seven weeks, and sixty-two weeks," that is, all together sixty-nine weeks (Dn 9.25). It could in no way be reasonably understood that here he meant a christ different from the one that he above called the holy of holies. The text, then, has this meaning, "from the issuing of the command or the permission to rebuild Jerusalem to leadership under Christ will be sixty-nine weeks."

5. But why does he now say sixty-nine, when above he said seventy, and so implying that the seventy weeks include within their end the death of Christ, about which he later says, "Christ shall be slain" (Dn 9.26)? He wishes, then, for us to understand that from the aforementioned issuing of the word to rebuild Jerusalem down to the reign of Christ, there are seventy weeks inclusively; and from the same starting point down to the same reign of Christ, there are sixty-nine weeks exclusively, because after the end of these weeks the reign of Christ is shown, that is, his preaching and the display of miracles by which he leads his own from this world to the Father. Beyond the end of the seventy weeks, however, the manifestation of Christ in the flesh and with men is closed. He puts seven weeks first and then sixty-two as is proper to Hebrew, which puts the lesser number before the greater, just as we say the opposite, putting the greater number before the lesser.[44] For example: we say that Abraham lived 175 (CLXXV) years; they, on the contrary, that Abraham lived for the years five and seventy and one hundred (VLXXC). But according to this it seems that this prophet ought to have said that down to Christ, the ruler, there will be "weeks nine and sixty," and not "seven and sixty-two." But perhaps he said this on account of the mystery of the number seven, or for some other reason that I confess I do not know. So, then, the seventy weeks must be reckoned from the rebuilding of Jerusalem.

6. But because the Temple had been built by Solomon at first—and this was the greatest and the principal step in the

---

44. See Jerome, *Commentary on Daniel* 9.

building of Jerusalem—someone could understand the rebuilding of Jerusalem to be what was begun under Cyrus and completed under Darius forty-six years later. In order to prevent someone from making this mistake, the angel specified which rebuilding ought to be understood, namely, that which was accomplished by Nehemiah, as was said above, in a difficult and brief time. This was the building of the wall and street, a rebuilding that was begun under Cyrus and finished under Darius. It is as if he said, "The seventy weeks are from the issuing of the command to rebuild Jerusalem; I say they are from the rebuilding in which the street and walls will be built again in difficult times, that is, from the rebuilding which was accomplished by Nehemiah." For that one, as history shows, was done in difficult times. But the other one, begun under Cyrus and finished under Darius, was finished over a great length of time.

7. The verse that follows—"after sixty-two weeks Christ shall be slain" (Dn 9.26)—has the same sense as "after seven and sixty-two weeks," that is, in the seventieth week. This abridged way of speaking seems to have a suitable explanation: namely, that if something should be said to be about to happen after some numbered length of time, and if this number consists of two numbers, a smaller one and a larger one, and if the one who is making the prediction wants to add something to the same length of time, he need repeat only the second number given, that is, the greater one. For example, someone could say, "After three and ten years there will be an earthquake, and after ten years such-and-such city will be overthrown," all the while wishing to imply that such cities will be overthrown at the same time as the earthquake. In the same way it must be understood that Christ will be killed after the sixty-two weeks, which Daniel earlier numbered with the seven weeks that he mentioned first; and those who would deny Christ will not be made sharers in the effect of his death.

8. And so that we would have a certain sign after the killing of Christ, Daniel added that the people along with their future leader will destroy the city and the sanctuary as a sign that Christ is he who had to be killed in the seventieth week, after the completion of sixty-nine weeks. And no one doubts that this

prophecy was fulfilled through the Roman people with their leader Titus to avenge the blood of the Lord Jesus.

CHAPTER 9

1. So, then, it is clear by this sign that the Lord Jesus, for whose murder Titus and the Roman people destroyed the city of Jerusalem and the sanctuary, truly is the Christ foretold and promised to the fathers. And so that no one doubt that the foretold destruction is the one accomplished by the Romans, Daniel adds some characteristics of that destruction, namely, that at the end of the destruction the conquered Jews were dispersed throughout all regions, and that this desolation was established and confirmed down to the end of time. And so that Daniel clearly and fully imply the effect of the death of Christ in believers, he says that one week (which can only be understood as the seventieth week, which must be figured along with the seven and the sixty-two weeks, and which he omitted) will confirm for the many (that is, not for all, but for the believers) that the covenant, which because of its excellence is called a gracious covenant, is promised to be firm, as the covenant made with Abraham that in his seed all nations would be blessed, and as that made with David that his seed would reign on his throne for ever. For to confirm the promise is to show the thing promised as really present.

2. The verses that follow have been made clear enough by the above words of Bede. We have also here two arguments against those who say that the christ has not yet come, and that the seventy weeks have not yet been completed. The destruction of the Jewish people and of the sanctuary that has already happened and that has lasted already for almost 1200 years down to our own time, has openly refuted them, since this destruction was prophesied to come when the seventy weeks were finished. Besides, when it is said that in the middle of the seventieth week sacrifice and offering will cease, it clearly implies that they were to endure up to that time. But they ceased in fact in the aforementioned destruction accomplished by Titus. For after this the Jews were not able to offer sacrifices and to make the offerings

that were commanded to be offered in the sanctuary, that is, the Temple. Therefore, they could not extend the mid-point of the seventieth week beyond that time, and so goes the argument that all the weeks passed long ago and the holy of holies already came.

3. In him who is promised to Abraham, in whom all the nations are blessed, and who is the expectation of the nations, God and man come together. Even if someone would be so bold that he would not wish to concede by the aforementioned arguments that he is God, at least he would concede that he is the greatest and best man, without any sin or lie, descendant from Abraham through Isaac, Jacob, Judah, Jesse, and David, who unifies all the nations in a harmonious way of life by a most equitable justice, who rules over all and has dominion without end, who was conceived and born of the Virgin, who is perfect from his conception in wisdom and virtue, who was born in Bethlehem when the leadership and principate of the Jews failed, dispirited by insults and despised, who suffered and was killed in the way that Isaiah and the Psalmist describe at the time Gabriel announced to the prophet Daniel, a time which history has shown to be during the reign of Tiberius Caesar. But it is impossible that all these things come together in any man but the Lord Jesus, son of Mary.

4. For all these things have not yet come together in another person; nor could they come together in anyone else, because the time of their fulfillment, foretold by the angel Gabriel to Daniel, has already passed more than twelve hundred years ago. But in the Lord Jesus, son of Mary, the wife of Joseph, all these things have been fulfilled as the histories testify. For one must trust history when it comes to individual past events. Therefore, he is the expectation of the nations, he in whom all peoples are blessed. The same is God and man, one in person.

5. His works and sufferings testify, it is clear, that he performed truly human and divine acts. For what he did in healing the incurable and in raising the dead only God could do. And the saints who performed miracles of this sort performed them, not in their own name, but in the name of Jesus.

6. Again, as we said above, he was true and without any lie.

He therefore asserted truthfully and not falsely that he forgave sins, and consequently, that he was God. Therefore, he truly was God, because he did not falsely assert that he was. Again, he himself said, "I and the Father are one" (Jn 10.30). And again, The Father remains in me, and he does these works. You do not believe that "I am in the Father, and the Father in me" (Jn 10.38). Therefore, the Lord Jesus Christ himself is the prophet who, the Lord said through Moses, would rise up from the brothers of the Jews and who, the Lord commanded, would be heard just as the Lord himself. Indeed, this prophet can only be understood to be he who was promised to Abraham, in whom all the nations are blessed. Therefore, this authority, that has been brought in to prove the cessation of the Laws, has the force of a true testimony, because the Lord Jesus Christ nullified them, both by his teaching and by his example. These points, and the many others mentioned in Part One, also confirm our faith, by which we believe in the Lord Jesus Christ.

7. It is shown by these authorities that Jesus, the son of Mary, who suffered under Pontius Pilate, is the Christ promised in the Law. Josephus's authoritative text (in Book Seven of the *Antiquities*) and that of the Sybil, which Lactantius gathers and Augustine recalls in Book Eighteen of *The City of God*, show the same thing.[45]

8. Josephus, then, in the aforementioned book, when he had reported the deeds of Pilate, said:

There was in those times a wise man named Jesus, if it is right to call him a man. For he was a doer of wonderful deeds and a teacher of those men who gladly hear the truth. He attracted followers, many of the Jews, and many of the Gentiles. He was the Christ. Although Pilate had decreed that he must be crucified, because of an accusation of the leading men of our people, those who loved him from the beginning did not abandon him. For he appeared to them on the third day, living again. The divinely inspired prophets had foretold that these and innumerable other miracles would happen concerning him. But to this day the name and race of Christians, who have been named after him, remain.[46]

---

45. See Josephus, *Antiquities of the Jews* 18.3.63–64; Lactantius, *Divine Institutes* 4.18–19; and Augustine, *The City of God* 18.23.
46. Josephus, *Antiquities of the Jews* 18.3.64–65.

9. The Sybil also says:

He will afterward come into the hands of the unfaithful. They will give to God blows with unholy hands, and they will spit out venomous spit with impure mouths. But he will only give his holy back to the whip. And he will receive blows and be silent, lest someone should recognize that he comes as the Word or whence he comes, so that he may speak to those below and be crowned with a crown of thorns. For food they gave him gall; to drink, vinegar. They will show him this table in hospitality. For you foolish people did not understand your God, when he played with the minds of mortals; rather, you crowned him with thorns and mixed for him horrible gall. But the veil of the Temple will be rent; in the middle of the day, dark of night will be very great for three hours. And he will die and be in death for three days, when he undergoes the sleep of death. And then he will return from below and come to the light, the first to be called back from the dead when the beginning of the resurrection has been shown.[47]

47. Augustine, *The City of God* 18.23.

# PART THREE

### CHAPTER 1

MANY TRUTHS CAN be shown also by reason concerning those matters which have been shown already by the authority of Scripture. And, when the historical truth of the Gospels is assumed, one can conclude that the man who is called Jesus, the son of Mary, wife of Joseph, is true God and true man, the Christ promised in the Law. The blessed Augustine, Gregory, and Anselm (most of all in his book entitled *Why God Man*) show more clearly than light that the one who liberates man, fallen into guilt and punishment, the one who leads man through the Passion of the cross back to the glory that he had lost by sinning, must be God and man, one in person. And here and there all the expositors of the sacred page reasonably declare that the restoration of fallen man must happen through the Passion of the God-man.

2. Nevertheless, whether God would become man even if man had not fallen, none of the sacred writers determine in the books of theirs that I have previously looked at, unless my memory fails me. But rather, they seem to imply that if man had not fallen, God would not have become man; and therefore God only became man to restore lost man. There seem, nevertheless, to be valid reasons to show simply that God would have become man even if man had never fallen. On account of this, we will omit for the moment those reasons by which the sacred writers prove that God must become man in order to restore lost man and will ask whether God would have become man even if man had not sinned.

3. It seems that the argument can be made in the following way. God is supreme power, wisdom, and goodness, and he is

better than can be even thought. Therefore, he makes the universe as good as it can be; that is, he pours into it as much goodness as it is capable of. For if the universe were capable of some degree of goodness which he did not pour into it, he would not be supremely generous and so not supremely good.

4. In addition, goodness exerts itself, insofar as it can, for the benefit of all. Therefore, if, when it could exert itself for a greater benefit, it instead exerts itself only for a lesser benefit, it is not perfect or supreme goodness. Therefore, supreme goodness pours in as great a good as it is capable of. But the universe is capable of this good, namely, that it have a part of itself as the God-man (if indeed he ought to be called a part). For it can have nothing of which it is not capable, and it has this good now. Therefore, it is capable of this good, and was not made capable of this good by the fall of man. Therefore, it is simply capable of this good, and, hence, the universe simply cannot not receive this good from the highest good. So, then, even if man had not fallen, the universe would not lack so great a good.

5. But perhaps someone would think that the universe was made capable of this good in the fall of man. I do not see how this idea would be rationally supported. For how was human nature not as capable of personal unity with the divine nature before the corruption of human nature as after it? On the contrary, if one or the other states of man has a greater possibility for union, the union of the divine nature and an incorrupt human nature in a personal unity would be more possible than that of the divine nature and corrupt human nature. For, as Master Peter Lombard said in his *Sentences*, "The Son of God assumed flesh and soul, but with the soul mediating the flesh. The Word of God was united to the flesh through the mediation of the intellect."[1] Therefore, if it happens that there is no difference in the human soul and intellect assumed by the Word of God, whether man had remained without sin, or had fallen, the soul would be equally assumable by the Word in each case.[2] In man's sinless condition the soul did not have a lesser

---

1. Peter Lombard, *Sentences* 3.2.
2. See John Damascene, *On the Orthodox Faith* 47.

union with the flesh than it has now; rather, it had a stronger union to the extent that the possibility of not dying differs from the necessity of dying. Therefore, either the assumption of the flesh by the Word through the mediation of the soul was more possible when man was in Paradise than it would be now, or at least it was as possible as it would be now.

6. In addition, the corruption of guilt and of punishment is not an essence but the privation of an essence. But how could the privation of essence, which certainly is evil, be the cause of so great a good as the capacity to be assumed by the Word of God or to be united with the Word of God?

7. Again, this ability to be assumed or united is either essence or the privation or negation of essence, for everything that is understood is called one or another of these. But who would say that this capacity for unity is the negation or privation of essence? If, therefore, it is essence, in no way is the privation of essence the cause of it. So then, human nature has not been made capable of union with the divine nature in a personal unity because of the fall of man; rather, it was simply and always capable of this union. And so, as was said, the universe cannot fail to receive this good from the highest good.

8. On this point, let us suppose that man had not fallen and that God did not become man; the created universe would not be as good, as perfect, as beautiful, as it is now, would it? In no way does it seem that it would be as glorious, for every creature, insofar as it is merely a creature, cannot be adored. But the flesh assumed by the Word, although it cannot be adored according to its own nature, as John Damascene says, it is nevertheless adored in the incarnate Word of God not because of itself, but because of Word of God united to it in *hypostasis*.[3] And we do not adore the flesh alone but the flesh of God, that is, God incarnate. Wood alone, for example, is not inaccessible to the touch, but united with fire, it becomes charcoal. It is inaccessible to the touch not because of itself but because it has been united with fire. It is not the nature of wood to be

---

3. See John Damascene, *On the Orthodox Faith* 61; *On the Two Wills in Christ* 9; and *Treatise against the Heresy of the Nestorians* 2.

inaccessible, but that of charcoal as it is wood on fire. Created flesh, therefore, that has been assumed by the Word of God, on account of the Word of God united to it in *hypostasis*, has that which can be worshiped; and the glory of being able to be worshiped incomparably exceeds every created glory. Although, therefore, the flesh of Christ must be counted among creatures, creation has, in the flesh of the adorable Christ, a glory beyond estimation greater than it could otherwise have, if the Word of God had never become incarnate. Consider this analogy: wood on fire has inestimably more brightness and craftiness than it could have were it not on fire. And all matter that can catch on fire has been more brightened in one piece of wood on fire than it could be made bright in some other way without fire (although other woods are not in themselves able to catch fire). Just so, the whole of creation was glorified in the flesh assumed by the Word; it was, if I may put it this way, on fire with the divinity of the Word that assumed it, even though other creatures could not "catch fire" in this way. And it was more glorified by the Incarnation than it could have been without it. And because this catching fire, if I may so put it, of the flesh assumed by the divinity of the Word that assumed it is a greater good than an evil could be evil (insofar as an evil can be compared with this good), the whole of creation will be better than it could in any way be without this good. Either, then, one must say that God would have become man even if man had not fallen, or that the whole of creation is now inestimably better than it would have been if man had not fallen.

9. Again, when God, who is supremely generous and from whom envy is supremely banished, creates every kind of creature that can exist (in order to show that he, who must be participated in by every possible nature, himself shares with each inasmuch as its nature can receive it), and does not leave even the nature of the insect or of some kind of fly or reptile uncreated, how will he not all the more make one person to be God and man, that is, one Christ, because one Christ, God and man, is an incomparably greater good than all of creation by itself? He does not omit the nature of the insect lest the whole of creation be imperfect and less honorable; would he omit Christ,

the greatest honor for all creation? For although the person of Christ has always existed—because the Word of God, which is Christ, was always with the Father, one God with the Father—nevertheless, according to John Damascene, Gregory the Theologian, Cyril, and Athanasius, neither he who is Word from God without humanity, nor, of course, he who was born of a woman as a man not united to God the Word, is called Jesus Christ.[4] But at the point when the Word was made flesh, they say that he is called Jesus Christ, and not before this point. And the Lord Jesus Christ did not receive a common species; there is certainly one Lord Jesus Christ, who does not have a species in common with others, and who did not always exist as Christ Jesus. How could he, being such, be omitted in such a way that he would never have existed if man had not sinned, when even the lowest species of reptile would not have been omitted?

10. In addition, if there were not one Christ, that is, God and man in one person, the Church would not have the head which it now has, nor would it be as the Apostle says, "The husband is the head of his wife as Christ is the head of the Church" (Eph 5.23); and again: the head of a man is Christ, and the head of Christ is God, but the Church would be headless and so would man.

11. In addition, if the God-man, who suffered, through himself justifies fallen man, and if this cause is precisely proportionate to this effect, then, if you take away the "fallen" and the "suffered," the precise cause of man's justification, the God-man, will, it seems, remain. For if man had not sinned, he still would not be able to be just by himself, but would always need someone who is just by nature to justify him.

12. But perhaps he would say that God justifies rational creatures by himself, and the "suffering God-man" leads "fallen man" back to justice in such a way that not only "suffering," but "suffering man" corresponds to "fallen," and "God" to "man." It is as if the suffering God-man is God insofar as he justifies man, and suffering man insofar as he justifies fallen man, inasmuch as

---

4. See John Damascene, *On the Orthodox Faith* 79, citing Gregory of Nazianzus, *Oration* 30.22; Cyril of Alexandria, *To Theodosius, On the Right Way* 28; idem, *To the Queens, On the Right Way* 13; and Athanasius, *Against Apollinaris* 21.

he is fallen. According to this line of thought, then, this person, the suffering God-man, as suffering man rescued and pulled us out of injustice, and only as God formed us with justice. But, then, in order to bring about justice in man, Christ as suffering man does nothing, because of one thing: there is always a single cause, and justifying God always corresponds to the just rational creature. Therefore, that "suffering man" is added effects nothing at all for justification, but only serves as the correlate to the fall, that is, to the rising up from the fall and to cleansing from the filth into which man fell by sinning; only as God does Christ form man in justice.

13. What the Apostle says about Christ seems to contradict this line of thought, that for us he was made by God to be wisdom, justice, holiness, and redemption.[5] Therefore, he redeems, sanctifies, and infuses justice and wisdom according to his becoming, not because as God he infuses holiness, justice, and wisdom; rather, he does this only through the assumed man, because of whom he is the mediator between God and man. What the Apostle says to the Romans seems to agree with this: "Then as one man's trespass led to condemnation for all men, so one man's act of righteousness leads to acquittal and life for all men. For as by one man's disobedience many were made sinners, so by one man's obedience many are made righteous" (Rom 5.18–19). Here the Apostle seems to say clearly that the form of justice flows into us through Christ, a man just and obedient to the Father. Dionysius seems also to agree with this when he says in the first book of the *Hierarchy* that the first supercelestial essences and the supreme hierarchies, which have been made worthy of the communion and strength of Jesus, "formatively represent the divine likeness not in images that are made of the sacred; rather, they themselves truly approximate the divine likeness in their first participation in the knowledge of its divine lights. And because the divine likeness has been given substantially to them, these kinds of beings share, insofar as they can in their pre-operative power, in its divine properties and in human virtues."[6] Another translation has

---

5. See 1 Cor 1.30.
6. Ps.-Dionysius the Areopagite, *On the Celestial Hierarchy* 7 (*versio Eriugenae*).

"philanthropic," that is, "compassionate," instead of "human." A *philanthropos* is called, as it were, "a lover of men."

14. So then, if the formation of justice always happens in one way, because the cause of one thing is always one, justice always and simply descends from God through Christ, the God-man, into every rational creature who is made just. On account of this, it seems, angels and men are not justified from the beginning except through the Son of God, God and man. But if someone should say that this, then, cannot be—because the Son of God was not God and man from the beginning—by this argument he would have to say that Abraham, Isaac, and Jacob were not justified in Christ, God and man, because Christ did not yet exist as God and man. But it is agreed that all the fathers of old were justified in Christ, God and man, dwelling in their hearts through faith, and they were not justified otherwise. Why, then, are angels and men in paradise not similarly justified from the beginning, in Christ dwelling in them from the beginning through faith?

15. Again, the Passion of Jesus Christ is the satisfaction for our offense, but it is one thing to be satisfaction for an offense and another thing to be the infusion of justice, or justification, because if man had not sinned, there would have been justification but no satisfaction. If, then, we should suppose that God is the precise and proportionate cause of justification, without any mediation, and the Passion, that of satisfaction, then the humanity of Jesus Christ would be only materially necessary for the Passion, that is, it would exist only so that God the Son could suffer in it and by his Passion make satisfaction for the offense of the human race. But this does not seem fitting.

16. Again, we are sons of God by adoption, and men, it seems, would have been adopted sons of God through grace, even if man had never sinned.[7] But now we are sons of adoption because we are "one (thing) in Christ," as the Apostle says, or as the Greek letters have it, "one (person) in Christ": "one in Christ," who is a natural son (Gal 3.28).[8] But the conformity alone of our will

---

7. See Rom 8.15; Gal 3.26; and Eph 1.5.

8. "One (thing) in Christ" renders *unum in Christo;* "one (person) in Christ" renders *unus in Christo;* the Greek has εἷς ἐστε ἐν Χριστῷ, though ἕν is a variant reading for εἷς. See also Grosseteste, *Hexaëmeron* 1.1.1.

with the will of Christ does not bring about this unity by which we are one thing or one person in Christ; rather, along with this conformity there is the unity of nature which we share with Christ. For Augustine says, "We receive this adoption because the unique Son of God did not spurn participation in our nature when he was made of a woman so that he may be not only the only-begotten who has no brothers, but also the 'first-born among many brethren'" (Rom 8.29).

17. Again, Augustine says about Christ that he was sent by God to take on flesh from our race and according to our nature, so that he, who shared in our mortality out of love, might make us to share in his own divinity by adoption.[9] So, then, unless the Son of God share in our nature, we would not share in his divinity by adoption, nor would we be his brothers or the adopted sons of God the Father. But, as has been said, even if man had not sinned, we would nevertheless be, so it seems, sons by adoption. Therefore, even if man had not sinned, the Son of God would have become man; or we must say that we would not be sons of adoption if man had not sinned. Indeed, conformity of wills does not alone bring about some kind of sonship; rather, among equals it brings about friendship and society, and among unequals it brings about obedient servitude. Therefore, the condition of man would be much worse if he had not sinned, for it would not be possible for him otherwise to pursue the great and inestimable good of being an adopted son of God. But it does not seem appropriate that the human race be in a better condition by sinning and that it receive the possibility for a greater good than it could have had if it had not sinned. For if the Son of God would not have become man unless man had sinned, and man could not be a son of God by adoption unless the Son of God by nature become man, by sinning, then, man was made able to become an adopted son of God.

18. Again, the Church together with its head, Christ, is one Christ, just as Augustine and Gregory show in many places.[10]

---

9. See Augustine, *Homilies on the Psalms* 118.

10. See Augustine, *Sermon* 40; *Homilies on the Psalms* 18, 21, 40, 44, 132; and Gregory the Great, *Pastoral Rule* 3.23; *Book of Letters* 2, ind. 10, *Epp.* 47 and 5, ind. 13, *Ep.* 43.

But if the Son of God had never had to become incarnate, the Son of God would never have become Christ. Therefore, the Church together with the Son of God would not have been one Christ, and so the Church would lack the greatest good, if man had not sinned, for it would not be one Christ with the Son of God.

19. But let us suppose that man had not sinned and that the Son of God would not become man. I ask whether the Church could be said to be one person with the Son of God, just as it is now said to be one person with Christ.

20. Again, before he fell Adam prophesied the marriage of Christ and the Church, when he said, "Therefore a man shall leave his father and his mother and shall cleave to his wife, and the two shall become one flesh" (Gn 2.24). The Apostle says about this, "This mystery is a profound one, and I am saying that it refers to Christ and the church" (Eph 5.32). But Adam did not prophesy without knowing what he prophesied, for the opinion of those who say that the prophets did not know what they foretold through the spirit of prophecy has been rejected. Therefore, he knew what he prophesied, and believed before his own fall in the marriage of Christ and the Church. He understood that the marriage of a man and a woman was a sacred sign, and so a sacrament of the marriage of Christ and the Church. But he did not foresee his own fall nor the fall of the human race in him. So then, while he knew and believed nothing about the sin of the human race, which was about to happen, he believed in the marriage of Christ and the Church. Therefore, even if man had not sinned, the marriage of Christ and the Church would happen, and so the Son of God would be Christ, that is, one in person, God and man.

21. Again, marriage is indissoluble because it is the sacrament of the indissoluble union of the humanity and divinity of Christ in a personal unity, and the sacrament of the indissoluble marital bond between Christ and the Church. But marriage was indissoluble from the beginning before sin. Therefore, from the beginning there was an indissoluble sacramental bond between the assumed flesh and the deity. The indissoluble marriage of Christ and the Church would have taken place if man had never

sinned. Therefore, the cause of this indissolubility would also have existed if man had never sinned, and God would have become man even if man had never sinned. Otherwise, marriage would not be *simply* a sacrament in its own right; rather, it would be a sacrament *because of man's sin,* and would not have as great a dignity as it now has if man had not sinned. And these conclusions do not seem fitting. There would be no Church that has Christ as a spouse who is one flesh with her, although she now enjoys this good, as the Apostle says:

For no man ever hates his own flesh, but nourishes and cherishes it, as Christ does the Church, because we are members of his body and of his bones. "For this reason a man shall leave his father and mother and shall cleave to his wife, and the two shall become one flesh." This mystery is a profound one, and I am saying that it refers to Christ and the Church (Eph 5.29–32).

22. Again, Augustine says in *On the Difference between the Soul and the Spirit,*

For there are two senses in man, one interior and one exterior, and certainly each sense has its good in that in which it is perfected. The interior sense is perfected in the contemplation of divinity; the exterior sense in the contemplation of humanity. For God was made man in order to beatify in himself the whole man, to convert man wholly to him, and to be man's whole delight, because he was seen by the sense of the flesh through flesh, and by the sense of the mind through the contemplation of God. This was the whole good of man, so that whether he turns inward or outward he finds pasture in his Maker, pasture outside in the flesh of the Savior, pasture inside in the divinity of the Creator.[11]

From these words of Augustine it seems that it can be expressly argued that God would become man even if man had not sinned. For the whole man would not be beatified in his soul through the contemplation of God, and in his flesh through seeing the flesh of assumed humanity, unless God became man. Therefore, man's full happiness demands that God become man; if we assume, then, that man had not sinned, God would nonetheless have become man, or man would never have been fully beatified. And because man, perfected in body and at the

---

11. Ps.-Augustine, *On the Spirit and the Soul* 9; see also Augustine, *Enchiridion* 26.

same time in soul, naturally desires the perfection of the exterior corporeal senses, he would in no way be fully happy unless his exterior corporeal sense—whose act does not consist chiefly in the restoration of defects—be perfected by the act of sensory perception.

23. But if someone should say that man could have perfect beatitude by contemplating one thing with the mind and by sensing another through the flesh, it must be said to him that the attention of his soul would be divided among several things, and so lessened in each of them. Perfect beatitude could not be this way because it demands the conversion of the whole attention of soul to the highest good. Therefore, if the exterior sense were not perfected in a sensible perception or if it were perfected in something other than God, there would be no perfect beatitude.

24. For this reason, the flesh of the Lord Jesus Christ will be manifested after the resurrection as more splendid and beautiful than the sun and every bodily creature, because in comparison with the splendor of the flesh of Christ, the sun will seem not to shine. When it will be glorified, the eye of our flesh will be able to see the splendor and beauty of the flesh of Christ. Therefore, if God had not become man, there would exist a greater splendor and beauty than can be found in mere visible creation, a greater splendor and beauty for glorified man's eye to see. For some mere corporeal creature could not have as great a beauty and splendor as the glorified flesh of the Lord Jesus Christ has. There, then, could be in us forever a vain and perpetual imperfection and a perpetual desire for something which we could nonetheless never obtain, and so there would be in us a perpetual misery. Besides, if Christ, who as man is a creature, is more beautiful as a man than a mere creature could be (just as charcoal aflame is more beautiful than mere wood could be), then unless God become man, the whole of creation would not be perfected in beauty.

25. Again, the universe, that is, the world, is one. But all unities are united in some one principle, as all the members of the body are united in the heart. Therefore, creation has some one principle in which all are united. But this one principle cannot

be a mere man, because an angel is equal to him and so also is another man. It cannot be an angel, because man, according to the dignity of his rational nature, is equal to an angel. And no other creature can be the unifying principle because every other creature is less than a man and an angel. A unifying principle must be more worthy than the others; this unifying principle, then, can be only the God-man. It could not be a God-angel, because all other natures have something in common with man, but not with angels. On account of this they could be more united in man than in an angel.

26. Again, "one" is spoken of in a threefold way, namely, one in number, one in species or nature, and one in genus, and the unity according to genus is the weakest and has the least true unity. In order that, then, all of creation not be one according to the weakest kind of unity, it is necessary to investigate whether there is a unity in creation other than that according to genus. It is not consistent with reason that the universe, because it is most perfect and most beautiful, participate only in the weakest kind of unity. Because perfection and beauty consist in unity, in greater unity there is greater perfection and beauty.

27. In addition, if we include God, who is the source of everything in the universe, because he could not share a common species or genus with some creature, we cannot say that the universe participates in generic unity. Therefore, it is simply impossible, it seems, to reduce the universe to complete unity in any other way unless we understand that the angel was created first by God from nothing and that it cannot be united to a body in a personal unity nor participate with a body in any unity except perhaps in generic unity. The rational soul and the angel, however, share a natural unity in rationality and intelligence, and by this sharing they have an indissoluble bond and a connection of natural unity. But the rational soul cannot be one with a body in species or nature. Nevertheless, the rational soul was made fit to be the perfection of an organic body, and it is united to the body in a personal unity. So, then, the angel and the rational soul have been joined in a natural unity, but the rational soul and the human body come together in a personal unity. The human body, however, has natural communion with all cor-

poreal natures, because the celestial bodies and the element of fire are united in the nature of light; fire and air are united in the nature of heat; air and water in the nature of humidity; and water and earth in the nature of coldness. But the human body consists of the four elements, on account of which it is united with them in nature, and accordingly with the celestial bodies which are united to fire in the nature of light. The human body is united, consequently, with all the elemental natures that are united with the elements themselves. The rational soul is also united with the sensible soul of brute animals in the sensitive power, and with the vegetative soul of plants in the vegetative power. Therefore, man is united in nature with every creature.

28. But up to this point the created universe has no unity with the Creator; nor can the Creator have, as has been said, unity with creation in genus on the one hand or species or nature on the other hand. But nonetheless, the Creator could have the unity with creation that would result from his assumption of the creature into a unity of person. If, then, God should assume man in a personal unity, all creation has been led back to the fullness of unity; but if he should not assume man, all creation has not been drawn to the fullness of unity possible for it. If, therefore, we leave aside the fall of man, it is nonetheless fitting that God assume man into a personal unity, because he could do it and it would not be inappropriate for him to do it; but even more, it would be appropriate, because without this the created universe would lack unity. But if this were done, all creation would have the fullest and the most fitting unity, and through this all natures would be led back into a circular fulfillment; because without God assuming man into a personal unity, one finds in the above-mentioned way a certain joining of angels and men. But this is not yet a connection of God to man, the last creature, or to the angel, the first creature. But when man has been assumed into a personal unity, the circular connection is then complete, because man and God are one in person, and the God-man, insofar as he is man, is one with the angel in nature.

29. Likewise, in the assumption of man by God the Word, the circle of human generation has been completed and the

straight line that is the series of human generation has been turned back into a circle. For I can say this: Seth is from Adam, and Enosh is from Seth, Kenan is from Enosh, and so in a line descending down to Jesus. And I can turn back and say, Adam is from Jesus, for this man, when Jesus was manifested, created Adam. Because, then, it is better that both the created universe and the series of human generation be united in such a circular period than that they be deprived of this union, it would also be possible for God to perfect them in this way. And that these things are thus perfected seems to be manifest, because it is necessary that the perfection of this sort of circular period exist. For John Damascene says, "Providence is the will of God, on account of which everything that exists receives fitting direction. But if the will of God is providence, it is altogether necessary according to right reason for everything that happens by providence to be also what is best and what most befits God, so that it could not turn out better."[12]

30. Again, because the Son of God is of one nature with us, and conversely because in the sacrament of the Eucharist we become one with the very flesh that he assumed from our nature, we are naturally made to be one body in Christ, and we all are made one in the Father, Son, and Holy Spirit. Hence in his book *On the Body and Blood of the Lord,* Rabanus gives three reasons for the frequent repetition of the offering of the Eucharist. He says about the third reason:

> The third reason is that those who worthily receive this life are made to be reborn as one, so that Christ remains in them just as he already does through their baptism in him. And so Christ's prayer to the Father is fulfilled: "I do not pray for these only," he says, "but also for those who will believe in me through their word, that they may all be one; even as you, Father, are in me, and I in you, that they also may be in us" (Jn 17.20–21). This unity between the Father and the Son is not said to be in will alone, as the heretics have it, who labor over his statement "I and the Father are one" (Jn 10.30). Therefore, they try to confer a sense of unanimity, so that unity of will in Father and Son is not unity of nature, just as was said of the multitude of believers in Jerusalem, that they were "one heart and one soul" (Acts 4.32). But we, following the footprints of the fathers, must believe that God was substantially and

---

12. John Damascene, *On the Orthodox Faith* 43.

naturally begotten from God, that is, that the Father—and because of their unity of nature—the Father and the Son are shown to be one.[13] And Christ is in us today not only by an agreement of wills; rather, he is in us also by nature, just as we are rightly said to remain in him. For if the Word was made flesh, and we truly receive the Word as flesh in the food of the Lord, how is Christ not rightly thought to remain naturally in us, who as God-born-man took the nature of our flesh and made it inseparable from himself, and who added the nature of his own flesh to the nature of eternity under this sacrament of the flesh, that we must partake of? And therefore on account of this we all are one in God, Father, Son, and Holy Spirit, because the Father is shown to be in Christ and Christ is shown to be in us.[14] Hence comes our being naturally made one body in Christ. And if someone confesses that the Father is naturally in Christ, he confesses also that he is naturally in him, for the Word was made flesh to be one in him. As a result, natural unity appears through the sacrament of truth. Because of this, then, he says, "He that eats my flesh, and drinks my blood, abides in me, and I in him" (Jn 6.57). Truly, therefore, just as God the Father is in the Son by the nature of divinity, so God the Son is rightly said to be in us by the humanity of his flesh. And he is called the mediator between God and man, because through him we have the communion of unity with God, as long as he remains in the Father and also in us. On account of this the Father is persuaded by the Son in his humanity to be one in the aforementioned.[15]

So, then, if God had not become man, and even if man had not fallen, the Church and the situation in paradise would lack so great a good in lacking so complete a unity. And the Church could not exist in such a way that it could be better, for this would be unfitting, according to the aforementioned words of John Damascene.

CHAPTER 2

1. These and similar arguments seem to be able to show that God would become man, even if man had never sinned. Nevertheless, I know that I do not know whether this is true, and in no small way I am pained at my ignorance here. For, as I said

13. See Hilary, *On the Trinity* 8.5.
14. See Robert Grosseteste, *On the Eucharist* (Cambridge, Trinity College MS B.15.20, coll. 519–20).
15. Paschasius Radbertus (rather than Rabanus), *On the Body and Blood of the Lord* 9.4.

above, I do not recall seeing anything from our authorities on this question. Nor do I wish or dare to assert anything on so difficult a matter without express authority, because a verisimilitudinous argument can quickly deceive me who am of small mind and knowledge.[16] Nevertheless, if this is true, that God would have become man even if man had not fallen, every creature would fittingly strive for that man, who is the head of the Church.

2. For no one doubts that all things were made for man in his best condition. On account of this, the end of all created things in this sensible world is the Church triumphant, and in particular the end of all would be the single head of this Church. For this reason, both time and every creature await and, in their own way, sigh for the God-man, the head of the Church. When he comes, because he would be the chief end of all, it would be the fulfillment of time. For the true fulfillment of something is the end for which it was striving, and in this way the God-man himself would be the "firstborn of every creature" (Col 1.15), because in intention the end is prior to those things that are ordered to it. And according to this line of thought, just as the first (in time) Adam had been made into a living soul and would have produced offspring if he had remained such, so the last Adam was made into a life-giving spirit.[17] And just as through the first Adam, who was the root of the tree of human generation, all were generated unto natural life, so, through the last Adam, who was and is now, the fruit of that tree, all were regenerated unto vivified life by grace. And just as we see in the natural tree that the whole tree exists for the sake of the fruit (but in the fruit is the seed, and lest the seed exist in vain, it germinates and generates again), so in the tree of human generation the God-man was the fruit and the seed, who regenerated into a life of justice and glory those who were generated from the first root unto natural life.

3. In addition, this head of the Church, namely, the God-man,

---

16. For similar statements of humility, see Grosseteste, *Hexaëmeron* 1.12.4; 1.17.1; 3.7.1; 8.1.2; 9.2.6; 9.10.11.

17. See 1 Cor 15.45.

generated unto justice not only men but also angels, because the whole Church is made up of men and angels, and power ought to flow from the head to all the members. And the salvation of angels and men came about from the beginning because of faith in Christ, God and man. Accordingly—and this seems truer than the above-mentioned way[18]—the fall of the angel had happened because from the beginning it was proposed to the angel that the Son of God made man must be believed for justice and must be venerated and adored with that adoration that is *latria*. For if by this faith and not otherwise the angels had had salvation, this faith would not have been at any time denied to or kept hidden from the angels, but from the beginning it would have been proposed and manifest to them all. From the beginning, it seems, the Devil refused through pride to offer this faith, despised the man who ought to be adored above him, and disdained receiving justice from him. The Devil thought him unworthy, envied him, and coveted his singular excellence; through this envy, by which he envied the God-man and hated him, he was a murderer[19] from the beginning, because "whosoever hates his brother is a murderer" (1 Jn 3.15). So the Devil did not remain in the truth of faith and salvation offered to him.[20] The words of the Apostle to the Ephesians seem to show that all salvation, both of angels and of men, was from the beginning not only through God the Word but through the Word, at the same time God and man, that is, Jesus Christ. He says, "Blessed be God," down to "that are in heaven and on earth, are in him," Christ (Eph 1.3–10). In this way the simple meaning of the tree of life in the middle of paradise stands out.

4. According to this line of reasoning, if man had not fallen, there would have been, it seems, three sacraments in paradise and only three. There would have been marriage, the sacrament of the conjunction of Christ and the Church and of the union of the human and divine natures in a personal unity. There would also have been the Eucharist, according to the argument mentioned earlier, and, as a consequence, there would

---

18. See above, 1.5.7–1.6.11.     19. See Jn 8.44.
20. See ibid.

also have been the priesthood. There would have been, however, no baptism or circumcision, because everyone would be born in original justice, and, consequently, there would be no confirmation. Nor would there be penance, because no one would have sinned, or extreme unction, because no one would get sick or die. And so what Christ said would be simply true, even if man had not sinned: "He that eats me, the same also shall live by me. And unless you eat the flesh of the Son of man, and drink his blood, you shall not have life in you" (Jn 6.58), and the rest of what he said in the same place on this matter.

5. But no matter what is true about the Incarnation of the Word in the event of man not falling, we are now absolutely certain, after man's fall, that God has become man. Not only has authority shown this, but also necessary reason, which can be quickly and easily found, as was said, in Augustine and Anselm. We will pass over the proof of this by rational argument and move on to other matters. It does not appear to me, however, that there is a way to show by rational argument that the Word of God should assume flesh from Abraham, Isaac, Jacob, Judah, Jesse, and David. I do not know whether an argument of this kind can be found by man, but I know that it cannot at all be found by me. The argument, however, that the God-man was fittingly born of a virgin without the seed of a man is evident in Anselm, and it can be added to this that it would be necessary for the circular period of human generation to be perfectly completed. For at first man was made from neither a man nor a woman. Then woman was made from man alone. Then man and woman were made from man and woman. This is how the line of human generation goes forth, and the result is propagation from man and woman at the same time. Therefore, when the line of human generation turns back, it will be similar to the beginning and it could not be otherwise: as a woman came to be from a man without a woman, so a man comes to be from a woman without a man. And from this man will come neither man nor woman through the propagation of the flesh. From the first man, who was a virgin, was made a woman, who was a virgin. Therefore, the last man also ought to be a virgin from a woman who is a virgin, so that the beginning and end of the

period of human generation may fittingly correspond to each other. In its beginning and end the period of generation turns back on itself and is united by unbroken similarity.[21]

### CHAPTER 3

1. To prove, however, the place of Christ's birth does not seem easy. Nevertheless, in our own way we will try to offer some fitting arguments according to which it was fitting that Christ be born in the middle of the earth. Christ, indeed, is the heart and head of the Church. But the position of the heart is naturally in the middle of the body. Likewise, the position of a man's head is at the top and in the middle of the body. For it does not extend out in front of him or follow behind him as do the head and tail in the case of other animals, nor does it deviate to the right or left, but is placed in the middle between the shoulders. Christ's body, the Church, has been spread throughout the whole inhabited world. It was fitting, then, that Christ, the head and heart of the Church, be born and live in the middle of the inhabited world. According to the histories that mention the places of the world, Jerusalem and Judea are in the middle of our inhabited world. The prophet Ezekiel testifies to this when he says, "This is Jerusalem, I have set her in the midst of the nations, and the countries round about her" (Ezek 5.5). About the same place, a commentator says that Jerusalem is, as it were, the navel of the world, for on the East it is bordered by Asia, on the West by Europe, on the South by Libya and Africa, "on the North by Scythia, Armenia, Persia, and the rest of the nations of the Pontus. It has been positioned, then, in the middle of the nations, so that all the nations of the world might follow its example, because 'In Judea God is known: his name is great in Israel' (Ps 75.2)."[22] In a similar way, then, the life of Christ fittingly unfolded in the middle of all the nations, because it was offered to all as an example.

2. Again, Jerusalem was a fitting place for Christ, the head of the Church, not only because it is in the middle of the inhab-

---

21. See Appendix, Figure 2, p. 250.
22. Jerome, *Commentary on Ezekiel* 2.5.5.

ited world, but also because it is a quite high place. Hence in Scripture, the way to Jerusalem is always called "going up," and the way from Jerusalem "coming down."

3. Again, Christ's way of life, his teaching, and Christ himself are the light of the world. The nature of light is that it diffuses itself from its light-source equally in all directions, but the diffusion of light is vain where there is no receptivity to it. In order, then, that the diffusion of the light of Christ be both naturally in all directions and not vain in any direction, it must begin from the middle of the nations that are receptive to this light and diffuse itself into all nations everywhere. Let no one say that this argument is void because not all the nations believe, for we do not speak about the present time, but simply. Indeed as the Scriptures testify, the Church, spoken of simply and not at the present time, grows larger up until the end of the world, when the Father gives to Christ the nations as his inheritance and the ends of the earth as his possession.[23]

Again, Christ is the mediator not only between God and man, but also between all men, because he unites all men with each other in a unity of faith and morals. And what place is more fitting for such a mediator than the place that is in the middle of all men?

4. Again, Christ is the restoration and the restorer of all the natures of this sensible world and the one who makes void sin and cleanses it. But it is most fitting that the restoration of natures take place where all natures and the powers of natures meet at their strongest and where they produce the greatest effect of the operating power. Also, medicine is most fittingly applied against an illness in the place where the illness is more serious. But the illness of natures is their weakness and damage on account of man's sin. Therefore, where the powers of all corporeal natures meet more, there the natural good will be fuller, and at the same time, nevertheless, it will have more damage. For nothing prevents a greater good from being more damaged in regard to its fulfillment. Now, the sickness of souls is sin. Therefore, the medicine against the sickness of sin ought

---

23. See Ps 2.8.

to be in the place where the abundance of sin is greatest, so that "where sin abounds, let grace more abound" (Rom 5.20). And sin was accustomed to grow stronger in men where natural goods were more abundant. But in Jerusalem and Judea there was the greatest abundance of natural goods, as the Scriptures attest, for it is called a land flowing with milk and honey, and with an abundance of all things.[24] On account of this it is clear that there, more than anywhere else, the efficacious powers of nature come together and meet, and they bring into existence an abundance of natural goods. In that same place also the histories testify that there has always been the greatest abundance of transgression. Because of this, the restoration of natures, the cleansing of sin, and the justification of the human race more fittingly happened in that place than in others.

Anselm, Augustine, and the rest of the sacred writers show most evidently that it was necessary that Christ suffer for the fallen human race and enter into his glory with his body, the Church, through death on the cross, and that there is no other way suited to the liberation of the human race and satisfaction for sin.[25] Therefore, I omit here the proof of this.

CHAPTER 4

1. Reason also seems to demand that six thousand years from the beginning of the world is the appropriate time for the coming of Christ. Consider this analogy: the philosophers think that the length of time of the pregnancies of animals is determined by their life-span, and so the length of the pregnancy of an animal with a long life-span ought to be longer, and it ought to be shorter for an animal with a shorter life-span. So, then, it simply seems that the length of time of the production of something into being is proportionate to the length of time that it naturally remains in being, as if the length of time of production into being were determined by some fixed number of some cycle, as, for example, the length of time that a day remains naturally in

24. See Ex 3.8.
25. See Anselm, *Why God Man* 1.9; and Augustine, *On the Trinity,* Book 4.

being ought to be determined by a similar number of some cycle proportionate to a day, so that, namely, one day in the production of something would correspond to one week, or one month, or one year, or some such cycle in the length of time that it lasts. So, then, the length of time of the production of the world into being ought to be proportionate to the length of its duration.

2. The world was completed in six days, and on the seventh God rested from all his works. Hence a set of seven natural days pertains to the creation of the world and its being brought into being. Naturally, therefore, the length of the duration of the world (until the figure of this world passes, and there are a new heaven and a new earth)[26] ought to be proportionate to the first seven days and ought to run its course through some sevenfold understanding of time proportionate to a day. The shortest length of time proportionate to a natural day is the cycle of a week, and a week is reckoned as a day, just as was also touched upon above. The second cycle proportionate to the day is the month, in the space of which the moon returns to the sun. The third cycle proportionate to the day is the year, that is, the length of time of a revolution of the sun to the same point of the Zodiac, and in this time by the approaching and receding of the sun are summer and winter, as it were, the day and night that make up a natural day. The proportion of a day to a year and a year to a day is considered in Ezekiel, to whom it is said, "You shall take upon you the iniquity of the house of Judah forty days: a day for a year, yea, a day for a year I have appointed to you" (Ezek 4.6). Similarly in the book of Numbers it is said, "Your children shall wander in the desert forty years, and shall bear your fornication, until the carcasses of their fathers be consumed in the desert, according to the number of the forty days, wherein you viewed the land: a year shall be counted for a day" (Nm 14.33–34).

3. Because the world is most perfect, it would not be fitting, it seems, that the age of the world run its course and be determined by the cycle of some other light than the sun, which is the greatest and most perfect of lights. And the sun cannot make its circuit around a greater space than the Zodiac. Hence, if we take

---

26. See Rv 21.1.

a proportional day from the motion of the sun and from the length of time that passes during its motion, a day greater than the solar year cannot be found. For some solar cycle (which can be called a "solar day" proportionate to a natural day) seems not to be determined by the return of the sun to the same planet, as a month is determined by the return of the moon to the sun. Indeed, in the return of the moon to the sun it is possible to find the proportional properties of the natural day. Likewise also in a solar year, but it is not possible to find this in the return of the sun to Mars, Jupiter, or Saturn. And so, the greatest day, which is taken from the sun through the amount of space or time passed from the sun, is the solar year. Therefore, there can be no greater proportional solar day than the year, except through the increase of the oneness of the same day.

4. Oneness is increased when ten, one hundred, or one thousand is put in the place of oneness, because, just as the mathematicians say, the first oneness is simplicity, the second oneness is ten, the third oneness is one hundred, the fourth oneness is one thousand. Indeed, beyond ten there is no number, but only the replication of number. And in this replication, ten first takes the place of oneness, then one hundred, and thirdly one thousand. Therefore, the first increase of the proportional solar day, which is a year, will be the space of ten years; the second, of one hundred years; and the third, of one thousand years. If, therefore, one thousand solar years should be the most perfect proportional solar day, it is fitting that the age of the world, because it is perfect, be numbered and determined by this most perfect day. According to the number of days in which the world was brought into being and established, the natural age of the world ought to run through seven thousand solar years, and each thousand years ought to have a proportionate day to which it corresponds in the foundation of the world. And down to the sixth age of the world and the sixth millennium this has been found to be so by the sacred writers, and it has been written on by them in their exposition of the book of Genesis.[27] It was fitting, then, that just as on the sixth day of the foundation

---

27. See Robert Grosseteste, *Hexaëmeron* 8.30.2–7.

of the world the first Adam was made into a living soul, so in the sixth millennium the newest Adam would be made into a life-giving spirit.

5. That a thousand years in the age of the world corresponds to one day in the foundation of the world Peter seems to imply in his canonical letter when he spoke about the end of the world against those who most recently were saying when his promise and coming would be. Peter said, "But of this one thing be not ignorant, my beloved, that one day with the Lord is as a thousand years, and a thousand years as one day" (2 Pt 3.8).

6. The millennium seems to be the most perfect solar day because it is a cubic and solid number of ten. No dimension can be added to its solidity, because it has a third dimension, and there is no fourth dimension in the nature of things. A linear number, however, like ten, and a surface-number, like one hundred, are lacking in dimension. The fulfillment of this day must not be sought except in the fulfillment of number, as far as indeed the space passed through by the sun cannot have a greater completion than the traversing of the Zodiac, as has been said.

7. No one should think that these sorts of arguments taken from the properties of numbers are futile, since Augustine says that the world was made in six days because seven is the perfect number.[28] But perhaps someone will say that, according to the aforementioned argument, the world will endure without qualification for seven thousand years, and thus the time of Christ's coming in judgment and the end of the world is known, although the Lord spoke to the contrary to the Apostles, "It is not for you to know the times or moments, which the Father has put in his own power" (Acts 1.7). And again in Matthew, "But of that day and hour no one knows, not the angels of heaven, but the Father alone" (Mt 24.36). And Augustine, commenting upon Psalm 89, reprimands those who say that the end of this age can be established in six thousand years, in the same way as six days.[29] And again, Augustine in the eighteenth book of *The*

---

28. See Augustine, *Literal Commentary on Genesis* 4.7; *The City of God* 11.30; and Grosseteste, *Hexaëmeron* 9.1.1.

29. See Augustine, *Homilies on the Psalms* 89.5.

*City of God* says, "In vain, then, we try to figure out and establish the years that remain in this age, when we have heard from the mouth of truth that this is not ours to know, and when some have said that four hundred years could be completed, and others that a thousand years could be completed, from the Ascension of the Lord to his last coming."[30] It would be lengthy and unnecessary to show how each of these proves his opinion; because, of course, they use human conjectures, nothing certain is offered by them from the authority of the canonical Scriptures.

8. We, however, say that to want to calculate the duration of the world is audacious and impious. God forbid that someone of the faithful would presume to do this. Nevertheless, it is not far from reasonably probable that the natural duration of the world would be seven thousand years, or, as some have wished to say, the space of six thousand years. Consider this analogy. According to doctors the natural life-span of a man is seventy years; nevertheless, many die before the seventieth year, and many also live beyond it. There are very few who die at the determined natural end of human life, and none of the doctors presumes to say how long anyone would live, although he would say that the natural end of life is at the completion of the seventieth year. In the same way, although the natural end of the world would be perhaps six or seven thousand years, nevertheless, because the world was made for man, it ought to be finished—inasmuch as it was made for man—when the number of men that are to be saved is fulfilled along with the body of Christ, which is the Church.[31] If we reckon by universal nature, then the world will end when the body of Christ is completed; but if we reckon by a proper, particular nature, it will end perhaps much earlier or much later. But because there cannot at the same time be a reckoning according to particular nature and one according to universal nature, the one according to universal nature takes precedence. Just as the common good must always be preferred to a private good, so at the beginning of the world, "the waters that are under the heaven," which by

---

30. Augustine, *The City of God* 18.53.1.
31. See Col 1.24.

their own nature ought to have covered the whole earth (because it is the lighter element), were "gathered together into one place: and . . . the dry land appeared" (Gn 1.9); this happened for the sake of the common good, namely, to make the earth inhabitable. So, then, because no one knows the day or the hour of the completion of the body of Christ, that is, the Church, at whose completion the figure of this world will pass away and there will be a new heaven and a new earth—because of this there is no one who can determine when the end of the world will actually happen, even though the natural end of the world can be determined.

### CHAPTER 5

1. Therefore, from the aforementioned arguments and those that we have purposely omitted (because they have been fully treated previously by others), it can be gathered that God and man are one in person, whose birth is from the Virgin, to whom it belongs to redeem the human race by his Passion, who lived and worked salvation in the middle of the earth, who will come in the sixth millennium, that is, the sixth age. When, therefore, six thousand years had already passed, Christ, who is one in person, God and man, came. The first coming of Christ must not be awaited in the future, unless someone should say that there can be another christ, namely one in person, God and man. In the six thousand years already passed, no one has been discovered in the histories who worked the divine deeds and suffered the human, who suffered a most disgraceful death in the middle of the earth and was born of a virgin. No such person has been found except Jesus the Son of Mary. Therefore, the Lord Jesus, Son of Mary, is truly the Christ, one in person, God and man, who frees the human race by his Passion.

2. Lest someone await another christ in vain, and in order to make clearer that the Lord Jesus, Son of Mary, is the Christ, let us offer the arguments that we can to show that there could not be several christs, that is, several christs who, being one in person, are God and man. Indeed no one doubts that there are several christs, that is, several who are anointed among kings

and priests. If there were several christs (that is, several christs who, being one in person, are God and man), this would happen with several persons of the Trinity assuming man. For a single person could not assume many men because, as has been shown in the *Sentences*, a person cannot assume a person, and a nature cannot assume a person, but a person can assume a nature.[32] When a single person assumes a single nature, there comes forth only a single person in and from two natures. And even if the same person [of the Trinity] were to assume the same nature twice, or three times, or more, there would always be a single person, the same one God and the same one man. He who existed beforehand was not one man at one time and another at another time, because he who existed beforehand was always one person in one nature.

3. It is unfitting, however, for several persons of the Trinity to assume a human nature, first, because the one God would be many men. For let us suppose that the Father became man, and that the Son became man; just as Peter and Paul are two men because they are two persons in whom humanity is multiplied, so also Father and Son would be two men because they would be two persons in whom humanity would be multiplied. For although the divinity would remain undivided and un-multiplied in the two persons, because of its supreme simplicity which is altogether unable to be multiplied, nevertheless the humanity must be multiplied in two persons since it is fittingly made to be multiplied in a multitude of persons and individuals. Therefore, the one God, namely, the Father and the Son, would be many men.

4. Again, the Son-man now has two wills, one uncreated and one created, and likewise two knowledges, and two powers, but on account of the unity of the person of the Son of God there is only one willer, one knower, and one who is powerful. Just as this is so with the Son, it would be likewise with the Father, if he became man. He would have two wills, two knowledges, and two powers, one uncreated and one created. Therefore, just as Father and Son are one willer, one knower, and one who is power-

---

32. See Peter Lombard, *Sentences* 3.5.

ful, because the uncreated will, the uncreated knowledge, and the uncreated power are undivided in them, so also Father and Son would be two willers, two knowers, and two who are powerful, because the two created wills and two created knowledges and powers are in two persons. For plurality in knowledge and in person, insofar as it does not result in several knowers, brings about one knowledge much more strongly than unity of knowledge in a plurality of persons. Just as, therefore, Father and Son are one God and one knower, so they would be several men and several knowers, one God, several knowers. And because the Son by his created will wills everything that he wills with his uncreated will, he in like manner by his created knowledge and power knows and is able to do everything that he knows and is able to do by his uncreated knowledge and power. Because of this he is all-willing, all-knowing, and all-powerful in his created will, knowledge, and power. The same would be true of the Father if he became man; he would be all-willing, all-knowing, and all-powerful in his created will, knowledge, and power. So the one God would be several all-willers, all-knowers, and several who are all-powerful. Authority demonstrates that the Son-man is all-powerful in his created power and in a similar way all-knowing and all-willing. For he himself says in Matthew, "All power is given to me in heaven and on earth" (Mt 28.18). Explaining this verse, Bede says, "In the Church we know that salvation has been accomplished by the victory of Christ, about which he says, 'All power is given to me in heaven and in earth' (Mt 28.18); this is not that power that he always had, but that which he took in the Church at the time when he, as the head in the members, wanted to have it. And so concerning this created power he says, 'All power is given to me.'"[33]

5. And Rabanus, explaining the same verse, says that Jesus speaks these words not about his divinity co-eternal with the Father, but about his assumed humanity, the assumption of which made him a little less than the angels. In the resurrection of this humanity from the dead, he was crowned with glory and honor and established above the works of the Father's hands. All

---

33. Bede, *Explanation of the Apocalypse* 2.12.

things were put under his feet; even death itself, which seemed to prevail over him for a time, was drawn under his feet.[34]

And so that no one think that he cannot be called all-powerful because of this created omnipotence, let him hear John Damascene when he says:

> He, being one, God and man, willed according to his divine and human wills. Because of this, the two wills of the Lord differ from one another not in natural opinion but rather in natural power. For his divine will was without beginning and was the founder of all things, impassibly having the consequent power; but his human will had its beginning in time; it sustained natural passions that could not be corrupted. Though it was not naturally omnipotent, it was omnipotent inasmuch as it was made to be truly and naturally God the Word's.[35]

6. Again, if both the Father and the Son became man, there would be several men to whom worship is owed, and because several men are several things, there would be several things to which worship would be owed. We, then, would be the worshipers of many and would offer divine worship to many.

7. Again, just as now the Word of the Father, God and man, is the head of the Church, so also the Father would be the head of the Church if he became man, and there would be several heads of the one body; and this is monstrous.

8. Again, just as now the Son, God and man, is the spouse and husband of the Church, and the Church is his wife and spouse; so also, if the Father became man, he too would be the husband and spouse of the Church, and the Church would be his wife and spouse, and there would be several husbands of the one wife. For the Son is the spouse of the Church not as God but as Christ, namely, as one in person, God and man.[36] On account of this, because there would be several christs, there would also be several spouses of the one Church. Marriage among men is a sacrament of the marriage of the Church and her husband, Christ. Because of this, just as in the marriage signified [Christ and the Church] there would be one wife and several husbands, so in the marriage that is the sign [human marriage] it would be

---

34. See Ps 8.6; Heb 2.6–9; and Rabanus, *Commentary on Matthew* 8.27.
35. John Damascene, *On the Orthodox Faith* 62.
36. See Eph 5.25–33.

necessary that there be one wife and several husbands; and this is most foul. For in some way a man could have several wives, because one man can make several women fruitful, so that they can be pregnant at the same time; but one woman cannot be impregnated at the same time by several men.[37] Therefore, such a marriage would not serve fruitfulness, but rather desire.

9. Again, because the natural Son of God the Father assumed our nature, and we were made one whole Christ with him, we are also sons, though adopted, of God the Father.[38] Therefore, similarly, if the Father had assumed our nature, and we had become one Christ with him, we would be all fathers of God the Word by adoption. Likewise, if we suppose that the Holy Spirit had assumed our nature and we were one whole Christ with him, we would be by adoption the Holy Spirit of the Son and the Father. Every single man, then, who would be of the body of Christ, would possess a trinity of adoption. Anyone at all would go into the three persons, for the following reason. As it is now, anyone who is just goes into the person who is the whole Christ, the Son, God and man, along with his body, which is the Church; so it would also be that a just man would go into that person who would be the Father-Christ with his body the Church, and into that person who would be the Holy Spirit-Christ with his body, the Church. And this would be inappropriate. Indeed, one person cannot pass over into other personhoods of the same kind, nor participate in many personhoods of the same kind, because what is singular cannot become more singular in the same kind of thing.[39]

10. Again, just as that man shown to be the Son-man is the natural Son of God the Father; so also, if the Father became man, that man shown to be the Father-man would be the Father of the natural Son of God. And if the Holy Spirit at the same time be-

---

37. See Robert Grosseteste, *On the Ten Commandments* 6.
38. See Rom 8.14–16.
39. Grosseteste is saying here that, e.g., one human person cannot go into another human person, as a divine person could not go into another divine person. But a human person can go into a divine person. A human person made one with the person of the Father could not also be made one with the person of the Son, for the persons of the Father and the Son cannot be made into one person.

came man along with them, the man shown to be the Holy Spirit, would be the natural Holy Spirit of the Father and the Son. The three persons would also be three sons of men, and only one of them would be the Son of God and the Son of man. Hence this person would be greater than the other persons in sonship, because they would not be the Sons of God but only sons of men. And it is unfitting that one of the persons would have precedence over the others in a property shared by the three persons.

11. Again, the Son-man now prays to God the Father until he will have handed over the kingdom in the end to his God and Father.[40] Similarly, therefore, if the Father became man, the Father-man would pray to God the Son, and the Holy Spirit-man would pray to God the Father and God the Son. And so every person would pray to another and would be prayed to by another for the same thing, nothing other than the salvation of the Church.

12. Again, the Son-man prays to and honors God the Father. Therefore, God the Father is prayed to and honored by the Son-man. But whatever is attributed to God is also attributed to the man on account of the unity of person. Therefore, the Father-man is prayed to and honored by the Son-man, and likewise the Son-man is prayed to and honored by the Father-man.

13. Again, a single Christ most fully suffices to renew all things, for which it was fitting that God became man. Therefore, a second christ would be altogether superfluous. And it cannot be said that some christ would not do all the things for which it was fitting that God became man, because if he did not do some of these things, then his power would be partly or wholly useless and vain, and so would not be utterly separated from vice. So, then, these consequences and very many more unfitting consequences of this sort (and perhaps they are much more evident than the ones mentioned) would follow if there were several christs.

CHAPTER 6

1. Therefore, we firmly and faithfully confess a single Christ. The deeds and sufferings of the Lord Jesus, Son of Mary (about

40. See 1 Cor 15.24.

which it is necessary to trust history) declare most clearly that he is the Christ, God and man. For he performed works proper only to God; the work of creation is God's alone, and the Lord Jesus also did it. The coin which was found in the mouth of a fish and which Peter gave for the Lord Jesus and for himself, he himself created, just as the expositors say about that text, and this seems not to have been otherwise.[41] For fishes do not take into their mouths anything from the outside except what nourishes them. Therefore, although the fish had found in the sea the coin that was made, it is not nourished by metal, and would not have taken it into its mouth. The coin, then, had come into the mouth of the fish only by the creation of Jesus the Word. But if someone should firmly resist this interpretation and not concede that Jesus created that coin for himself by his word, he could not deny that the prescience by which he found the coin was the power of divinity alone.

2. But perhaps someone will say that he foreknew in the same way that the Prophets foreknew, not because they were God, but through the spirit of prescience and prophecy that they received from God. And perhaps someone will say also that he worked miracles only as one of the holy men. On account of this, we first endeavor to show only that his works were works proper to divine power. After this is demonstrated, in our own way we will show that he did not perform these deeds by his ministry alone—as many saints have resuscitated the dead by their ministry and performed other deeds by authority that are possible to God alone. Rather, we will show that he performed those deeds with authority and power, that he could not perform them except as God. Whatever, then, is thought about the coin—whether it had been created at that time or not—at any rate no one can deny that the illumination of the blind, and especially of the man born blind, the opening of deaf ears and mute mouths, the healing of the lame, giving power to the limbs of paralytics, the cleansing of leprosy, and the sudden restoration, by word and command, of natural defects of this sort that could not be repaired by the work of nature or medicine, all of these deeds are the works proper to the power of the Creator. Indeed, it belongs to the same power,

41. See Mt 17.26.

on the one hand, to create and perfect something, and, on the other hand, to restore that same thing, imperfect and corrupt, to perfection. Therefore, when the Lord Jesus performed the aforementioned works, he performed works of creative power.

3. Also, the multiplication of a few loaves of bread and small fish, to whose power does this work belong if not to him who said in the beginning, "Let the earth bring forth the green herb, and such as make seed," and so on (Gn 1.11)?[42] Also, by the power of whose word is one grain of seed multiplied into innumerable crops? What power can immediately change water into wine, except that which changes the water that is pulled through the grape-vine into wine?[43] But if it is necessary to attribute one or another of these works to a greater power, the conversion of water into wine without delay in jars seems to belong to a greater power than that conversion which is accomplished after a time in the grape-vine. So then, if the conversion that is the work of the grape-vine belongs to the first creative power, also that which happened in the jars was the work of the same power.

4. Again, to what power could belong the work of raising the dead and especially the man who was dead for four days and stinking, except to the same power which "formed man of the slime of the earth: and breathed into his face the breath of life, and man became a living soul" (Gn 2.7)?[44] For to readapt immediately a rotten body for the reception of union with the soul and to call back the soul from hell and unite it to the body is beyond every strength of a created power. It is clear, therefore, that the many deeds which Jesus, the Son of Mary, performed, were the works of the creative power.

5. Again, the knowledge of the secret thoughts of human hearts and the knowledge of individual future contingent events is the work of divine providence. Indeed, a man who knows these sorts of things through the spirit of prophecy, does not know them through himself but through the light and in the light of divine providence. For God alone through himself searches and knows these kinds of secrets of the heart.[45] But the Lord Jesus

---

42. See Mt 14.19; 15.34–36.  43. See Jn 2.7–10.
44. See Jn 11.39.
45. See 1 Chr 28.9; Ps 7.10; Rom 8.27; Rv 2.23.

knows the secrets of the heart and foretold individual contingent future events. So then, he worked deeds of providential power.

6. Again, he himself forgave sins. Indeed, when he said to someone, "Your sins are forgiven you," others thought that he said this as a lie and that he blasphemed (Mt 9.2). He immediately proved the invisible work of forgiveness by a visible work, when he said to them, "Why do you think evil in your hearts? What is easier: to say, Your sins are forgiven you: or to say, Arise, and walk? But that you may know that the Son of man has power on earth to forgive sins, (then said he to the man sick of palsy,) Arise, take up your bed, and go into your house. And he arose, and went into his house" (Mt 9.4–7). He showed, therefore, through a work of visible healing, which itself belonged to the divine power alone to bring about, that it was not foreign to him to perform a divine work. But he who could cure the body in a supernatural and divine way could also heal the soul in the same way. And it does not seem true that if he had lied in saying, "Your sins are forgiven," he would have been so effective in saying, "Arise, and walk" (Mt 9.2, 5). But if he was telling the truth and not lying, he forgave sins by power and authority and not by a ministry as do the prelates of the Church to whom it has been said, "Whose sins you shall forgive, they are forgiven them" (Jn 20.23). For he said, "That you may know that the Son of man has power on earth to forgive sins" (Mt 9.6). But if someone should say that he had a conferred power only, just as a minister has, and that he was not powerful through himself, it would follow that he was a liar in the way in which he proved that he had the power to forgive. For the manner and evidence of the proof implied more that he forgave powerfully, as God, than that he forgave only from a conferred power, as a minister does. The Lord Jesus, therefore, performed works of renewal in the spirit of the mind, and those are the works of divine kindness alone. For the works of renewal and justification in the spirit of our mind are greater and more worthy than the works of creation. Hence, the works that are greater could not belong to a lesser power.

7. He performed works that belong to the governing power when he commanded the winds and the sea, when he made the

sea able to be walked upon by himself and Peter, when he commanded the demons.

8. He also performed the glorifying work of raising bodies to life, when on the mountain he transformed himself between Moses and Elijah in the sight of three disciples. But most evidently, it seems to me, he showed himself to be God when he died on the cross. For to separate one's human soul from one's healthy human body and heart is beyond every created power, because the soul naturally desires to be joined to its body, and it abhors nothing so much as separation from its body through death. Hence it is naturally inseparable [from the body and heart] while it is in the heart and while the vigor of life has not yet died. It is not, then, within the power of man to divide his soul from his body while it is healthy and has the vigor of life. Rather, it does not belong to a lesser power to separate one's soul from a healthy body than to unite it to an organic body. Therefore, it is a work proper to divine strength and creative power to separate by one's own will one's soul from one's healthy body. And so when the Lord Jesus hung on the cross with a then-healthy body and breathed forth his own spirit by will, he performed a work divine and proper to divinity alone. Because he died with his innards and vital parts healthy and while his natural vigor remained, it can be shown that he died after spending only three hours on the cross, that he died even though he was healthy and whole when he was crucified, even though he was affixed to the wood of the cross by nails that pierced only his hands and feet, even though his body was not otherwise wounded and blood did not flow out from his innards through another wound.

9. For the piercing only of his hands and feet could not empty his blood from his heart and innards in so brief a time, nor could it extinguish so quickly the vigor of life of a strong, young, and healthy man. There is testimony that he did not die on account of a great loss of blood through the nail-wounds: when his side was opened with a lance after he died, blood came out from his innards (although dead bodies even without the loss of blood, if they are wounded after death, do not usually flow with blood because the blood is cooled and coagulated). In addition, he shouted with a loud voice when he expired;

his shout was not an inarticulate groan, but a loud extension of the voice, literate, meaningful, and humbly praying to God the Father, when he said, "Into your hands I commend my spirit" (Lk 23.46). If he had been a mere man, and if blood and the vigor of life had failed within him, he would not have been in any way able to shout so. Therefore the vigor of life had not been removed, or he was more than a mere man, or at the same time there was no loss of the vigor of life and he was more than a mere man. If he was more than a mere man, then we have the proposition that he was God, because nothing is naturally superior to man except God. But if the vigor of life had not yet been exhausted in him, he did not die by the violence of a wound but by the power which can unite the soul to the body and separate the soul from a body that has not yet fallen away from nature and the vigor of life. And this power is not human but only, as has been said, divine. Hence the centurion saw that he had thus shouted and expired, and said, "Indeed this man was the Son of God" (Mk 15.39).

10. Again, his dominion over the elements of the world and his suffering the elements in his Passion attest to his divinity. For the sun was obscured beyond its natural course, since at that time it could not naturally be eclipsed, as the moon was in the fourteenth day of its cycle and in the opposite part of the sky from the sun.[46] Besides, no solar eclipse makes darkness throughout the whole land, and not even over some of the land for three hours.

11. But in the Passion of the Lord Jesus darkness came over the whole land from the sixth to the ninth hour. In addition, the earth was shaken, graves opened, stones split, the veil of the temple torn, and although earthquakes happen in the usual course of the elements, nevertheless the one that happened then seems to be outside the course of nature because the obscuring of the sun, as was said, happened outside the natural run of things. When the bodies of the saints who had fallen asleep came out of their graves and appeared, it was likewise outside the course of nature. Where would the elements more

---

46. On the fourteenth day the moon is full; a lunar eclipse of the sun requires a new moon.

fittingly suffer beyond the course of nature (and in a certain way die), than in suffering and dying along with their Creator and Lord, who suffered and died? The sun also, according to the secular philosophers, cannot lack light in itself by any operation of nature. For when it is eclipsed by the interposition of the moon, it does not in itself lack light, but is naturally impassible in respect to darkness. Therefore, in that darkening of the sun was the passion of the naturally impassible. This did not happen except by a divine ordinance and providence according to which nothing happens in vain. The providence of God, then, wanted to teach the human race something by that darkening of the sun. But what did it quite evidently say, as it were, by the passion and darkening of the visible and naturally impassible sun, except the Passion and death of the true Sun, invisible, impassible, and immortal? Then the impassible suffered, and the immortal died; and he could not do this except as the God-man, impassible and immortal as God, but passible and mortal as man. One does not read in any history about the passion and death of anyone (except that of the Lord Jesus) when the sun was darkened, especially anyone who performed some divine works. The Lord Jesus was, therefore, by the testimony of the sun, the impassible one suffering and the immortal one dying. The earth (which was unmoved because it was not removed from its place as a whole, but rather was shaken), the split stones, and the temple whose veil was torn—what else do they speak of except the motion of the immutable, the splitting of stability, and the revelation of heavenly sacraments?

12. In addition, the resurrection of the Lord Jesus—just as he had foretold—his frequent appearances to his disciples, his Ascension before them into heaven, the sending of the Holy Spirit, and the speaking in all languages after he was received: what else do they attest, except that the Lord Jesus himself was not a mere man, but at the same time God and man?[47] No one can deny that the Lord Jesus performed divine, nay, most divine, works in the flesh, except someone so bold that he refuses to accept authentic histories. But if the histories about the Lord Jesus were false, because they were written soon after his death,

---

47. See Acts 1.3; 1.9; and 2.1–4.

they would not at all have been accepted from the beginning, as the memory of him was still recent.

13. The deeds that the evangelical history narrates are absolutely true, and even those who do not believe in Jesus do not deny this. They do affirm, though, that he is not God, even though he performed deeds of this sort. But, as has been said, it will by no means be possible to deny that the works that he did were divine and proper to divine power. But perhaps certain people say, as I said above, that he did these works not by power, as God, but by ministry, as a mere man, a friend of God and pleasing to him. But if they concede that he was pleasing to God, they must also concede that he was truthful and not a blasphemer. But he said that he was God. So, then, he said these words truthfully and did not blaspheme. Therefore, he was God, just as he himself says about himself, "I and the Father are one" (Jn 10.30). And again, "The Father is in me, and I in the Father" (Jn 10.38). And again, "Philip, he that sees me sees the Father also" (Jn 14.9). And again, "You believe in God; believe also in me" (Jn 14.1). The only conclusion could be that he is one God with God the Father.

14. Again, he says in another place, "Before Abraham was made, I am" (Jn 8.58). And again, when the Jews had asked him who he was, he responded, "The beginning, who also speak unto you" (Jn 8.25). And many things of this sort. Therefore, he was either a liar, a blasphemer, and a man inflated with diabolical pride, who claimed divinity for himself; or he was true God. But if he had been so opposed to God, how could he have performed such divine deeds? If he had been so proud, how could he have undergone such humiliations, when he foreknew them and had the power to avoid them? If he had been so mean, how could he have performed acts of such kindness? But if someone should say that he hid hypocritically the pestilence of his soul, it has to be responded to him that it would have to have come out at some time. It must be confessed, then, that he was either true God or the worst man. The enemies of faith in him, however, would not confess him to be the worst man, and his deeds testify to the contrary; all must confess him to be true God, if they yield to the truth.

15. Again, that he performed his deeds with the power of God is clear from that fact that others in his name performed similar deeds and even ones greater than the many performed by him. It is impossible to cast out demons, to heal all manner of illnesses, to raise the dead, and to command the elements in the name of a blasphemer, or even in the name of someone other than him who naturally has power over demons, illness and health, the dead and the living, and the elements of the world. For to do these deeds in his name is to do them by his natural strength and power. All these deeds, then, were frequently performed in the very name of the Lord Jesus.

16. Because this is clearer than light from innumerable accounts—and they even still may often happen—it is most manifest that the Lord Jesus was not a blasphemer, but that he himself said truly that he was true God. The argument for the truth of the faith is not small, the faith in Jesus which is held and by which it is believed that he is the Christ, God and man, who was promised in the Law. The argument is what Gamaliel said in the council of the elders about the preaching of faith in him through the Apostles, "For if this council or this work be of men, it will come to naught. But if it be of God, you cannot overthrow it" (Acts 5.38–39). For if what was preached and received concerning faith in the Lord Jesus for over 1230 years were a falsity of human invention, then how had it become so strong among the wise and the foolish, the poor and the rich, the weak and the powerful, every sex, every age, every condition? How did it become so strong especially when falsity is dark and tends to disappear by its nature? Faith in Jesus, however, grows and is strengthened, and this is the firmest sign that this faith is the light of the countenance of God "signed upon us" (Ps 4.7).[48] So, from the aforementioned it must be firmly held and confessed that there is a single Christ, that he is our God, Jesus, the Son of the most blessed and glorious Virgin Mary, who suffered under Pontius Pilate and was crucified, and that there is no other name in which the human race must be saved.[49]

---

48. See Roger Marston, *Quodlibetal Questions* II, q. III, I, 1 (p. 106).
49. See Acts 4.12.

# PART FOUR

### CHAPTER 1

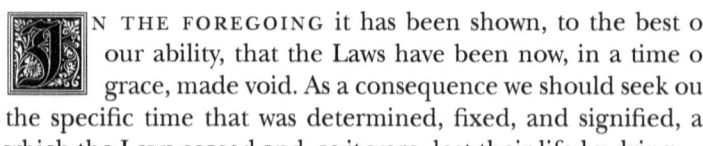N THE FOREGOING it has been shown, to the best of our ability, that the Laws have been now, in a time of grace, made void. As a consequence we should seek out the specific time that was determined, fixed, and signified, at which the Laws ceased and, as it were, lost their life by dying.

2. It seems, then, that this time was the birth of John the Baptist, or the time when John began to preach, or the time when he died, since the Lord said, "For all the Prophets and the Law prophesied until John" (Mt 11.13). But if the Laws died at one of these three times, Christ himself and his disciples kept and observed dead Laws, since Christ and his disciples ate the Paschal lamb after the death of John.[1] And the Paschal lamb, immolated on the day of the supper before the Passion of the Lord Jesus Christ, would lack life; it would lack the pious signification of the sacrifice of the body and blood of Christ offered on the altar of the cross. But this is manifestly most false. So the Laws lived with a life of pious signification after John.

3. Likewise, all prophecies first find their fulfillment when the Lord said, "It is consummated," bowed his head, and handed over his spirit (Jn 19.30). Hence Rabanus, in his book *On the Cross* places the number six (which is the first perfect number) formed in the manner of a triangle at each of the corners of the cross,[2] as a sign of the then-perfect consummation. After

---

1. See Lk 22.15.
2. A "perfect number" is one that is equal to the sum of its divisors (not including the number itself as a divisor). So the divisors of 6 (aside from 6 itself) are 1, 2, and 3, which, added together, make 6. Another example is 28: its divi-

this was done,³ he then said, "Notice how the number six fittingly includes the four corners of the Lord's cross and shows the complete perfection of the work that was carried out, because on the cross the Creator of things issued a judgment on his consummation, when, after he took a drink, he said, 'It is finished.' Indeed, it was rightly written that it was finished at that time when the human race was liberated. The Passion of Christ benefited not only men (because they obtained the grace of redemption) but also the heavenly crowds of angels (because in him they attained the fullness of their number)."⁴

4. Therefore, the Law and the Prophets extend not up to John but beyond him, up to the Passion of Christ. Thus, "all the Prophets and the Law prophesied until John" (Mt 11.13) must be understood, it seems, to mean that they prophesied up to Christ, who came in the time of John. As Rabanus says, "When, therefore, it is said that 'all the Prophets and the Law prophesied up to John,' it applies to the time of Christ; and so John showed that he had come, who they said would come."⁵ It is as if the Lord said, "The foretelling of prophets was finished in what John showed."

5. But this seems to contradict the fact that many prophecies seem to pertain to the time even after the Passion of Christ, because many prophets foretold the Resurrection of Christ, his Ascension into heaven, and his coming to judge the good and the evil and after judgment to assign them to their state. Many prophecies, therefore, prophesy not up to John or up to Christ, but beyond John and Christ. All prophecy, then, is not ended, it seems, with John or Christ, that is, in the time of John's or Christ's appearance. And so, all of the Law seems not to be ended, because the Law and the Prophets, as Christ's above-mentioned words indicate, seem to be coterminous.

6. Again, he says, "The Prophets and the Law prophesied"; so,

---

sors (aside from 28) are 1, 2, 4, 7, and 14, which, added together, make 28. On the number six, see also Augustine, *On the Trinity* 4.4, 7–6, 10.

3. See Appendix, Figure 1, pp. 247–49, and PL 107:242C.

4. Rabanus, *On the Praises of the Holy Cross* 1.23; see Grosseteste, *Hexaëmeron* 9.8.4.

5. Rabanus, *Commentary on Matthew* 4.11.

then, the Law prophesied. This verse means one of two things. Either the sense is that the events that the Law and Prophets prophesied are finished and consummated at the appearance of John; or that the act of prophesying lasted only until John, although many of the events prophesied by the Law and the Prophets happened after John. But the first sense seems false from what has already been said, for many of the events that the Prophets prophesied are at this point still to come. For example, there is the prophecy of Isaiah that if the number of the sons of Israel is as the sand of the sea, then a remnant will be saved.[6] Other things that are to be believed about the salvation of the people of Israel at the end of time were prophesied along with the things about the Antichrist, the end of the world, the resurrection, and the age to come. Certain events, which were signified beforehand by certain Laws, are at this point still to come—for example, the loss of all corruption and mortality in the resurrection of the saints, which is signified beforehand by circumcision, and that full rest to come after the resurrection and God's rest from every work, when the kingdom of saints is completed, which are signified by the Sabbath.

7. The second sense also seems to be false, because many prophesied after John. As Rabanus says, "'All the Prophets and the Law prophesied until John' does not exclude prophets after John, for we read in Acts of the Apostles that Agabus and the four virgin daughters of Philip prophesied, but at a time when the Law and Prophets, which were written and which we have read, prophesied about the Lord whatever they prophesied."[7] Therefore, not every act of prophecy ended in John's time. So neither the events prophesied by the Law and the Prophets nor the prophetic act itself of the Law and the Prophets seem to have taken their end and consummation at the appearance of John or the Lord. Nevertheless, the aforementioned words of the Lord himself, when he said on the cross, "It is consummated" (Jn 19.30), and the authority also of Rabanus prove that all the things prophesied by the Law and the Prophets have received their consummation in the suffering Christ.

---

6. See Is 10.22.  7. Ibid.; see Acts 11.28–30 and 21.9.

8. In order to solve this contradiction as well as our limited abilities will allow, we say that the prophetic act of the Law and the Prophets lived up to the birth of John. For from the beginning of the world up to the birth of John, the prophets did not fail to prophesy the reconciliation of the human race through the Passion of the Son of God. Hence Zechariah, the father of John, said when John was born, "As he spoke by the mouth of his holy prophets, who are from the beginning" (Lk 1.70). At the birth of John, that prophesying began to die, and it continued to die more and more up to the time of the Passion of Christ. When Christ handed over his spirit on the cross, all prophecy was ended and fully dead, and all the things prophesied were consummated in that moment.

9. In order to prove these points, it must first be considered that something can die successively and over an extended period of time. This is clear in the case of many men in whom the vivacity of the senses or the vigor of life gradually fail until certain members of the body become thoroughly unsensing and immobile. After these become so, other members do the same, and thus gradually at some point sense and motion fail in the whole body. What is this drawn-out failure of the body but a truly drawn-out death, if sense and vital motion are parts of life, and if each is a kind of life?

10. It also must be considered that not every foretelling of a contingent future event is properly, principally, and especially called prophecy. That, however, which does not come by the Holy Spirit is called divination and not prophecy. But that which does come by the Holy Spirit and does not concern the salvation of the human race by the mediation of Christ, can indeed be called prophecy, but not properly, principally, and especially. For the sense most properly given to the word "prophecy" includes in its meaning not only the foretelling of a future event, but also the foretold event's inscrutability to the mind of man. Nothing, though, is as far from human wisdom's power of discovery as the restoration of the human race by the Son of God, God and man, who suffered on the cross. Therefore, no foretelling of a future event is as principally and especially prophecy as that which foretells this restoration, which is especially inscrutable to

every human wisdom. And so only those who foretold this restoration through the Holy Spirit are principally and especially called Prophets.

11. Along with these first two points, it must also be considered that the death of Christ was the reconciliation of the human race with God the Father and the restitution of all creatures to their best and final state of being, which they lost when man sinned. The creatures of the world were made so that they might easily serve man in his perfect obedience to his Creator, and they could not do this after man was disobedient to God by sinning. They could not do it until man perfectly obeyed God in the obedience of Christ. In Christ, therefore, offering his life unto death and thereby reconciling the human race to God the Father, all things were consummated, even those which are to happen at the end of time.

12. This will be able to be more easily understood from an analogy. Let us suppose that some soldier wronged his king and was guilty of injuring his majesty. Let us also suppose that on account of his guilt he was deprived of land, camps, and other possessions. Then the same soldier was reconciled when satisfaction was offered to his king and accepted by the king; and after the reconciliation he would receive back land, camps, and other possessions, and those which had fallen into ruin and been damaged would all have to be repaired. Let us suppose also that in this reconciliation the cause of the restitution and future restoration is infallible. Would it not be rightly and truly said at the time of the reconciliation, "Now all of that soldier's belongings have been restored to him; his possessions that were damaged are now repaired; whatever he earlier had lost, at the time of reconciliation he regained; that reconciliation repaired all of his damaged possessions"? In addition, if someone long beforehand had foretold this reconciliation, this restitution of possessions after the future reconciliation, and this restoration of damaged belongings, would it not rightly be said at the time when the reconciliation was accomplished, "At this time all things have been consummated and perfected," which that someone long before this time foretold? And so by the same right and true manner of speaking, it was most truly said that all things had been re-

paired by the Passion of Christ, and that all of these that have been prophesied by the Prophets and the Law were consummated at the same time. For in that very reconciliation by the Passion there was an infallible cause of repairing all things.

13. Besides, the Son of God, God and man, who joins the human race to God the Father by his perfect love and obedience, is the head and end of all creatures, and all creatures, whether past or future, depend on this mediator who by his mediation unites the creature and the Creator, and they are, so to speak, his appendages. But the very appendages, even though they yet be in the future, are perfected in the existence of the principle as the source and cause from which they necessarily follow. The principle itself is also the fullness and perfection of all the appendages dependent upon it. For where else do the appendages have perfection except in that on which they depend? As cause, therefore, as source, and as form, the principle is the fullness and consummation of its appendages.

14. In Christ, then, who suffered and reconciled the human race, on account of which all things were made, all things are consummated, as he is their cause, source, and form. This is true even of those things which are yet to happen in this age or in another. Hence Rabanus, in the words we cited above about the consummation of things by the Passion of Christ, says that the angels attained the fullness of their number in Christ, although it is nevertheless clear that their number is not yet filled up; rather, the completion of their number is in the future, at the general resurrection.[8] For the crowd of past creatures that precede the coming of Christ and the crowd of creatures that follow after the coming of Christ shout, "Hosanna to the Son of David" (Mt 21.9); they, as it were, seek from him and in him their salvation and consummation. For "Hosanna" means "I beseech you, save me." All that is prophesied, whether it is already past or is yet to happen, was consummated when Christ handed over his spirit on the cross, as he himself testified.

8. See 4.1.3.

## CHAPTER 2

1. What is yet to happen, in respect of the showing forth of the thing to be consummated, had at that time already happened, in respect of its consummation; what was yet to be done, in respect of being brought into existence, was at that time already done, in respect of the source of its cause. Therefore, no prophecy extends beyond the Passion of Christ, and so nothing prophesied is consummated after that point. For although something is yet to exist and must be brought into existence, nevertheless it already existed and was made, as has been said, through its consummation.

2. Hence, even those who after Christ foretold something about the end of the world and the future kingdom—as Paul and John (in Revelation) did about the Antichrist—even they are not called prophets, meaning "foretellers of future events"; rather, it is said that a revelation of things hidden has been made to them, and the consummation of these things, which has already happened, even though their act of existence is yet to exist, is most mysterious and very far removed from human wisdom. Hence, they are more announcers of an event that has already happened than foretellers of the future. And so every act of prophecy, in the proper, principal, and specific sense, comes to an end in the suffering Christ. Because everything that pertains to the salvation of the human race must be spoken by the Holy Spirit, it has already happened in its consummation and something very mysterious and very far removed from human investigation has already been displayed, manifested, and known in the arrival of the thing itself. But, as we said above, prophecy in its proper and principal sense signifies the foretelling through the Holy Spirit of a future event very remote from human investigation. Therefore, the prophetic act, in its proper, principal, and specific sense, altogether ended and itself died when Christ died, and all that had been prophesied was at that time consummated, as has been said. So the Law and the Prophets do not prophesy after Christ died, both because the events prophesied do not await further consummation and because the prophetic act at that time altogether died.

3. The prophetic act of the Law and the Prophets began to die and what was prophesied began to be consummated when John the Baptist was born, because insofar as the presence of Christ the mediator had come, the prophetic foretelling of that presence was dying; and insofar as his presence had come, whatever had been prophesied beforehand partook of its consummation. And with the ever-growing manifestation of his presence, the prophetic act and foretelling died more and more, and whatever was prophesied about our salvation partook more of its consummation. But when the course of Christ's life was complete and the human race was reconciled by his death, the prophecy of the Law and the Prophets, as has been said, was completely dead, and all that had been foretold by the Law and the Prophets was consummated. At the birth of John, though, the presence of Christ began to be manifest, and the presence of Christ was manifested more and more by all John's actions. For although when John was born, Christ had not yet been born, nevertheless the birth of John manifested the presence of Christ.

4. For John was the forerunner and herald of Christ, and by his birth, as if by the voice of a forerunner and herald, he announced the birth of Christ. Hence there is the verse in Matthew which says, "Are you he that is to come, or look we for another?" (Mt 11.3), and Gregory in his *Homilies* says about this verse, "He seeks to know if he who had come into the world by himself would also by himself go down to the prison of hell. For coming before Christ, he had announced him to the world, and by dying he went before him to hell. He says, therefore, 'Are you he that is to come, or look we for another?' Speaking openly he would say: 'Just as you deigned to be born for men, make known whether you also deign to die for men, so that I who am the forerunner of your birth may be also the forerunner of your death and may announce in hell that you are about to come as I announced to the world that you had come."[9] From Gregory's words it is clear that John more announced by his own birth the birth of Christ, as if by the voice of a herald, rather

---

9. Gregory the Great, *Homilies on the Gospel* 1.6.

than prophesied his future presence. Again, as Ambrose says in his commentary on Luke, "John heard in his mother's womb the greeting of Mary."[10] And as the evangelist at the sound of Mary's greeting says that "the infant leaped in [his mother's] womb" (Lk 1.41), it is clear that he announced the presence of Christ by this leaping. John, therefore, announced that Christ was present though still in the Virgin's womb by leaping in his mother's womb, as it were by the voice of a herald, and he no less shouted the presence of Christ in the womb of the Virgin and his manifestation from the womb by his own birth, again, as it were, by the voice of a herald. In addition, John himself says about himself, "I am the voice of one crying out in the wilderness; prepare the way of the Lord" (Jn 1.23).[11] Because, then, John himself is a voice, the whole John shouts by all his actions and by his whole way of life. He holds the office of the voice, the office of a herald's and forerunner's voice—it is clear—because he is the herald and forerunner.

5. Again, he is the voice of the Word, that is, of Christ, who is the Word of the Father. But the voice naturally precedes the whole word and manifests the whole word. John, then, announced and manifested the birth of Christ the Word, as a voice precedes a word. Consider this analogy. When some king, who at present is sitting on his throne, plans to go outside to the people, the voice of a herald shouts, "Prepare the way and the place for the king who is coming; for, behold, he comes." The voice of the herald is a certain indication of the presence of the king who up to that point was perhaps quiet on the throne. In the same way when our Lord was up to that point quiet on the throne of the virginal womb, the very birth of John as if a herald's voice commanded to prepare a way for the Lord and rather indicated the presence of the Lord than foretold him. For a herald is halfway between someone who foretells something to be completed and someone who announces something already completed, but he is closer to the one who announces something present than to someone who foretells the future. Hence, John was, even by

---

10. Ambrose, *Commentary on the Gospel according to Luke* 2.23.
11. See Is 40.3.

his very birth, more a proclaimer of Christ than a prophet, and yet he was not an evangelist. So, then, just as the morning star indicates the present day rather than announces a future day, and just as the herald's voice that orders subjects to prepare a way for the king cries out that he is present rather than that he is to be expected in the future, so John proclaimed by his birth that Christ was present, rather than announced that he was to be expected in the future. Insofar as the birth of John was the proclamation of the presence of Christ, prophecy at that time began to die and what was prophesied partook already of its consummation. When, consequently, the presence of Christ became ever more manifested, prophecy ever more died, and what was prophesied was ever more consummated.

6. Therefore, up to the birth of John, prophetic action lived fully, and what was prophesied did not yet partake at all of its consummation. But at the death of Christ prophetic action fully ceased, and what was prophesied received the fullness of its consummation; the former was finished by ceasing; the latter, by being consummated. In the time, though, between the appearance of John and the death of Christ, prophecy through the Law and the Prophets lived in one sense and died in another; and what was prophesied about the plan of salvation for the human race had been in one sense consummated and in another sense yet to be consummated. On account of this, the Prophets and the Law prophesied up to the birth of John when prophetic action was fully alive and when what was prophesied awaited its whole consummation. From the birth of John to the death of Christ, however, dying prophecy lived and living prophecy died.

### CHAPTER 3

1. Because, then, the Laws, insofar as they were Laws, were signs, the shadow, and foretelling of their perfect consummation in the death of Christ, the very moment of the death of Christ was the designated and determined time when the Laws ceased and, as it were, lost their life by thoroughly dying. Because, therefore, the death of Christ was the complete death of the Laws, it seems, as Jerome thinks, that to keep the Laws after

the time of Christ's death would be ruinous for everyone.[12] The words of Augustine, though, seem to resound to the contrary when he says that the Laws had to be kept by the Jews for some time after the death of Christ until they could be buried with honor.[13]

2. But surely there is no unharmonious dissonance (as opposed to harmonious dissonance) between those two sacred writers, between those two flutes of the Holy Spirit? If experts in the art of music can, by their art, make two flutes to be harmoniously dissonant and dissonantly harmonious, it is much more likely that the Holy Spirit, the Maker of all, who has all strength and foresight over everything, make these two flutes to resound with a harmonious dissonance. And it is not fitting that so great an artist as the Holy Spirit omit some kind of artful modulation in the song of divine praise. Therefore, that artist makes not only a harmonious harmony to sound through such flutes but also a harmonious dissonance and a dissonant harmony, because dissonant harmony is an artful melodious modulation. Indeed, all musical harmonies, except where there is tonal identity, are dissonant harmonies, such as the octave, the fourth, and the fifth; but just as it happens that dissonance is apparent and harmony hidden to the heavy sense of bodily hearing when two flutes are dissonantly harmonious, so it happens that the dissonance of these spiritual flutes is clear to the hardened hearing of our mind, while the tempered harmony beneath dissonance remains hidden.

3. So, then, the clear dissonance resonated in their words: after Christ the Laws are to be observed by no one; after Christ the Laws are to be observed by the Jews for a time. If there is harmony in these words, as it appears likely to be, it is not evident but hidden, and we must investigate more carefully. Even if we cannot in all cases and everywhere reduce their clear dissonances to a hidden harmony, we ought, nonetheless, to do this wherever we can. And perhaps it will not be possible in all cases, because just as the prophetic spirit was not always present to the Prophets, so perhaps the Holy Spirit did not always dictate everything which those two saints wrote, but abandoned them sometimes

---

12. See Jerome, *Commentary on the Letter to the Galatians* 1.2.11.
13. See Augustine, *Ep.* 82.16.

to their own voices so that some useful benefit might come to us from their dissonance.

4. It must be observed that the sacred writers often did not intend to assert something but rather to show that it is possible; and their propositions often are not as much about existence as about possibility, even though they seem to us to be assertions offered about existence.

5. They propose many propositions as an exercise. As Gregory of Nyssa says about himself, "We do not propose what occurs to our mind as an assertion but enjoin it upon our kindly hearers as an exercise."[14] Often, then, they seem to contradict each other in assertions when their words are rather about the possibility or likely probability of something. The Holy Spirit in the song of divine praise often sounds like dissonant harmony; this is clear from the books and words of the sacred page according to the bodily sense. It is most certain about these books that there is nothing in them that is repugnant or contradictory on the level of meaning, even though in them the words often sound contradictory and dissonant at face value. For at face value, what is more contradictory than to divorce one's wife for any reason at all and not to divorce her except on account of only adultery?

6. Again, what is more contradictory than, on the one hand, "tooth for tooth" and "eye for eye" (Ex 21.24), and, on the other hand, "do not be mindful of the injury of your citizens" (Lv 24.20) and "do not [at all] resist evil" (Dt 19.21).[15] Such apparent contradictions are innumerable in the Scriptures, and, nevertheless, it is certain that according to their interior meaning they agree entirely. But perhaps someone may say: If there is a latent agreement between Jerome and Augustine, how did Augustine not see that Jerome's meaning and intention agreed with his own, and vice versa, when each considered the writings of the other and investigated the words of the other diligently and without ill will? Therefore, it seems more likely that Augustine would perceive that the meaning of Jerome's words

---

14. Gregory of Nyssa, *On the Creation of Man* 17.15; see Grosseteste, *Hexaëmeron* 4.1.4.

15. See Lv 19.18; Mt 5.39.

agreed with his own, and vice versa, than that someone among us would, since we are much less perspicacious than were Augustine and Jerome.

7. But to this we say that each investigated the other's words as words of man, not as words of the Holy Spirit offered through the mouth of a man. For they knew what was written, "You shall not praise a man while he lives" (Eccl 11.2). While they both lived—and as long as it was not clear that both were saints—it was right that they treated what each other said only as human words that called for investigation. But we, for whom it is certain and evident that the Holy Spirit spoke through them, ought to treat the words of both as offered by the dictation of the Holy Spirit. Each did not write to the other and respond to all of the other's writings and objections, unless perhaps they wrote several letters to each other which have yet to come into our hands. So, then, it is for us to try to recall these two flutes of the Holy Spirit to harmony as and where we are able, although we are, perhaps, not able everywhere.

CHAPTER 4

1. It must be considered that, as was said above, the Laws, because they are Laws, are witnesses and signs, shadow and prophecy, that foretell and precede as forerunners the future Passion of Christ. Therefore, he who intends to keep the Laws, as Laws, intends to keep them insofar as they foretell the future Passion of Christ. But he who keeps and observes them with this intention by his action and observance says that Christ is to come. So he who keeps them after Christ with the aforementioned intention, by his word and by the meaning of his action speaks a lie and a heresy; he is thus enclosed in infidelity and mortal sin.

2. Again, the Laws, because they had Christ beforehand in their signification, and because the whole salvation of the human race is in the offering of Christ, brought salvation to those who kept them. They could not have brought salvation, however, except by participation in him who alone is true salvation and the reconciliation of the human race to God. But they could have participated in him only by signifying him before-

hand. Therefore, he who intends to keep the Laws as salvific, intends in them to participate in the Mediator through their signification of him. And so, by the meaning of his own work and intention, he who keeps the Laws as salvific after Christ is a heretic and an infidel. Therefore, after the consummation accomplished by the Passion of Christ, it is ruinous to keep the Laws as Laws and as salvific. And so the text is true that says that the Laws, kept with the intention that they had as Laws, are simply ruinous for all after the Passion of Christ. It is so whether or not someone seeks salvation from them. Nonetheless, so long as someone keeps the Laws and intends to keep them in the way in which they ought to be kept because of their institution, he necessarily announces by the intention of his action that Christ is to come. The one who does this after Christ is a heretic.

3. Again, he who treats the Laws in the aforementioned way treats something dead as if it were alive; and this is entirely wicked. But let us suppose that someone's teacher, leader, and instructor died. Likewise, let us suppose that some man's wife, or some wife's husband, or a son's or daughter's mother died. If the survivor were to cast off immediately his dead and to shudder at touching him as if touching something impure, would he not act impiously and incur the guilt of ingratitude for the benefits that he earlier received and the guilt of neglected friendship? It is fitting, then, for the survivor in the time right after death to deal with his dead dutifully and piously and to show gratitude for past benefits and friendship. But when the cadaver of the dead man begins to decay, stink, and corrupt those still living, the duty to bury it must be delayed no longer. But the cadaver must be buried with the honor it is owed, and never removed from its tomb. Therefore, in the time right after death it is impious both not to take care of the dead by a failure in human duty and to remove a rotten or burned cadaver after burial.

4. Therefore, in the time just after the death of Christ, when the works of the Law were dead, the Jews, to whom the Law had been a teacher, leader, and instructor, as a wife to her husband, a husband to his wife, or a mother to daughter, ought to have handled these works as dead and out of pious duty to remem-

ber the benefits and friendship that they received from the Law while it was alive.[16] But they could handle the works of the Law only by doing them. So they were bound to keep the Law for some time after the death of Christ as if offering human funeral rites. But the Gentiles, who had no such union of this sort of kinship with the Law, were not bound to offer this kind of funeral for it.

5. To keep, then, after Christ the Law as Law—that is, as living a life of pious signification as a shadow, testimony, and prophecy of the coming Christ, and as salvific through its signification of Christ, who alone is true salvation—is altogether wicked, because this is to deny Christ and to preach another still to come, just as at present the unfaithful Jews do. There can be no dispensation for the Laws to be kept licitly in this way, because there can be no dispensation for denying Christ and preaching a christ other than the Lord Jesus.[17]

6. So, then, when Peter abstained from profane foods or when Paul circumcised Timothy or tonsured himself according to the Nazirite Law, they did not keep the Laws by some intervening dispensation of the aforementioned sort.[18]

7. There does not have to be some intervening dispensation in order to keep the Laws as an observance of the funeral rites for its recent death, because to treat them in this way would be not only permitted but also obligatory. How, then, according to Jerome, did Peter and Paul keep the Laws by some sort of pretense permitted by a dispensation?[19] There is no way, is there, other than the two aforementioned ways in which the Laws were observed after Christ, that a dispensation could excuse someone keeping the Laws? That is, there is no way, is there, in which the Laws were observed other than one of the two aforementioned ways in which the Laws were observed by many after the death of Christ?[20] For, as in what was said above, and as is clear from the histories and authoritative writings, there were in the primitive Church those who believed in the Lord Jesus Christ

---

16. See Gal 3.24.  
17. See Acts 10.14.  
18. See Acts 10.14; 16.3; and 18.18.  
19. See Jerome, *Ep.* 112.  
20. That is, either the Laws were kept as Laws, and so wickedly; or the Laws were kept as funeral rites.

but who thought that faith in Christ did not alone suffice to save anyone, unless at the same time the ancient Laws were kept and observed. As Augustine says, "It was contrary to the truth of the Gospel that those who believed in Christ thought that they could not be saved without those old sacraments. For at Antioch the circumcised believers held this, and Paul perseveringly and bitterly fought against them."[21] And again he says, "Those who thus wanted the Laws to be observed, had reported this about Paul, as if there could be no salvation for believers in the Gospel without them."[22] It is just as we read in Acts of the Apostles, "Some who were coming down from Judea said to the brethren: That except you be circumcised after the manner of Moses, you cannot be saved" (Acts 15.1).

8. These men, then, because they believed that the Christ had already come, did not intend to keep the Laws as prophetic and foretelling of the coming of Christ nor as salvific because Christ was signified in them. Nor did they intend to handle the Laws as something that had to be quickly buried in a dutiful funeral, because they thought that they were always to be kept. They believed, therefore, that the Laws were not commanded by God for a time, but that they had to be kept for all times. They believed that they had been bound and obliged by the authority of the Lawgiver to keep the Laws for all time as if they had been simply commanded for all time. Hence they believed that they were promised salvation by the obedient observance of the Laws as if by the obedience simply to commands, and they believed themselves to be transgressors by disobedience if they did not observe them. So, then, they did not know of the life, strength, end, consummation, and death of the Laws, since by their obedience alone to the Lawgiver they received them as simple commands of simple deeds, that had to be observed by all and that hold the reward of salvation by the obedient observance of them. The command given to Adam that he not eat of the tree of the knowledge of good and evil had to be observed because of the authority of the Lawgiver. The command was meritorious for the one who observed it because of the good of obedience, and ruinous

21. Augustine, *Ep.* 82.8. See Gal 2.11–21.
22. Augustine, *Ep.* 82.9.

for the one who transgressed it because of disobedience, even though to eat of that tree and to abstain from eating of it were in themselves indifferent. Both could always have been permitted, if only the command had constrained Adam in another way. In a similar way, then, they believed that the Laws always had to be observed because of the authority of the Lawgiver.

9. But to believe this about the Laws was wrong, and it was not permitted for them to keep the Laws because of this belief; so much is clear enough from what has been written above. Nevertheless, let us suppose that some such persons would altogether withdraw and fall away from faith in Christ unless they were permitted to keep the works of the Law because of this belief. And let us suppose also among these persons someone to whom all look as a teacher and leader, to whom God has committed their pastoral care. Let us suppose further that if this pastor should not perform along with his flock these old works as if they ought to be kept by the command of God and as if they were necessary for salvation because commanded, then his flock would abandon completely their faith in Christ. What, then, should such a pastor do? If he keeps the Laws in such a way, he commits a sin. If he does not keep them, he loses the flock entrusted to him, and if he kept his flock, he could gradually call it back from error and lead it back to the way of truth.

10. Surely he must think of a middle way, if there can be one, by which he neither loses his flock nor himself commits a sin. And so he can proceed along this middle way, openly doing the works of the Law in the presence of all his subjects while in his mind intending to keep them not as living Laws, nor as prophetic of some future event, nor out of the pious duty to bury them, nor because they ought to be done simply on account of a command, but only as actions and things that are in themselves devoid of meaning. Thus he would sustain the weak by performing the Laws lest they fall away completely from the faith and rush into the pit of all manner of infidelity. He would silently hide, though, the manner and intention with which he performed the works of the Law. For to hide the truth and be silent about it is not in itself sinful.

## CHAPTER 5

1. Likewise, it is not sinful to perform the mere works that were the sort of works found in the Law, for if any plain and simple abstinence from flesh is not sinful, then the mere slaughtering of animals is not sinful either. Therefore, to perform these bare works and to be silent about the manner and intention with which they are performed is not sinful. Just as Abraham licitly said that Sara was his sister and did not say that she was his wife, so Peter licitly could keep those works and be silent about the manner, reason, and intention he had in mind when doing them.[23] The analogy can be extended. From Abraham's words Pharaoh assumed that Sara was his biological sister and not his wife, even though Abraham did not wish to communicate this, but rather wished to communicate that she was related to him by a relation that is rightly called by the name "sister." Abraham wanted to hide the truth from the king because it was not useful for him to know it. Nevertheless, Abraham well figured that the king would infer a falsehood from what he said, a falsehood that Abraham himself did not wish to communicate. In the same way because of Peter's works, the Jewish Christians could think that Peter kept the Law as something that was still obligatory by the command of the Law and as something meriting salvation by the obedience of the one who keeps it. And they would not think that he kept the Laws to bear their weakness. Nevertheless Peter did not want to indicate this to them by his actions, but he wanted to hide the truth from them, because the knowledge of it was not useful for them. He wanted to communicate in a general way that he kept the Law for the sake of salvation. Indeed, he did this for the sake of their salvation, but still he did not want to reveal his intention to them. He knew, however, that they believed that he kept the Laws as if there were an obligation to keep them by the command of the Law. So, then, it can be called a pretense that he wanted to hide from them a truth that would not be useful for them to know and that he signified a general truth from his action, even though he knew that they would interpret it as a specific falsehood.

23. See Gn 12.11–19; 20.1–13.

2. Indeed, a real pretense intends that a falsehood be believed and that the truth be hidden or disbelieved. But Peter intended to hide the truth, and he knew that a falsehood would be believed because of his actions, although he did not intend that a falsehood be believed from what he did. Therefore, he had all the simulation that was possible in a perfectly and simply spoken pretense, except the sin. So what Peter did can be called a pretense. Nevertheless, even this sort of pretense (which is not a pretense in the proper sense) must not be done except when a good recompense is hoped for. But, just as Bernard says, "'a faithful ... servant, whom his lord has appointed over his family' (Mt 24.45; Lk 12.42) knows how to use a dispensation where he can have a good recompense."[24] Because, then, Peter hoped for a good recompense—namely, the support of the weak lest they fall completely from the faith, before finally returning to sincerity of faith—he could engage in a so-called pretense as a dispensation.

3. It is clear enough from Jerome's words that Peter's pretense, about which Jerome speaks, is not a pretense in the proper sense, a pretense that intends to bring about belief in something false. In his commentary on the letter to the Galatians, Jerome justifies the pretense of Paul and Peter, when he says:

> that a useful pretense must be assumed at times. Jehu, the king of Israel, gives us an example. He could not kill the priests of Baal unless he had pretended that he worshiped an idol. He said: "Gather for me all the priests of Baal. For if Ahab served Baal a little, I will serve him much" (2 Kgs 10.18).[25] And consider David, when he changed his appearance before the face of Abimelech, who sent him away. It is no wonder, however, that just men pretend to do some things for a time on account of their own salvation and the salvation of others, when even our Lord himself, who did not have sin or sinful flesh, assumed the pretense of sinful flesh in order to condemn sin in the flesh and in himself to make us the justice of God.[26]

4. So, from Jerome's words, the pretense of Peter and Paul clearly was only some action that had the likeness of something but not the reality, just as the flesh of the Lord Jesus had the

---

24. Bernard of Clairvaux, *On Law and Dispensation* 2.3 (*Opera omnia* III, 256).
25. My translation.
26. Jerome, *Commentary on the Letter to the Galatians* 1.2.11.

likeness of sinful flesh. Nevertheless, because his flesh was not sinful but rather had a likeness to sinful flesh without being sinful, Jerome says that the pretense of sinful flesh was assumed. It is similar also with David: he did not intend, when he changed his appearance, to make Abimelech believe that he was insane, but he intended to hide the truth from him, which the servants of Abimelech or Achish were speaking, when they said, "Is not this David, the king of the land of Israel? Did they not sing to him in their dances, saying: Saul has slain his thousands, and David his ten thousands?" (1 Sm 21.11) David wanted to hide this truth from Achish lest his identity become clear and Achish kill him. Thus, according to Jerome, Peter and Paul did something that had the likeness of something whose reality it did not have. Nevertheless, they did not intend by their actions that the underlying reality, which in fact was not there but rather lacking, be believed to be there, just as Christ did not intend that his flesh be believed to be sinful though he had the likeness of sinful flesh. And so there is now one clear way in which the Laws can be kept after the Passion of Christ by the pastors of souls, namely, as a necessary and useful pretense granted by a dispensation.

5. Again, Peter and Paul could have carried out those recently deceased Laws among their weak brethren with a secret intention of carrying out the obligatory funeral rites while at the same time intending, as was mentioned above, to support the weak brothers lest they withdraw completely from faith in Christ unless their pastor keep the works of the Law with them. Thus the pastor would perform works that bear a likeness to works that are necessary for salvation because of a command, without intending, though, that his weak brethren believe by his actions that these kinds of works are necessary for salvation. Rather, he would wish to support the weak until the opposite belief, that is, that they are not necessary for salvation, could be more fittingly formed in them. In this way a pretense by dispensation, of the sort mentioned above, would intervene. To handle the Laws, however, with the obligatory funeral rites required no dispensation.

6. Again, let us suppose that someone who preaches faith in

Christ and the making void of the Laws at the time of grace through Christ, is believed to destroy the Laws, as if they had never been necessary or useful, but had always been sacrilege, like things that are offered to idols and demons. If this belief were confirmed, it would taint the credibility of the preaching, for it would be believed that he preached that the old fathers were sacrilege, that the Old Laws had never lived a life of pious signification, and that they did not foretell and testify to later events. And this belief would undoubtedly turn many away from hearing and receiving the preaching of such a preacher. What, then, would this sort of preacher rather do to render groundless this false and ruinous opinion that has arisen about him than keep these very Laws in the presence of all who think falsely about him, and so by his very action show that what they think and have heard about him is false?

7. Therefore, to keep the Laws after Christ in order to show that they were not sacrilegious before Christ and that they are now preached to be void but not because they were sacrilegious, was quite appropriate and permitted to the preacher of the Gospel. Nevertheless, no one was allowed to keep the Laws after Christ out of human fear. Even though someone understand that the Laws do not confer salvation, he may not keep them out of fear of those who believed the Laws necessary for salvation and were compelling them to be so kept. It is just like the fact that no one is allowed to sacrifice to idols, even though in his mind he holds the truth of the Christian faith. It is, then, clear from what has been said that to keep the Laws after Christ—that is, the Laws as prophecy, shadow, and sign of the christ to come and of the salvation of the human race through him, in the way that they were kept by the holy fathers of old who lived before Christ—and to keep the Laws after Christ as they were instituted by Moses and to treat them as if they were still alive with pious signification, to do this is all together sacrilegious and heretical. Again, to keep the Laws after Christ as if they were eternal commands that ought still to be kept because they were commanded is erroneous and illicit, because, as was shown above, they had the force of a command only up to Christ. Again, it is not allowed that someone, even if he be com-

pelled out of human fear, keep the Laws as if they were necessary for salvation when he knows that it is true they have no life or force after Christ. There are, therefore, three ways in which to keep the Laws after Christ is ruinous for all.

8. Nevertheless, to handle the Laws soon after their death with the funeral rites that they are owed until they should be buried with honor is not only allowed but obligatory for those for whom the Laws had earlier lived. Again, a thoughtful pastor is allowed to keep the Laws after Christ, secretly intending them as indifferent actions or secretly intending to perform their funeral rites, but with the outward likeness that implies that they are necessary for salvation; the thoughtful pastor may do this lest his flock rush into all manner of infidelity. Again it can suit the office of true preacher to keep the Laws so that it may be shown that the reason why they are void is not because they were once sacrilegious, and so that the belief that they are so preached may be done away with. There are, then, also three ways in which it was once allowed for some to keep the Laws after the Lord's Passion.

9. Because, therefore, in some ways the Laws were ruinous for all after Christ and in other ways they were licit for some, or even obligatory, was there really a true and substantive contradiction between Augustine and Jerome on the observance of the Laws after the Passion of Christ, with the result that one must concede that one or the other of them had uttered a falsehood, as our gloss on the letters of Paul seems to concede?[27] Or rather was there an apparent contradiction and a true harmony in substance and meaning, and so a certain dissonant and musical harmony?

CHAPTER 6

1. But the words of Jerome seem to sound a real contradiction with Augustine, for in a letter to Augustine, Jerome writes:

What Christian could patiently hear what is contained in your letter: "Paul was a Jew, but when he became a Christian he had not abandoned

27. See *Glossa ordinaria* on Gal 2.12–15.

the sacraments of the Jews, which his people at a necessary and Lawful time had fittingly accepted. And so he undertook to celebrate them, when he was already an apostle of Christ, in order to teach that they were not ruinous for those who wanted to keep them as they had received them from their forefathers through the Law." I, on the contrary, would say and proclaim boldly, even if the world shouted in protest, that Jewish rituals are both ruinous and deadly for Christians, and whoever observed them, whether Jew or Gentile, fell into the pit of the devil. "For the end of the Law is Christ, unto justice to every one who believes" (Rom 10.4).[28]

Jerome introduces many other authoritative texts in the same letter and after a few lines says, "To observe the rituals of the Law cannot be a matter of indifference, but is either good or evil. You say that it is good; I assert that it is evil, and evil not only for Gentile believers but also for those believers from the Jewish people."[29]

2. Here, then, is the dissonance, obvious to all, between two flutes of the Holy Spirit. But without the precedent of a better opinion, I think that there was a hidden agreement in meaning in this disagreement at the level of words. But the meaning which Augustine understands his words to have, Jerome did not yet understand them to have. For Jerome's thought was that to observe the Laws together with the sacraments of the New Law, and to mix the rituals of the Law with the Gospel of Christ out of the belief, namely, that no one can be a true Christian without this mixing of the old with the new, was ruinous for all, Jew and Gentile, after the suffering of Christ. It is clear that Augustine's meaning was the same, although Jerome believed, when he wrote the aforementioned letter, that Augustine thought just as did the heretics Cerinthus and Ebion, "who, although they believed in Christ, were anathematized by the Fathers only because they mixed the rituals of the Law with the Gospel of Christ, and so confessed the new without leaving behind the old."[30]

3. This also can be clear from Jerome's words in the same letter. For he says to Augustine:

---

28. Jerome, *Ep.* 112.14.   29. Ibid., 16.
30. Ibid., 13.

The meaning of your whole discourse (which you drew out by a very long arrangement) is that Peter did not err when he thought that the Law must be kept by the Jewish believers. Rather, he deviated from the right path when he forced the Gentiles to become Jews, though he forced them not by the command of his teacher but by the example of his way of life. And Paul did not say one thing and do another, but asked why Peter forced those who were Gentiles to become Jews. This, then, is the heart of the matter, or rather of your position: that after the Gospel of Christ, believing Jews do well to keep the mandates of the Law, that is, if they offer the sacrifices that Paul gave up, if they circumcise their sons, if they keep the Sabbath, as Paul observed in relation to Timothy and as all Jews have done. If this is true, we fall into the heresy of Cerinthus and Ebion, who believed in Christ but were anathematized by the fathers because they mixed the rituals of the Law with the Gospel of Christ, and thus confessed the new without leaving behind the old. What should I say about the Ebionites, who pretend to be Christians? Up to today throughout all the Jewish synagogues of the East there is a heresy that is called Minean, and it is still condemned by the Pharisees, who declare to the people that these heretics are Nazarenes. They believe in Christ, the Son of God, born of the Virgin Mary, and they say that he suffered under Pontius Pilate and rose again; in whom we also believe. But so long as they want to be both Jews and Christians, they are neither Jews nor Christians. Therefore, I ask that you, who want to heal our little wound, which is the hole, or rather the prick, of a pin—I ask that you heal the wound that is your opinion, a wound which is inflicted by a spear, and if I may say, a massive catapult.[31]

4. Again, in the same letter he says to Augustine, "If I am not mistaken, here you forbid one thing and fall into another. For while you fear Porphyry the blasphemer, you rush into the trap of Ebion, when you side with those of the Jews who believe that the Law must be observed."[32] From Jerome's words it is clear that he believed that on the question of the observance of the Laws after Christ, Augustine thought just as did Cerinthus, Ebion, and those who thought that the grace of the Gospel did not suffice for salvation without the rituals of the Law. He believed, I say, that Augustine thought this (either on his own or relying on someone who had held that opinion earlier), for he thought that the heresy of Ebion could be brought against the words of Augustine. For Jerome had not yet read the letter of Augus-

---

31. Ibid., 12–13.
32. Ibid., 16.

tine in which Augustine responds to the above mentioned letter of Jerome and reveals his thoughts on the observance of the Laws after Christ, namely, that they had to be observed by the Jews because they were dead and had to be honored by funeral rites until they could be honorably buried.[33] Augustine thought that they could also be kept in order to commend the old sacraments lest it be believed that they must be condemned just like the idols of the Gentiles.

5. Also in this epistle, Augustine chides himself for not explaining his meaning more fully in the earlier letter, from the words of which Jerome thought that Augustine thought as Ebion and Cerinthus did. Augustine says that he had explained his mind and thought on the observance of the Law after Christ much earlier, when he wrote against Faustus the Manichee.[34] Again, that Jerome did not understand Augustine's mind in this regard and did not contradict his understanding is clear from Augustine's words in the same letter, in which he responds to the words of Jerome quoted above. For Augustine says:

Believe what I say about my own mind—I, speaking before God, demand it by the Law of charity. It never seemed to me that Jewish converts to Christianity ought to celebrate the old sacraments with any intention or purpose whatsoever or that it is permitted for them in any way. For I have always thought that about Paul, from the time that his letter was made known to me—just as it seems to you that at the present time the Laws cannot be kept as a pretense by anyone, although you believe that the Apostles did this. Accordingly, just as you, "on the contrary, would say and proclaim boldly, even if the world shouted in protest, that Jewish rituals are both ruinous and deadly for Christians, and whoever observed them, whether Jew or Gentile, fell into the pit of the devil," so I completely confirm these words and add that not only he who really kept the Laws fell into the pit of the devil, but also he who pretended to keep them.[35]

6. From these words and those that follow in this same letter, Augustine makes plain enough that Jerome understood him to think that Jewish rituals were allowed to be observed by Jews not only in the primitive times of the Church but also in his own

---

33. See *Ep.* 82.
34. See Augustine, *Against Faustus the Manichee* 1.19.17.
35. Augustine, *Ep.* 82.17–18.

time. How far this was from the mind of Augustine can escape no one who has read this letter to Jerome. Therefore, Jerome and Augustine thought in harmony with each other, that the Laws after Christ were ruinous for everyone, if they were kept out of the belief that in the Gospel there is no salvation without the observance of the Laws. But Augustine's aforementioned position was not yet clear to Jerome. Hence, he did not contradict Augustine's mind and meaning, but he contradicted a false opinion which he had conceived from Augustine's words. Augustine's words on the surface sounded like this false opinion, and these words had come into the hands of Jerome before they had been explained. Therefore, Augustine agrees with Jerome in this regard at the level of meaning, and Jerome does not contradict Augustine at the level of meaning, for Augustine's meaning had not yet been, as has been said, known by Jerome. If it had been known by him, I think he would have agreed most easily.

7. It also seems to me that Augustine did not understand Jerome's mind on the question of pretense allowed as a dispensation; rather, he thought that Jerome wanted to say that a pretense is a lie that is allowed by a dispensation. Thus he writes against Jerome as if against someone who is defending a lie and a lying pretense, as if against someone who admits a lie into the Sacred Scriptures. Jerome responds to this when he says, "Do not think that I am the teacher of a lie, I who follow Christ who says, 'I am the way, the truth, and the life' (Jn 14.6). It cannot be that I, a worshiper of truth, submit my neck to a lie."[36] As is clear to anyone who wants to look at Jerome's and Augustine's explanations of the letter to the Galatians, they evidently offer irreconcilable interpretations of what Peter did at Antioch (namely, that, before certain men from James came, he ate with Gentiles, although when they had come, he withdrew and separated himself from them, because he feared those who were of the circumcision) and of Paul's reprimand of Peter for doing this.

8. Nevertheless, the meaning of each was in itself possible. For it could have been as Jerome thought, and it could have

---

36. See Jerome, *Ep.* 112.18.

been as Augustine thought, but what they both thought could not have happened. Hence, if in the matter of individual contingent events they were not so much announcing and asserting what happened as indicating what was possible, then in this regard there is between them a harmonious dissonance. The aforementioned words of the letter to the Galatians can fittingly echo either Jerome's or Augustine's interpretation, and we have shown this in our own way in the small book that we wrote on the same letter.[37] It cannot be doubted that by the ordination of the Holy Spirit, these two flutes were either made or allowed to be dissonant, either everywhere harmoniously dissonant or in this place dissonantly dissonant, because their dissonance and that of many others exercises our abilities; each, because of the opposing words of the other, explained to us his own mind and meaning more fully and illuminated for us the teaching of truth, snatching us from many errors. For if Augustine had not objected to Jerome's pretense by dispensation as if it were a lying pretense, though excusable because of the dispensation, and if Jerome had not responded to Augustine's objection by saying that he in no way defends or admits lies, we would probably believe that a dutiful lie could be allowed by a dispensation, and we would not understand what Jerome meant by a pretense allowed by a dispensation. Likewise, if Jerome had not objected to Augustine's words on the obligation to observe the Laws after the Passion of Christ, Augustine would not have made clear to us as plainly as he did what he meant, namely, that the Laws could be kept by the Jews for a time as the funeral rites for the Law, until they were honorably buried. And lest the Laws seem to be condemned as sacrilegious, lest they be believed to be like the condemned idols of the Gentiles, Augustine says that they were handled and observed by Saint Paul, when "he circumcised Timothy,[38] fulfilled his vow at Cenchreae,[39] or undertook the celebration of those rites with those who had taken a vow,[40] when he was admonished by James in Jerusalem."[41] Likewise, in

---

37. See Grosseteste, *Commentary on the Letter to the Galatians* 2.11–19.
38. See Acts 16.3.
39. See Acts 18.18.
40. See Acts 21.26.
41. Augustine, *Ep.* 82.8.

the differences of interpretation found in the expositions of the relevant text in Galatians, there are manifest to us many things that suit pastoral diligence and the truth of life, and they would not be manifest if the various explanations had not been made. So, then, either the dissonant or harmonious dissonance of these flutes produces for us these kinds of benefits and many harmonies necessary for the Church.

### CHAPTER 7

1. The ritual Law—it is clear from what has been said—is with the death of Christ fully dead in its life of piously signifying the future reparation of the human race through Christ and in its obligatory fleshly and literal observance according to the precept and institution of the Law. So, then, the ritual Law differs now in the time of grace from the way it was in the time before grace, as the dead differs from the living.

2. Concerning the moral Law, however, that is, the Decalogue and the moral norms that follow from the Decalogue, it can be doubted whether it is different now in the time of grace than in the time of the Mosaic Law. For it seems it would be not at all different then and now, because the whole moral Law now and then must be understood in the same way, explained in the same way, and kept in the same way. It is meritorious in the same way for the one who keeps it and blameworthy for the transgressor, and then and now it likewise has the obligation and form of a command. For if someone should say that the moral commands in the time of the Old Law restrained only the hand but not the heart, but now restrains both the hand and the heart, this will be proved false for him, because the Old Law in Deuteronomy commands the love of God "with [one's] whole heart, and with [one's] whole soul, and with [one's] whole strength" (Dt 6.5) and the love of one's neighbor as oneself.[42] The lawyer in Luke and in Matthew also testifies to this, when he said that this twofold love is the fullness of charity.[43] Love, though, is a movement

---

42. See Lv 19.18 and Mk 12.30–31.
43. See Lk 10.27 and Mt 22.37.

and action of the heart and the truest and strongest check on every evil, for "love is strong as death" (Song 8.6). Because, then, the Mosaic Law commands love, it commands the restraining not only of the hand but also of the heart from evil. In addition, the Mosaic Law commands "You shall not covet"; but it can be held with Augustine that, although concupiscence is sometimes said to be of the flesh, nevertheless coveting itself pertains to the heart and is a work of the heart. This command, then, restrains not only the hand, but also the heart. So the moral commands equally restrain the hand and the heart in both the Old Testament and the New. There seems, therefore, to be no difference of moral precepts in the Old and the New, and the Decalogue does not seem to be different in any respect now in a time of grace than in the time of the Old Law.

3. But against these arguments, it seems, the authority of Paul and of the saints who explained his letters shouts. For he says to the Romans, "The Law works wrath" (Rom 4.15); and again, "The Law entered in, that sin might abound" (Rom 5.20). And no one doubts that he is saying these words about the Mosaic Law, and that they apply also to the ritual Law. The Apostle, nevertheless, wanted to include in these words not only the ritual Law but also the moral Law under the name of Law. This is clear from the authoritative exposition of these verses.

4. Jerome, in fact, explains this verse ("the Law entered in, that sin might abound" [Rom 5.20]); he says, "Lest they say, 'but the Law forgave us our sin,' [Paul] does not say, 'it came to forgive,' but to make transgressions manifest."[44] Jerome's words, then, clearly say that the Law, which "entered in, that sin might abound" (Rom 5.20), makes transgressions manifest. But the ritual Law did not make transgressions manifest, because the ritual Law concerns matters that are in themselves neither just nor sinful, but because they are only commands, they are to become just on account of the force and authority of the precept. Hence such commanding does not make transgression manifest, but in the commanding it is established that what is commanded is just and that the opposite of the command is unjust

---

44. Jerome, *Commentary on the Letter to the Romans* 5.20.

and a transgression. The moral Law, however, because it concerns matters that are in themselves naturally just, and because something is just, it is for that reason a precept and a command, and not the other way about (that is, when something is commanded, and for that reason just, as with ritual Laws)—the moral Law alone makes transgressions manifest, which would be transgressions even if there were no commands written or promulgated about them. Indeed, the ritual Law, by the act of commanding, established what was just and unjust, and makes something to be a transgression. The moral Law alone, however, makes manifest what is naturally in itself just or unjust and a transgression. Therefore, according to Jerome, even the Law of moral commands is expressly included in the phrase, "the Law entered in, that sin might abound" (Rom 5.20).

5. Again, Ambrose explains this verse of the Apostle and says, "If there had been no Law, sin would lie hidden. But through the Law, man knows the various kinds of sins and the crime of transgression."[45] So, then, according to Ambrose the moral commands are also included here under the name of Law. These commands make sins manifest, which would also be sins, though hidden, even if the commands had not been promulgated or written. Again, on the same verse of the Apostle, Ambrose says that here the Apostle indicates what was produced when the Law was given, not what the Law, which was given, did. The Law was a help to human nature: "as if it were seeds of justice sown in our nature, the Law was added to bring about the fruit of justice, and by its authority and teaching our natural powers of mind advanced."[46]

From Ambrose's words it is clear that the Law, which "entered in, that sin might abound" (Rom 5.20), is the natural law that was about to be written down and delivered in commands to advance the natural powers of our minds, which had become dull. Seeds of natural justice, though, were naturally sown into our minds in order to bear the fruit of justice. For it was not the

---

45. Ambrose, *Commentary on the Gospel according to Luke* 6.35.
46. Ambrosiaster, *On the Letter to the Romans* 5.20; see *Glossa ordinaria* at Romans 5.20.

seeds of positive justice or ritual Law that were naturally sown in us, since only the seeds of natural justice were naturally sown in us.

6. Again, a teacher who commented upon the letters of Paul says that the following texts must be understood to concern the commands of the ritual Laws according to the letter and the letter of the moral Laws without grace: the text from Ezekiel, "I gave them statutes that were not good" (Ezek 20.25); the one from the Apostle's letter to the Hebrews, "the Law brought no one to perfection" (Heb 7.19); and from Romans, "the Law works wrath" (Rom 4.15), and "the Law entered in, that sin might abound" (Rom 5.20).[47]

7. Augustine, too, explains this verse—"the Law entered in, that sin might abound" (Rom 5.20)—in his letter to Optatus. He says, "it was necessary, then, that by an additional command ("you shall not covet" [Ex 20.17]) the crime of transgression penetrate the proud heart, and so guilty illness would seek the medicine of grace rather than the health that comes through the Law."[48] Therefore, the command, "You shall not covet" (Ex 20.17), which clearly concerns the moral and natural law, is included in the name "Law," taken in the sense of entering "that sin might abound" (Rom 5.20).

8. Again, the Apostle to the Romans showed that we are dead to the Law, and he showed this using the analogy of a wife who has been freed from the Law of the husband because her husband is dead. And so, this command, "you shall not covet" (Ex 20.17)—which means "for I had not known concupiscence to be a sin, if the Law did not say: You shall not covet" (Rom 7.7)—is included in the very Law to which he says that we are dead. So he calls the Law to which we are made dead the Law of sin and death. Therefore, because the command, "You shall not covet" (Ex 20.17), concerns the moral Law, we are made dead to the moral Law given through Moses, and it is even a Law of death and sin. The gloss of the Master on this verse testifies to this truth. He explains that "the law of the Spirit"—that is, the

---

47. See Peter Lombard, *On the Letter to the Romans* 5.
48. Augustine, *Ep.* 190.2.7.

Holy Spirit, who teaches what must be done and what not, who is the Giver of life—"has delivered me from the law of sin and of death"—that is, from the Law of Moses who through sin, that is, through transgression, is the cause of death.[49]

9. Again, about the verse from [First] Corinthians, "The letter kills, but the Spirit gives life" (1 Cor 3.6), Augustine says, "Notice what is meant by the letter that kills, and on the contrary what is meant by the Spirit that gives life: the letter is certainly the Decalogue, which was written on those two tables, because 'the Law entered in, that sin might abound' (Rom 5.20)."[50] It is clear from Augustine's words that "the Law, which entered in, that sin might abound" (Rom 5.20) includes the Decalogue.

10. Therefore, it is sufficiently clear from these authorities that not only the ritual Mosaic Law but also the moral Mosaic Law works wrath, makes transgression to abound, works every concupiscence, and makes sin come alive. It deceives and kills. It is a Law of sin, death, and weakness. It is the power of sin and leads no one to perfection. The Apostle says all this about one and the same Law. But the moral Law, the Decalogue, including even all the moral commands that depend on the Decalogue, does not work such things and is not such things now, in the time of grace. The moral Law, therefore, is different in the time before grace from now in the time of grace in the above-mentioned ways. For then it had all the aforementioned properties, and now it has none of them. Indeed, who would concede that the Decalogue now works wrath, or now makes transgression to abound, or the other things listed above that the Decalogue used to do, according to the testimony of the Apostle?

11. But it seems that the following response could be made to this argument, which seems to prove that the Decalogue then and now is different in the aforementioned ways: the properties that characterize the Law of old, and that now do not characterize the Law, are accidents not of the Law itself but of those to whom the Law was given in ancient times and to whom it is now given. For the ancient people, to whom Moses gave the

---

49. See *Glossa ordinaria* at Rom 8.2.
50. Augustine, *On the Spirit and the Letter* 1.14.24.

Law of the Decalogue, was hard and proud; it relied on its own powers, and on account of this the moral Law of the Decalogue worked in that people wrath, concupiscence, an abundance of transgression, and all that the Apostle enumerates.

12. But the new people, to whom is now given the command of charity and the Decalogue in the command of charity, is humble and relies on grace alone; on account of this it receives from the command of charity and of the Decalogue an abundance of justice. Consider the following analogies. Weak eyes are hurt and darkened by the sun, but healthy eyes are joyfully and delightfully illuminated by the same sun which acts uniformly and indifferently, insofar as the sun itself is concerned. Similarly, the uniform heat of the same fire cleanses gold and consumes lead, hardens clay but melts wax. Therefore, when the sun is said to darken the sight of some and to illuminate that of others, and when the same fire hardens some things and softens others, these differences are not said to exist in the sun and in fire, nor do they somehow change the sun and fire; rather, there are only differences in the things that the sun and fire work on. Likewise, then, they say that the Law of the Decalogue worked wrath in the ancient people and justice in the new. This happens so only because of the difference between the old and new people and not because the moral Law was different in the past than it is now.

13. But from the words of the Apostle, this response is clearly false, for he says, "If there had been a law given which could justify entirely, verily justice should have been by the Law" (Gal 3.21). So, then, the Apostle plainly implies that the Mosaic Law could not justify, but, if the aforementioned differences come about only because of the recipients, it would be false that the Law could not justify when it was working wrath and the other things that the Apostle lists, just as it would be false to say that the sun cannot illuminate when it darkens weak eyes, for it can illuminate if a healthy eye is present to receive its light, and just as it would be false to say that fire cannot cleanse or solidify, when it consumes lead and softens wax. For, according to this false way of thinking, the Law could justify someone if he were humble and receptive of justification. It is clear, though, that

there were some humble and even just men among the ancient people. The Law, then, must be different now than it was of old and not only because of the recipients, but because of the Law itself; otherwise, Paul implies something false, namely, that the Mosaic Law could not justify.

14. In addition, consider this analogy. If there is one healthy eye present among many who have weak eyes, the sun illuminates the healthy eye while the rest are darkened, and it would be false if someone said that the sun illuminates no one. So also because there were some humble men among the ancient people, if the moral Law were not at all different then and now, it would be false that the Law did not lead anyone to perfection in the ancient times, for it would have led the humble to perfection while it worked wrath in the presumptuous, just as the sun illuminates the healthy eye while darkening the weak.

CHAPTER 8

1. The Law of the Decalogue, then, is different then and now not only because of differences that come from the variety in those who received the commands of the Decalogue then and now, but also because of some difference whereby the Decalogue itself is different now from when it had been given by Moses. So, then, we must ask what this difference is.

2. To investigate this matter, first we must consider the fact that perfect and meritorious carrying-out of any command whatever proceeds from knowledge that loves what is right because it is right. For no one unknowingly acts well, even if what he does is good. Likewise, duty does not make an action good, but a good and upright end that is intended and loved. Augustine shows this against Julian.[51] Therefore, a good and wise legislator by speaking and commanding Law intends to mandate that the Law be kept out of a knowledge that loves what is right because it is right and out of a love of knowing why it is right.

3. Nevertheless, it is not within man's power to do by himself what is right out of a knowledge that loves what is right because

51. See Augustine, *Against Julian* 4.3.21.

it is right; rather, it is necessary that the help of grace come. For only the rational mind conformed to eternal wisdom and goodness, which, because of its adherence to God, is one spirit with him—as it is written, "he who is joined to God is one spirit" (1 Cor 6.17)—can do what is right on its own account out of a loving knowledge, because eternal wisdom and goodness are working in it. Only the humble mind is adaptable to the reception of cooperating grace, not because it is humble before it receives grace, but because it is humble at the very time when prevenient grace is received, which a mind cannot receive while it is still swollen with self-presumption. So, then, the humble mind is open to eternal wisdom and goodness, that is, grace; but he who presumes its reception is not.

4. It must also be considered that the Word of God says some things from a voluntary and loving understanding, that is, from a word of good pleasure, wherein for him to say something is for him to do it. For, because he speaks in this way, he accomplishes something by speaking. But other things he speaks from knowledge alone, such as the evils that men do; he eternally knows them and eternally speaks them, but, nonetheless, by so speaking he does not bring about what he speaks. Therefore, for the sake of brevity, let us call it a word of good pleasure, when the Word of God brings about what he speaks, and a word of mere knowledge when the Word does not bring about what he speaks.

5. Again, the life, form, and consummation of the word that is expressed outwardly is the interior word of the speaker, that is, the interior understanding of the mind that is signified by the outward sound. Whenever, then, a word proceeds outwardly from an interior word of good pleasure, even then the life of the external word is the same interior word of good pleasure. But whenever it proceeds outwardly from an interior word of mere knowledge or understanding, then the life of the exterior word is a half-full life, an imperfect life, because mere knowledge is an imperfect life in respect of the lover's ordered knowledge.

6. Again, when a legislator or prophet promulgated the commands of the Lord, either by speaking a word outwardly or by

writing, he spoke the eternal Word of God in their minds and formed an interior word in them, from which proceeded the external word. So the life and form of the commands of God, which are outwardly expressed by the mouths of those in whom God has spoken, is the eternal Word of God who moves and forms in them first an interior word of the mind and then an external word through the mediation of the interior word.

7. Again, let us suppose that there are two weak men and one who commands that something be done, that neither of the weak men can accomplish by himself, though they could accomplish it with the help of the commander. And let us suppose that one of the weak men knows his own weakness and humbly awaits the help of the commander. The other weak man, however, presumes upon his own powers as if he could keep the command without help. He does not seek out the help of the commander, but says by his presumption that he who should fulfill the command is not lacking, but only he who orders it. Is it not just and right that the humble weak man be given at the same time the command and the help of the commander, whereby he can keep it, and that the weak man who presumes upon his own powers be given the command alone without the added help of the commander? The result would be that he would be goaded by the command toward what must be done, struggle, and fail to do it, and in this failure perceive and mourn his own weakness. Thus he would humbly run to the source of help and seek out his help, without which he has already learned that his attempts are vain. And so he will be justly crushed by the weight of the command and mercifully restored to the power of acting when help is conferred after it is humbly sought out. If, then, the operating and the co-operating of this sort of commander were a word of good pleasure, he would propose to the humble, weak man a command from a word of good pleasure that brought about in him whom it commanded the strength to do the work of the command. But to the weak man who presumed upon his own strength he would propose a command from a word of mere knowledge, that does not confer the strength to do what was commanded. He would, then, command one and the same thing to both, and nevertheless, the command offered

to the humble weak man would live and be informed by the perfect life of the interior word of perfect good pleasure. But the command offered to the proud, weak man would live and be informed by the imperfect and half-full life of the interior word of mere knowledge.

8. When the aforementioned arguments are taken together, it can already be seen that the command of the Decalogue, inasmuch as God offered it through the mouth of Moses, lived and was informed not with the life of the eternal Word, but with the life, I say, of the word of mere knowledge. Only the precept was in the command thus given; the help and strength to keep the command was not conferred in the very command. The same command of the Decalogue, however, given through the mouth of Jesus Christ in the flesh, lives, is informed, and is consummated by the full life of God's eternal Word of good pleasure; it has in the very command the help to bring about what is commanded in him whom it commands. For through the mouth of Moses, God gave a command to the old people, which presumed upon its own power and proudly said, "He who should fulfill the command is not lacking, but he who orders it." But through the mouth of Jesus Christ in the flesh, a command was given to a humble people that relies only on the help of grace and that says, "Command what you wish, and do what you command."[52] So, then, the Decalogue commands one and the same thing through Moses and Christ, namely, to keep a command out of loving knowledge because it is right. Nevertheless, this neither the new or old people could do without the help of grace, but because the new people is humble and does not presume upon its own powers, the command was rightly given to it as a command that lives by a word of good pleasure, by a word, I say, that not only commands but brings about what it commands. The presumptuous old people, though, was rightly given a command that lives only by a word of mere knowledge, by a word, I say, that only commands and does not bring about what it commands through good pleasure.

9. The moral Law, then, is different now from what it was of

---

52. See Augustine, *Confessions* 10.29.40; 10.31.43; and 10.37.60. See also Augustine, *On the Spirit and the Letter* 1.13.22.

old because of itself and not merely because of the recipients, because then it had been given and offered only from a word of mere knowledge, living by a half-full life, commanding only and not helping or cooperating so that the command could be kept. But now, in the time of grace, the moral Law has been given and offered from a word of good pleasure, living by the full life of the word of good pleasure, not only commanding but also cooperating and helping to accomplish the command, and being the strength to act in the one who is commanded.

10. And it was fitting that a Law that commands only and does not help to keep what it commands be given through a servant to stubborn servants, but that a Law that commands and cooperates be given to the humble through the Son who appeared in the humility of the flesh and was configured to the humble.

11. And no one can say that the moral Law, that is, the Decalogue with moral commands that depend on it, was not given and promulgated through the mouth of Jesus Christ in the flesh as it was through the mouth of Moses, because it is certain that Christ promulgated the commandment of love by the mouth of his flesh, and in this commandment the Decalogue is contained—just as in a living root that germinates and grows into a full tree—together with all the moral commands which can either exist or be thought of.[53]

12. John explains to us this difference between legislation through Moses, a servant, and through Christ, Son and Lord. He says, "Of his fullness we all have received, and grace for grace. For the Law was given by Moses; but grace and truth came by Jesus Christ" (Jn 1.16–17).

13. Citing this verse, Jerome says in his commentary on Galatians, "You will adore the Father in spirit and truth; receiving from the fullness of Christ, you knew that the Law was only given to the people through Moses, but it was not also kept. Through Jesus Christ, however, grace and truth are not only given but also effective."[54]

14. Origen says, "Just as Saint John says: 'The Law was given

---

53. See Grosseteste, *On the Ten Commandments,* prol. 5.

54. Jerome here contrasts the two verbs of Jn 1.17. The Law was *data* through Moses, but grace and truth are *facta* through Jesus.

by Moses, grace and truth came by Jesus Christ' (Jn 1.16), in whom the promise in the prophetic prefiguration and the reason for commands of the Law were fulfilled since he teaches true prophecy and makes the commands possible by grace."[55]

15. Again, Augustine in his book *Against Adversaries of the Law and the Prophets* says, "The Law, then, was given through Moses. But grace came through Jesus Christ, because by the charity diffused in our hearts by his Spirit,[56] what the Law commands is fulfilled. For it is commanded by the letter, but it is fulfilled not by the letter but by the Spirit. Hence it is written: 'You shall not covet' (Ex 20.17). Through Moses the Law is commanded, but through Christ comes grace whereby what is commanded is fulfilled."[57]

16. Again, Augustine says in his book *On Penance:*

"For the Lawgiver shall give a blessing" (Ps 83.8). The Old Law was given to reveal the wounds of sinners, which the grace of blessing heals. The Law was given to make the proud aware of their own weakness, to urge the weak to do penance. The Law was given that we might say in the valley of lamentation, "I see another law in my members" (Rom 7.23), fighting against the Law of my mind and capturing me in the Law of sin, which is in my members. When in this lamentation we shouted, "Unhappy man that I am, who shall deliver me from the body of this death" (Rom 7.24), "the grace of God, by Jesus Christ our Lord" (Rom 7.25) rescued us because he who raises the broken, frees those in shackles, and illuminates the blind heard us.[58]

17. Dionysius, too, in the second book of the *Hierarchies* says, "After the older tradition, the [New] Testament is rightly preached to the world. A divine and hierarchical order declares, I think, that the older tradition says that Jesus would perform divine activities, but the [New] Testament that he has performed them."[59]

18. From these authorities it is clear enough that the Old Law and the Decalogue given through Moses consisted of only a command and had, as has been said, as its form and life, a word

---

55. Origen, *Commentary on John* 6.
56. See Rom 5.5.
57. Augustine, *Against the Opponents of the Law and the Prophets* 2.3.
58. Augustine, *On Penance*, i.e., *Sermo* 351.1.1.
59. Ps.-Dionysius, *On the Ecclesiastical Hierarchy* 3.5, *versio Eriugenae*.

of mere knowledge that commands but does not bring about what it commands. The Decalogue in the New Law, however, has the form and life of a word of good pleasure that brings about the precept itself through grace. The authority of Ambrose makes the same point; he says, "'The Law works wrath' (Rom 4.15). It was given to make wrongdoers guilty not as an efficient cause, but because grace does not help. Again, the Old Law commanded with threats and did not offer the grace to keep the Law."[60] Again, Augustine says that because of the Law transgression is said to have abounded, not because the Law commanded transgression but because desire was increased by prohibition in the absence of grace. Then, as it were from its own power, it became full-grown vice. From these considerations it is again clear that the Old Law given through Moses commanded only and did not offer the strength to keep the commands that comes from grace.

19. About the New Law, however, the authorities say: the New Law commands works and obtains the accomplishment of these works by believing. It performs works out of the justice of the soul and offers the grace to do them. Again the Old Law says, "Do what I command." The New Law says, "Do what you command." Again, the authorities say that the old sacraments promised salvation, the new give it. So, along similar lines, moral precepts in the Old Law commanded, but in the New they accomplish what they command.

20. Again, Augustine, distinguishing the Old Testament from the New in his book *Against the Adversaries of the Law and the Prophets*, says:

It would be too much and too long to collect all the things that the blessed Apostle says on this matter when he distinguishes Law from grace, in that under the former the exalted are crushed while under the latter the crushed are exalted, and in that the former is good because it commands the good while the latter is good because it confers it. The former makes one hear what is just; the latter makes one do it. Under the former a sinner, and even a transgressor, lies convicted without any excuse of ignorance. But under the latter, which spares and assists, he is not extinguished, because he did evil deeds; rather, he is set aflame

---

60. *Glossa ordinaria* at Romans 4.15.

that he may do good. Why, then, is it a wonder if the Old Law brings death, since the letter kills by forbidding the evil that is done and by commanding the good that is not done? Why is it a wonder if, on the contrary, the service of the Life-giving Spirit is that we rise from the death of transgression, and that we not read about the justice of the matter on tablets, but as free people we have it in our hearts and way of life? This is the difference between the New and Old Testaments: in the latter the old man is constricted by the straits of fear, while in the former the new man walks freely in the spaciousness of charity.[61]

From these words of Augustine and the others cited above, I think it is already well enough shown that the form of the commands given through Moses is the word of mere knowledge, which only commands, while the form of the commands in the New Testament is the word of good pleasure, which brings about what it commands.

21. It can be gathered from the aforementioned that Christ fulfills the Law not only in that he kept it perfectly but also because he is the Father's Word of good pleasure, the life, form, and consummation of the moral commands, and the strength that works all the commands in the humble, who keep them in him, through him, and from him. They say with the Apostle that Christ speaks in them, and similarly that he does in them all the works that the moral precepts command. And because the word of good pleasure has in itself the love that is the strength to do what is commanded, the Apostle is right to say that "love therefore is the fulfilling of the Law" (Rom 13.10). So, then, the eternal Word is also the beginning of every good work, as it is written that the beginning of every work is the word.[62] In addition the life and form of every exterior word, that proceeds from ordered, loving knowledge is the eternal Word of the Father, Jesus Christ. Hence by a full and perfectly living word, "no man can say 'Lord Jesus,' but by the Holy Spirit" (1 Cor 12.3).

22. From what has been said already, it can be concluded that the whole Mosaic Law, the ritual Law as well as the moral Law—as it was given through Moses—is dead to us who are sons of grace, and we are dead to it, just as the Apostle says that we

---

61. Augustine, *Against the Opponents of the Law and the Prophets* 2.7.
62. See Grosseteste, *On the Ten Commandments*, Prol.; Jn 1.3 and Col 1.16.

are made dead to the Law. Nevertheless, the different parts of the whole Law are dead in different ways. The ritual Law died, as has been said, in the sense that it lost its life of piously signifying our future restoration through Christ and in the sense that it lost its life of obligatory literal observance, since it does not have the force or life of a command after Christ suffered. The Mosaic moral Law, though, died in the sense that it lost the life that it had as a word that only commanded, and this kind of life is a kind of death (and defect, imperfection, and shortcoming), when compared to the life of the word of good pleasure which brings about what it commands. The Mosaic Law died to these privations by the addition of the life of good pleasure. The ritual Law died the same death and was raised to the new life of the word of good pleasure, not because of literal ritual observance but because of its moral sense through allegorical interpretation.

23. It is clear also that the Old Law, insofar as it is the Old Law, cannot either perfect anyone or be perfected by anyone, since it lacks grace on the one hand, and, on the other, only commands and does not help to do what it commands. It cannot perfect because it does not cooperate or consummate through the justice which comes from grace and the word of good pleasure. The Old Law lacks these insofar as it is the Old Law. And so the one subject to the Law does not have what it takes to keep the Law.

24. It also follows that the Old Law, as Old Law, does not restrain the mind because it does not infuse the mind with the grace of good will, which alone checks disordered concupiscence. Nevertheless, it did restrain, as was touched on above, both the mind and the hand by commanding that both refrain from evil. It did not, however, restrain the mind and the hand by bringing about the very restraint.

25. In addition, it restrained the hand from evil by punishing exterior actions, but it did not restrain the mind in this way because the Old Law did not establish Laws that punish the hidden, interior sins of the mind.

26. It must also be considered that the moral Law, as has been said, passed from a kind of old death into new life when

Christ said, "A new commandment I give unto you: That you love one another, as I have loved you" (Jn 13.34). At that point, the old word, which gave commands, passed into a new word of good pleasure, which does what is commanded. For he who sat on the throne says, "Behold, I make all things new" (Rv 21.5). And the Apostle says to the Corinthians, "If any be in Christ a new creature, the old things are passed away, behold, all things are made new" (2 Cor 5.17). The old ritual Law, though, never lived the life of a word of good pleasure, because it was never promulgated through the mouth of Jesus Christ in the flesh. In the Old Covenant, the ritual Law had been given through Moses as a word that only commands, but in the New Covenant it never had the force of law in its bodily sense. Hence the ritual Law could not be kept meritoriously on account of anything that it had in itself. And so, in the commentary on the letter to the Romans it is said that the ritual works of the Law, even if they are performed in charity, did not justify, because they were never informed with the justifying grace of the word of good pleasure, which gives life to ceremonial precepts; nevertheless, the holy fathers meritoriously performed rituals because of the grace given to them from elsewhere.

27. Hence the rituals justified those who performed them, not because of themselves, but because of the grace received from elsewhere. For the ancient holy fathers belonged to the body of Christ and were free sons of grace. From the New Testament and from their head, Christ, they received all moral precepts inasmuch as they were not from the Old Mosaic Law, but from the New Law that was kept because of Christ. For, through Christ, the Head, whom they possessed in faith, the strength of grace flowed into them. From their Head they received all moral precepts inasmuch as they were promulgated through Christ and informed by a life-giving word of good pleasure. They kept these moral precepts by the grace that they received from Christ, and so they observed the ritual Laws meritoriously, but, as has been said, they did so not by the grace of the ritual Laws, but by what had been conferred in the moral precepts that were received from the New Law, but before the New Law.

28. Augustine shows clearly enough that the ancient holy fa-

thers belonged to the New Covenant and were free with that freedom by which Christ freed them and about which Christ himself says, "If the Son shall make you free, you shall be quite free indeed" (Jn 8.36).[63] Augustine says:

That faith, nevertheless, saves, and by it we believe that no man, great or small, however young, is freed from the contagion of that ancient death and the pledge of sin that he contracted from his birth, except through the one mediator between God and men, the man Christ Jesus.[64] Those just ones were saved by a most saving faith in the God-man because they believed that he would come in the flesh before he came in the flesh. Ours and theirs is the same faith, since what we believed has already happened, they believed would happen. Hence the Apostle Paul says, "Having the same spirit of faith, according to what is written: I believed, for which cause I have spoken; we also believe, for which cause we speak" (2 Cor 4.13).[65] If, then, the same spirit of faith was held by those who foretold that Christ would come in the flesh and by those who announced that he had already come, then the sacraments could be different at different times though they return most harmoniously to the unity of the same faith. It was written in Acts of the Apostles, with Peter speaking, "Now therefore, why tempt you God to put a yoke upon the necks of the disciples, which neither our fathers nor we have been able to bear? But by the grace of the Lord Jesus, we believe that we are saved, in like manner as they also" (Acts 15.10–11). If, then, those men, that is, the fathers, who could not bear the yoke of the Old Law, believed that they were saved by the grace of the Lord Jesus, it is clear that this grace made the just ones of old to live by faith, "for the just man lives by faith" (Rom 1.17).[66]

And in the letter to the Hebrews it was written, "the Law brings no one to perfection" (Heb 7.19); that is, it perfects no one by justification, for even if some were then perfect, they were not so because of the Law or through the Law but through faith in the one to come.

29. Again, Augustine says in his book, *On Christian Doctrine:*

He who serves or venerates something that signifies something else, but without knowing what it signifies, is a slave to a sign. But he who serves and venerates a useful, divinely established sign, whose power and meaning he understands, does not venerate what is seen and what passes, but rather that to which such finite signs point. Such a man is

---

63. See Gal 4.31.  64. See 1 Tm 2.5.
65. See Ps 115.10.
66. Augustine, *Ep.* 190.2.5–6. See Hab 2.4; Heb 10.38; and Gal 3.11.

spiritual and free. Already in the time of slavery—when it was not yet necessary that those signs be revealed to carnal minds that had to be subdued by the yoke of those signs—there were such spiritual men, Patriarchs and all the Prophets among the people of Israel, through whom the Holy Spirit bestowed on us the very help and consolation of the Scriptures.[67]

30. But if the ancient fathers, according to these witnesses, belonged to the New Testament and were free sons of grace, it can be doubted whether or not they were bound to the Law's rituals, by whose yoke slaves had to be subdued. It seems, though, that they were bound to observe and keep the ritual Laws because they belonged to the Old People in flesh and kinship, and because they dwelled with them. Although their way of life is heavenly, the saints of today are bound to live, as the Apostle says, in conformity with those who live according to praiseworthy, and not pernicious, rites and customs that pertain to the necessities of this life in the flesh and its maintenance.[68] They are so bound because in the body they live with earthly men on the earth. Just as it is with the saints of today, so it was with the saints in ancient times. Although their spirits belonged in freedom to the New Testament, they seem to have been obliged much more to observe the rites of the Law that pertained to the worship of God.

31. But if they were obliged to observe the Law, they seem to have been transgressors, because, as Peter says, the yoke and obligation to observe the Law is a burden which neither the Apostles nor their fathers were able to bear.[69] Jerome says in his commentary on Galatians, "There ought to be collected here how many commands in the Law there are that no one can keep."[70] And again, he says, "The Jews keep the precepts and teachings of men rather than the commands of God. They keep neither the corporal Law—for it is impossible—nor the spiritual Law, which they do not understand."[71] If, as the words of Peter and

---

67. Augustine, *On Christian Doctrine* 3.9.13.
68. See Phil 3.20.
69. See Acts 15.10.
70. Jerome, *Commentary on the Letter to the Galatians* 1.2.16.
71. Ibid., 3.6.13.

Jerome indicate, no one could keep the commands of the Law, if the holy men of old were obliged to keep the Law, they seem necessarily to have been transgressors. But who would dare to say this? For, if they were transgressors, how were they saints?

32. It seems that Jerome thinks that they were not obliged to observe the ritual Law, for he says in his commentary on Galatians that the men of old kept the Laws only on account of the weak, as when Paul cut off his hair.[72] And again he says that the ancient fathers kept the Laws only in the way of a dispensation; they were not under the Law, but it was as if they were under the Law, just as Christ did not have sinful flesh, but the likeness of sinful flesh, and just as the bronze serpent that Moses lifted up in the desert was not a real serpent, but the likeness of a real serpent. Moreover, the Apostle says to the Galatians, "but if you are led by the Spirit, you are not under the Law" (Gal 5.18). So, then, the ancient fathers, if they were led by the Spirit, were not under the Law; rather, if the saints were led by the Spirit, they were not, then, under the Law.

33. To this it must be added that, as has been said, the ancient holy fathers were free sons of grace and were not obliged to carry the burden of the Law and keep it as if they were slaves. Nevertheless, if they had not kept those Laws, they would have been transgressors of the Law, although as free men they were not obliged to keep it. This will be more easily understood by an example. Let us suppose some hard, proud slaves. Some yoke and servile burden is placed upon their hard necks to subdue them, and they are obliged by the condition of their servitude to bear this burden. Let us also suppose that a free man associates with them and lives with them. It is certain that that free man is not obliged to bear the servile burden and yoke. Because, though, he has been made a free man having once been a slave, he is obliged to observe the Law of liberty. But the Law of liberty and charity demands that you do to another what you want to be done to you, and that you do this freely, out of love, and not by coercion. According to the liberty of the Law of charity and grace, that free man is bound and obliged to carry

---

72. See ibid.; and Acts 18.8.

and lift, with the slaves with whom he lives and associates, the burden and yoke of slavery. In this way he lifts and lightens their burden, inasmuch as he can. But if he refuses to do this, he is a transgressor of the Law of liberty and grace and would rightly be beaten back into the condition of slavery. So he would be obliged to bear the servile yoke according to the Law of slavery, because he refused freely to lift it together with the slaves according to the Law of liberty. And so, if he does not carry the yoke out of liberty, he is obliged to carry it out of slavery. But again, if he refuses to do so, he is made a transgressor not only of the Law of liberty but also of the Law of slavery.

34. And so, in this way the ancient holy fathers were obliged to carry and bear, along with the slaves, the yoke of the ceremonial Law; they were obliged, I say, by the Law of liberty, and by its grace they were freed from slavery and became sons. They were not obliged, though, by the Law of slavery to bear this burden, as slaves are. Nevertheless, if they had not freely carried it along with the slaves, they would rightly be led back into slavery and be bound by the Law of slavery to bear the burden as a slave, which they had refused to bear freely. They would have thus become transgressors first of the Law of liberty and second, of the Law of slavery. So, then, no one who is subject to that yoke as a slave could ever bear the commands of the Law, inasmuch as they were a yoke imposed on slaves; rather, that yoke oppressed and crushed everyone who was subject to it in the manner of a slave. Hence no one could ever keep the Laws if they were imposed upon him as a servile yoke; those who were free sons of grace, however, could, by the strength and power of grace, bear the yoke that was imposed upon the slaves and carry it along with the slaves to provide some relief for them and help them lift the load. So, then, it is clear enough how the ancient holy fathers were free and not obliged to bear the yoke and burden of the rituals only because of the Law of liberty, and it is clear that if they, nevertheless, did not perform the rituals along with the slaves, they would be transgressors both of the Law of liberty and of the Law of slavery, because the desertion of the Law of liberty makes one a debtor to the Law of slavery.

35. It is clear, then, from what has already been said how the

saints of old bound themselves to the ritual Law, inasmuch as it had been given to crush the proud, to subdue the hardened, and to convict the presumptuous. For they were not under the Law thus given; rather, according to the Law of liberty, they carried out the Law thus given as if they were under it, as Jerome says.[73] In addition to the aforementioned manner in which the Law was given—as a yoke and burden that crushed, subdued, and convicted—it must be considered whether it had also been given as a permission, like the writ of divorce, which had been permitted because of the hardness of their hearts as if to allow an evil lest it become worse. John Chrysostom testifies to this, quoting the words of Christ to the Jews. He says:

> Often Moses commands for us an injustice as if it were just on account of your hardness. For example, he commanded the offering of sacrifices to God in the desert. And how does he say through the prophet, "I will not take calves out of your house: nor he-goats out of your flocks" (Ps 49.9)? But because your fathers had gone out of Egypt in body but not in soul (for they carry the whole of Egypt with them in their manner of life), Moses saw that they were inclined by carnal love to be zealous for sacrifices, and if he had commanded them to withdraw from sacrifices, they would not have listened to him, since a long-lasting passion for something is not cured by quick remedy. So he commanded them to sacrifice indeed, but no longer to the demons, as they did in Egypt, but to the living God. He permitted a lesser evil lest he lose the whole good. This is why he allowed them to issue writs of divorce, because he judged it better that marriages be dissolved by a permissive Law than that murder be committed out of hatred. He permitted you to commit evil acts, lest you commit worse ones. So then, by allowing you to do these things, he did not show to you the justice of God; rather, he took the guilt of sinning out of sin—as if you acted according to the Law—so that your sin not seem to be sin.[74]

And so it is clear that the saints of old were not under the Law thus given, that is, as permission for hardness of heart and an allowance of an evil lest it become worse; nor were they obliged to keep the ceremonial Law thus given, that is, as permission for hardness. Again, the Law had been given as a tutor, as Paul says to the Galatians, but it is clear that a mature and free son

---

73. The editors have here, "Locum Hieronimi non potuimus invenire."
74. The editors have here, "Locum Chrysostomi non potuimus invenire."

of advanced age is not under a tutor.[75] Therefore, the ancient fathers were not under the Law insofar as the Law was a tutor. The Law had also been given to check concupiscence. But the holy fathers, who had conquered concupiscence through charity, did not need the restraint of the Law.

36. But in addition to the reasons already mentioned for the giving of the Law, the ritual Law had been given also for the worship of God and to signify the future salvation of man through Christ. The ritual Law was prophetic, and that ancient people, according to its ritual acts, was prophetic. So, then, insofar as the Law was given for the worship of God and as a prophetic sign of man's future salvation, it seems that the whole prophetic people, as prophetic, was obliged to keep the ritual Law as prophetic. And so it seems that the saints of old were obliged to observe the rituals insofar as the rituals were prophetic of future salvation and established for the worship of the one God for a suitable time.

37. But if in this way they were obliged to perform the rituals, it can be doubted whether they observed all the ritual commands, whether they were transgressors by not observing all of them. For it seems, from the authority of the saints, that the whole number of ritual commands could be completely observed by no one both because of the burdensome irrationality of the actions that are commanded and because of the superfluous number of commands. On this matter, without the precedent of a better opinion, we say that the holy fathers, inasmuch as they belonged to the ancient prophetic people, were together with the people obliged to observe the ritual Law, insofar as it was prophetic and pertained to the worship of the one God. Nevertheless, because those saints were voluntarily observing the Law, out of the charity they received from the Law of grace and of the Gospel, they were not under the Law in the sense of being forced to observe it—nor was this Law instituted for the just. Rather, those saints were the doers of the Law, as free men, and they perfected the Law by means of the power and strength of the grace that they received from Christ, their head. Together

---

75. See Gal 3.24–25.

with the Apostle they knew that "I can do all these things in him who strengthens me" (Phil 4.13). And if by chance they could not keep all the commands of the Law because of the number of commands, they were not, nevertheless, transgressors. They were not transgressors because they kept as many of the commands as were sufficient to carry, out of the Law of liberty, the yoke, and thus to lighten the burden of the slaves, and because they kept as many as were sufficient to venerate the one God and prophetically signify man's future salvation.

38. For the numerical multiplication of the commands of their own ceremonial Law fittingly subdued the proud who presumed that they had abilities beyond those of men and even beyond those of holy men. And so, a burden was rightly imposed on them, a burden that exceeded the capacity even of holy men. Therefore, it does not seem that the multitude of commands, which exceeded the abilities of men, had been given to the humble; rather, only as many of the commands as were sufficient for the ultimate intention of the commands, that is, the veneration of the one God, the signifying beforehand of our salvation, and the knowledge of their own weakness, so that they humbly run to grace as if to the medicine for illness and weakness.[76]

76. See Grosseteste, *On the Ten Commandments*, prol.

# APPENDIX AND INDICES

# APPENDIX

## *Figure 1*

See translated text, pp. 194–95, and Figure 1, p. 249. This figure is from Rabanus Maurus, *On the Praises of the Holy Cross* 1.23 (PL 107:239A–40B), and Grosseteste does not reproduce it. The text over which the figure is drawn reads:

> Nobilis ecce micat flos regis nomine pictus,
> Atque notis signant victoris facta potentis
> Cornua laeta crucis, trino sic condita versu:
> Quae numerant sex insigni quater arte monades
> Perfectumque decus ostendunt rebus inesse
> Omnibus, omnipotens quas condidit atque redemit.
> Clara dies illa est, qua conditor omnia finxit:
> Non minus haec lucet doctor qua cuncta beavit.
> Tum bona cuncta bonus complevit facta creator:
> Nunc pia cuncta pius opera benedixit amator:
> Quattuor ergo plagas laudat senarius orbis:
> Sex micat in numeris perfectus primus et ipse est,
> Dividit ipse diem totum, constringit et ipse
> Anni mensisque bisextilis atque quadrantis
> Hic numerator adest, attollens tempora nutu.
> Saecula fine capit, et claudit limite mundum,
> Vitam perpetuam tunc regna et lucida ductor
> Dat super astra piis, dimittens debita, vultu
> Indere consignans Jesus pia praemia, scis tu
> Ex omni mundo his quos tanta ad dona coruscans
> Conduxit fidei lux, vivus et indidit haustus.
> Verus amor decorat justi beat atque opus almum:
> Ergo plagis orbis consignat ab omnibus ast hic
> Adpositus numerus undique pergere plebes
> Ad crucis auxilium, pia numina poscere Jesus
> Perfectumque decus perfecto dogmate discant,
> Perfectae fidei quod facta benigna sequantur.
> Omnia nempe Deum verum haec testantur ubique:

> Perfectum perfecta quidem, formosa decorum
> Quae vertigo poli tornat, quae condit Olympus,
> Quae mare, quae tellus, quae caeli continet aula:
> Ast quoque nos homines in rebus portio parva,
> Rite crucem cantu salvantem et voce sonemus.
> Qui bene nos fecit, quique auxit, quique redemit,
> Carmine et in celebri crebros cantemus amores,
> Quos satis ipse opere sacro et tutamine nobis
> Jam impendit, suasit, jussit, ostendit, amavit.

Rabanus describes the letters found within the figure: "The four names of the heavenly conqueror are written in the four triangles around the cross, and the holy cross spreads out these names at its ends like a lily opening its leaves. Beginning from the middle of the cross, that is, from the two names Jesus Christ there are like leaves two names above and below the cross, that is, 'brave' [*fortis*] and 'courage' [*virtus*], and another two to the right and left, that is, 'victor' [*victor*] and 'famous' [*clarus*]. Thus there are found two verses written on the cross from one triangle to another. The text along the length is, 'fortis complevit Christus sua famina virtus'; and along the width is, 'victor consignans Jesus pia praemia clarus'" (PL 107:242C).

XIII figura. De numero vicenario et quaternario, deq; eius sacramento.

```
Nobiliseccemicat f l o s r egisnominepictus
Atq'enotisfignantvi c t o r isfactapotentis
Cornualaetacrucis r r inoficcondiraverfu
Qaenumerantfexinfigniqaterartemonades
Perfectumquedecuso f tendunt rebusineffe
Omnib:omnipotensquasconditatq:redemit
Claradiesillaestqa conditor omniafinxit
Nonminushaelucetd octorqacunctabeauit
Tumbonacunctabon:co npleuitfactacreator
Nuncpiecunctapiuso perabenedixitamator
Quattuoergoplagas l audatfenariusorbis
Sexmicatinnumerisperfect:prim:etipfeeft
Diuiditipfediemtot umconftringitetipfe
Annimenfifq:biffext i lisatquequadrantis
Hicnumeratoradefta t tollenstemporanutu
Saeculafinecapitet claudit l:imitemundum
Vitamperpetuamtunc regnae tlucidaducto r
Da u fuperastrapiisd mittensdebitavu t u
Inde r econfignansie fuspiaproemia f c istu
Bx o mnimundohisquos tantaddonacoru f c ans
Conduxitfideiluxvi uusetindidithauftu s
Verusamordecoratiu ftibeatatq:opusalmum
Ergoplagisorbiscon fignatabomnib:afthic
Adpofitusnumerusen undiqepergereplebes
Adcrucisauxiliumpi anuminapofcereiefus
Perfectumq;decusper fectodogmatedifcant
Perfectaefideiqodf actabenignafeqantur
Omnianempedeumveru mhaectef tanturvbique
Perfectumperfectaq idemformonfadecorum
Quaevertigopolitor natqaeconditolympus
Quaemareqaetellusq aecaelicontinetaula
Atquoquenoshominesinrebusportioparum
Ritecrucemcantufal uantemetvocefonemus
Quibenenosfecitquiq:auxitquiqueredemit
Carmineetincelebr c rebroscantem:amores
Qosfatisipfeoperefacroettutaminenobis
Iaminpenditfuafi r iuf fitoftenditamauit
```

FIGURE 1. The cruciform figure created by Rabanus Maurus and preserved in a German manuscript of 1503 (Graphic Arts Collection. Department of Rare Books and Special Collections. Princeton University Library. Used with permission)

See pp. 247–48, above, and pp. 194–95 in translated text.

## Figure 2

Illustration of the "circular period of human generation."

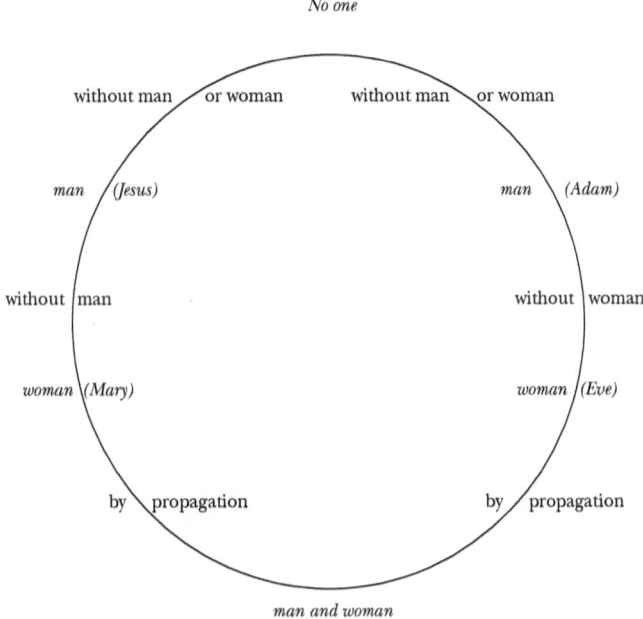

FIGURE 2. The "circular period of human generation"

This is mine, not Grosseteste's. See pp. 172–73 of the translated text.

# GENERAL INDEX

Abraham, 17, 30, 61, 63, 67, 84, 110–12, 115–16, 118, 123–24, 136–37, 149, 151–53, 161, 172, 192, 211
Adam, 18–19, 22, 54, 57, 59, 61, 65–68, 163, 168, 170, 172, 178, 209–10
Agnellus of Pisa, 9
Albert the Great, 21
Alexander of Hales, 21
allegory. *See* Scripture
angels, 49–56, 59, 105–6, 112, 126, 137, 161, 166–67, 171, 178, 182, 195, 199
Anselm of Canterbury, xvii, 20–21, 52, 54n32, 59–60, 155, 172, 175
Apostles, 27, 31, 35–36, 63, 87–88, 109, 126, 143, 178, 193, 196, 209, 218, 226, 238
Aquila, 130
Aristotle, 3, 5n7
Aston, T., xv
Augustine, xviii, 16, 20–22, 31–32, 36–37, 39–40, 44, 46, 64, 74, 78, 92, 94n66, 104–8, 122, 139, 153–55, 162–64, 172, 175, 178–179n30, 195, 204–6, 209, 215–20, 222, 224–25, 227, 230, 232–34, 236–38
Averroes, 5n7

Balaam, 119, 122
Barton, J., xiv
Bede, 139, 141, 143n38, 145–46, 151, 182
Benjamin, 73
Bernard, 71, 212

Bonaventure, 21
Boyle, L., xiv, xv
Brown, J., xv

Callahan, D., xvii
Callus, D., xiv, xvi, 3n1, 4, 9
Catto, J., xiv
Cheney, C., xiv
Church, 10, 12–13, 22, 27, 66, 90–91, 128, 136–37, 159, 162–64, 169–71, 173–75, 179–80, 182–85, 188, 208, 218, 221
circumcision, xvii, 17, 30, 61, 84–85, 96, 103, 105–7, 137, 172, 196, 219
Cobban, A., xiv
Cohen, J., xiv
concupiscence, 55, 57, 65, 222, 224–26, 235, 242
Congar, Y., xv

Dahan, G., xv
Dales, R. C., xviii–xv, 10, 11n27, 14–16, 23, 59n35
Daniel, 11n28, 102, 139, 141, 144–46, 148–52
David, 101, 108, 112, 115–17, 118–19, 122–23, 127, 146, 151–52, 172, 199, 212–13
De Jongue, M., xv
Devil. *See* Satan
Duffy, E., xv

Emery, K., xvii, 15n44

faith, 19, 27, 60, 67, 76–79, 81, 86, 93, 99, 103–6, 109, 121, 127, 129,

faith *(cont.)*
  137, 148, 153, 156, 161, 171, 174, 192–93, 209–10, 212–14, 236–37
fall. *See* sin
free choice. *See* free will
free will, 41–43, 55, 70–71, 73

Garreau, A., xv
Gieben, S., xiii–xv, 11n27
Ginther, J., xiii–xv, 4n5, 11n24, 12, 21
Goering, J., xiii–xv, 3–5, 7, 11n25, 12n33, 14n41
grace, 21, 27, 29, 39, 42–43, 63, 68, 71, 88, 90–91, 99, 103–5, 111–12, 115–17, 126, 161, 170, 175, 194–95, 214, 217, 221–22, 224–26, 228, 230–40, 242–43
Gregory IX, 6n10
Gregory the Great, 20, 35–36n8, 49, 52–53, 65–66, 74, 155, 162, 201
Gregory of Nazianzus, 159
Gregory of Nyssa, 205
Guerric of St. Quentin, 21

Hackett, M., xv
happiness, 18–19, 39–46, 49–50, 53, 106, 117, 164
Heffernan, T., xvi
Henry III, 14–15
Hill, R., 5n6
Hoesle, V., xvii
Holland, M., xv, 13n38
Holy Spirit, 51, 120, 130, 142, 168–69, 184–85, 191, 197–98, 200, 204–6, 216, 220, 225, 234, 238
Hood, Y., xv
humility, 41, 91, 98, 106, 135, 170, 231

idleness, 42, 105
Ignatius of Antioch, 13
Isaac, 67, 110, 118, 123, 137, 152, 161, 172

Jacob, 73–74, 94, 102, 110–11, 113, 115–16, 118–20, 123, 137–38, 147, 152, 161, 172
Jerome, xviii, 16, 21–22, 62, 104–6, 130n16, 149n44, 173n22, 203–6, 208, 212–13, 215–20, 222–23, 231, 238–39, 241
Jesse, 118, 120–21, 123, 130, 152, 172
Jesus Christ: Ascension of, 126, 135, 179, 191, 195; cross of, 71, 90, 125, 128, 131–32, 138, 155, 175, 189, 194–97, 199, 247–48; flesh of, 90, 96, 103, 149, 156–58, 163–65, 168–69, 172, 212–13, 230–31, 236–37, 239; God-man, 19–20, 22, 75–76, 110–13, 115, 117–18, 121, 123–24, 132, 152, 155–56, 158–61, 163, 166–67, 170–72, 174, 180–81, 183–84, 186, 191, 193, 197, 199, 237; hypostatic union of, 117, 132, 152, 155–59, 163, 166–67, 171, 180–81, 183; Incarnation of, 15, 19, 20–22, 37, 59–60, 65, 75–76, 88, 115, 117, 141, 155–59, 162–65, 167, 169–70, 172, 181–82, 185; marriage with the Church, 22, 163, 171, 183; Passion of, 19, 21–22, 34, 37–38, 65, 67–68, 71–73, 98, 109, 124–25, 127, 131–38, 142–43, 145, 147, 155, 161, 180, 190–91, 194–95, 197, 199–200, 206–7, 213, 215, 220, 241; Resurrection of, 104, 106, 135, 154, 165, 182, 191, 195
Jews, 14–16, 87, 94, 102, 105, 109, 124, 129, 132–33, 135–39, 143, 145–46, 151–53, 192, 204, 207–8, 216–18, 220, 238, 241
John the Baptist, 74, 120, 143, 194–97, 201–3
John Damascene, 13, 59, 107–8n87, 156n2, 157, 159, 168–69, 183
John Duns Scotus, 21
John Wyclif, 65n44, 79n51, 83n55, 87n60

# GENERAL INDEX

Joseph, husband of Mary, 130, 152, 155
Joseph, Patriarch, 63, 73
Josephus, 145, 153

King, E. B., xiii, 11, 14–16n50, 23, 59n35
Koslowski, P., xvii

Law: ceremonial, 31, 34–35, 39, 65, 88, 91, 98–100, 102, 236, 240–41, 243; of charity, 62, 96, 218, 239; of deeds: *see* Law, positive; eternal, 31, 84, 86, 96; of fear, 75; of liberty, 75, 108, 239–41, 243; natural, 18, 39, 45–49, 54, 60–62, 64–66, 70–73, 81, 86, 90–91, 223–24; positive, 18–19, 22, 44–49, 60–62, 65–66, 71–73, 86, 90–91; sacraments of, 18, 36, 72–73, 94–95, 97–99, 104–6, 209, 216, 218, 233, 237; temporal, 31, 84, 86, 91, 96–98; written, 19, 39, 45, 47, 63–67, 70–73, 81
Levering, M., xv
Lewry, P., xvi
Logan, F., xvi
Luard, H., xiii
Lucifer. *See* Satan

Mackie, E., xv, 5n7, 11n25
Manichees, 36
Mantello, F. A. C., xiii, xiv, xv, 5n8, 14n41
Marcellinus, 32, 92, 95
Marcionites, 36
Marshall, B., xvi
Maximianus, 107
McEvoy, J., xiii, xiv, xvi, 3–7, 10–13, 15
metaphysics of light, 10
Michael, Archangel, 23, 56
Moses, 27, 31, 63, 88, 103, 109, 126, 128, 153, 189, 209, 214, 224–25, 227, 230–34, 236, 239, 241

natural law. *See* Law
Noah, 18, 61, 63

obedience, 18, 31, 41, 43–44, 46–48, 50, 61, 90–91, 98, 126, 128, 160, 198–99, 209, 211
O'Carroll, M., xvi, 6
Oliver Sutton, 5n6
original sin. *See* sin

Panti, C., 5n7
Pantin, W., xvi
Patriarchs, 13, 73, 110, 238
Paul, Apostle, 27, 63, 88, 104, 106, 109, 137, 181, 200, 208–9, 212–13, 215, 217–18, 220, 222, 224, 227, 237, 239, 241
Paulinus, 106
Pegge, S., xvi, 14
Pelagius, 62n39
Perrier, E., xvi
Peter Lombard, 6n9, 156, 181n32, 224n47
Pinto de Oliveira, C.-J., xvii
pit of sin. *See* sin
Plato, 32, 33, 40, 91
positive law. *See* Law
Powicke, F., xiv, xvi
Prophets, 34, 36–37, 94, 104, 106–7, 109, 116–17, 129, 136, 139, 141, 146–47, 163, 186, 194–97, 199–201, 203–4, 232–33, 238
Ps.-Augustine, 44n15, 164n11
Ps.-Dionysius, 160n6, 232n59
Ps.-Jerome, 62n39

Quinn, C., xvi

Rabanus Maurus, xiii, 168, 169n15, 182–183n34, 194–96, 199, 247–49fig2
Rashdall, H., xvi
redemption, 38, 60, 65, 67–68, 70–71, 160, 195
restoration, 77–79, 90, 97, 141, 155, 165, 174–75, 186, 197–98, 235

resurrection, general, 39, 95, 140, 196, 199. *See also* Jesus Christ
Richard Fishacre, 21
Richard Rufus, 21
Robert Grosseteste, life, 3–10
Robert Grosseteste, works: *Commentarius in VIII libros Physicorum Aristotelis*, 10n21; *Commentarius in Posterium Analyticorum Libros*, xiii, 10, 33n7; *De accessu et recessu maris*, 10; *De calore solis*, 10; *De colore*, 10; *De cometis*, 5n7, 10; *De decem mandatis*, xiii, xvii, 6n9, 11–12, 50n23, 81n54, 184n37, 231n53, 234n62, 243n76; *De dotibus*, xiii, 12; *De iride*, 10; *De libero arbitrio*, 12; *De modo confitendi et paenitentias iniungendi*, xiii; *De motu supercelestium*, 5n7; *De ordine emanandi causatarum a Deo*, 12; *De spera*, 5n7; *De veritate*, 12; *Dicta*, 12; *Epistulae*, xiii; *Expositio in epistolam sancti Pauli ad Galatas*, xiii, 11n26, 220n37; *Hexaëmeron*, xiv, 11n27, 51n25, 63n40, 139n33, 161n8, 170n16, 177n27, 178n28, 195n4, 205n14; *Sermo ad religiosos*, xiv; *Speculum confessionis*, xiv; *Statutes of Lincoln*, xiv; *Templum Dei*, xiv
Robert Kilwardby, xvii, 15
Robson, M., xvi

Sabbath, 27–31, 80–85, 96, 98, 100–101, 105, 107–8, 140, 196, 217
sacraments, 18, 36, 88, 94
sacrifice, 93–94, 101–2, 107, 134, 139, 143, 151, 194, 214, 241
Sara, 108, 118, 211
Satan, 49, 52–53, 97–99, 104–6, 171, 191, 216
Sayers, J., xvii
Schenk, R., xvii, 15
Scripture: historical meaning of, 34, 80, 82, 87–88, 97, 121; mystical interpretation of, 29, 34, 82, 84, 97, 104
Seneca, 38

Septuagint, 31, 129–35
Shaw, J., xvii
sign, signification, 17, 27–30, 71, 76–77, 81, 84, 89–91, 99, 150–51, 163, 183, 193–94, 206–8, 214, 237, 242
Silver, D., xvii
sin: original, 19–20, 65–70, 90, 103, 124, 155–60, 167, 169–71, 175; pit of, 67, 70–73, 90
Smalley, B., xvii, 11n25, 12n30, 14
Smith, L., xvii, 6n9
Southern, R., xvii, 3n1, 4, 6n10, 8, 9, 14n41
spiritual sense. *See* Scripture
Srawley, J., xvii
Stevenson, F., xviii, 4n1
Stoneman, W., xv
Symmachus, 130

Tanner, N., xiii
temptation, 18, 48–51, 53–59
Thomas Aquinas, xvi, xvii, 11, 21
Thomas Chobham, 6n9
Thomas Eccleston, 9
Thomson, S., xviii
Tierney, B., xviii
Tillman, H., xviii
Tobias, 74

Unger, D., xviii

Virgin Mary, 22, 126, 130, 152–53, 155, 180, 185, 187, 193, 202, 217

Wasserstein, D., xviii, 14n41
Watt, J., xviii, 14n41
Wawrykow, J., xvii, 15n44
Weisheipl, J., xviii, 10
White, C., xviii
William of Auvergne, xvii, 6n10
William de Vere of Hereford, 4
written law. *See* Law

Zimmermann, A., xvii

# INDEX OF HOLY SCRIPTURE

*Old Testament*

Genesis
  book of: 11, 46–47,
    74, 177–78
  1.9: 180
  1.11: 187
  2.7: 187
  2.7–8: 48n20
  2.17: 44
  2.24: 163
  9.4: 31n2
  12.3: 110
  12.11–19: 211n23
  17.1–16: 118
  17.12: 17, 30
  17.13: 17, 30, 84n57
  17.19–20: 118
  17.21: 118
  18.17–18: 110
  18.18: 110
  20.1–13: 211n23
  21.10: 108
  21.12: 118
  22.18: 110, 148n42
  26.4: 148n42
  32.29: 113
  37.3: 73
  42.38: 73
  49.10: 115, 138, 147n41
  49.18: 116

Exodus
  3.8: 175n24
  12.22: 128
  20.12–13: 44
  20.17: 224, 232
  21.24: 205
  31.16–17:27

Leviticus
  17.10: 31n3
  17.11: 87
  19.18: 205n15, 221n42
  23.21: 31
  24.20: 205
  25.3: 140

Numbers
  14.33–34: 176
  19.1–10: 128
  21.8–9: 126n8
  24.17–19: 119

Deuteronomy
  4.24: 78
  5.14: 81
  6.5: 44n16, 221
  12.23: 31n3
  18.15: 20, 88n62, 100, 109
  19.21: 205
  22.10–11: 44
  27.21: 31
  27.26: 31, 86n59
  28.15: 31

Judges
  13.18: 113

1 Samuel
  16.7: 121
  21.11: 213

2 Samuel
  7.12–14: 122

2 Kings
  10.18: 212

1 Chronicles
  28.9: 187n45

Ezra
  7.4: 145n40

Nehemiah
  1.11–2.1: 141n35
  4.17–18: 142n36

Tobit
  4.16: 64n42
  6.15: 74

Job
  book of: 49n22, 52n29, 66n45
  14.4–5: 136
  25.4: 120
  40.14: 52

# INDEX OF HOLY SCRIPTURE

Psalms
  2.6–7: 112
  2.8: 137, 174n23
  2.8–9: 122
  4.7: 193
  7.10: 187n45
  8.6: 183n34
  15.2: 93, 94
  15.4: 94, 102
  21.17–19: 138
  23.8: 114
  26.4: 87
  38.3: 116
  39.2: 116
  39.7–8: 102
  39.9: 136
  44.3: 117
  44.7–8: 117
  44.8: 141
  49.8–14: 102
  49.9: 94, 241
  50.16: 87
  57.2: 64
  67: 105
  67.13: 137
  71.2: 112
  71.17: 112
  73: 105
  75.2: 173
  77: 106
  83.8: 232
  86: 117
  87.5: 138
  89: 178
  99.3: 79
  101.25: 74n50
  101.27–28: 94
  109.1: 119
  109.2: 119
  109.3: 119
  113.3: 107n82
  113.5: 107n82
  115.10: 237n65
  118.6: 82
  118.105: 70
  118.142: 33

Proverbs
  3.28: 38
  6.23: 70, 72
  8.12: 114
  8.14–16: 114
  13.12: 38

Ecclesiastes
  11.2: 206
  18.1: 112

Song of Songs
  4.2: 79, 80n53
  8.6: 222

Wisdom
  1.13–14: 33

Sirach
  49.5–6: 122

Isaiah
  book of: 11n28, 130n16
  1.11–14: 85n58, 101
  1.13: 82
  1.14: 137
  7.14: 113, 123–24
  8.16–17: 116
  9.1–2: 114
  9.6: 113, 115
  9.7: 115
  10.22: 196n6
  11.1: 120, 130
  11.3–5: 121
  11.6: 121
  11.9: 121
  14.13–14: 51n26
  14.14: 51n25
  25.6–9: 116
  25.9: 116
  26.18: 79
  38.10: 74
  40.3: 202n11
  40.6: 106
  46.8: 64
  52.13–53.12: 124–25
  52.15: 128
  53.1: 129
  53.2: 129–31
  53.2–3: 132
  53.3: 132
  53.4: 133
  53.5: 133n20
  53.6: 134, 135n21
  53.7: 134, 135n22, 136
  53.8: 135
  53.9: 118, 120n5, 135, 136
  53.10: 136
  53.11: 137
  53.11–12: 137
  53.12: 137–38
  57.19: 114
  59.20–21: 111n3
  60.17: 114

Jeremiah
  3.4: 114
  3.19: 114
  4.4: 78, 84
  5.14: 78
  6.11: 137n26
  6.20: 100–101
  7.22–23: 100
  9.26: 84
  13.18–19: 123
  23.5–6: 122
  23.6: 123
  31.22: 124
  31.31: 100
  31.31–32: 94n65
  31.31–34: 102
  31.33: 63n40
  33.15–17: 123
  38.31–32: 94n65

Lamentations
  2.6: 101
  3.24: 116
  4.20: 135

# INDEX OF HOLY SCRIPTURE

Baruch
  2.35: 63n40, 100
  3.36–38: 115

Ezekiel
  book of: 49
  4.6: 176
  5.5: 173
  20.12: 29, 84n56
  20.20: 29
  20.25: 100, 224
  28.12: 52
  28.15: 52
  36.26: 84

Daniel
  9.24: 141, 144, 147–48
  9.24–27: 139
  9.25: 141, 144, 149
  9.26: 142, 149–50
  9.27: 102, 143
  10.2: 145

Hosea
  2.11: 82, 85, 101
  3.4: 101

Micah
  5.2: 124
  6.6–8: 101

Habakkuk
  2.3: 117–18
  2.4: 237n66

Malachi
  1.6: 114
  1.10–11: 101
  4.2: 105n75

*New Testament*

Matthew
  Gospel of: 63, 183n34, 195n5
  1.20: 130n18
  3.16: 142n37
  4.1: 55n33
  4.11: 126
  5.18: 34
  5.39: 205n15
  7.12: 64n42
  8.20: 137
  8.26: 126
  9.2: 188
  9.4–7: 188
  9.5: 188
  9.6: 188
  9.33: 126
  11.3: 74, 201
  11.13: 194–95
  12.25: 125
  12.36: 42n14
  13.23: 137n25
  14.19: 187n42
  15.34–36: 187n42
  17.26: 186n41
  21.8–10: 127
  21.9: 199
  22.37: 221n42
  22.37–39: 96

  24.36: 178
  24.45: 212
  26.26–28: 133n19
  26.28: 134
  27.18: 131
  27.35: 138n29
  27.40: 132
  27.63: 133
  28.18: 182

Mark
  1.10: 142
  10.45: 125n6
  12.30–31: 221n42
  14.36: 136
  15.28: 138
  15.29: 132
  15.39: 190
  16.16: 134
  16.19: 126

Luke
  Gospel of: 202, 223n45
  1.34–35: 130
  1.41: 202
  1.70: 197
  3.22: 142n37
  10.27: 221n43

  10.28: 79
  12.42: 212
  22.15: 194n1
  22.19: 133n19
  22.26: 98
  23.34: 132, 138
  23.46: 190
  24.27: 109n1
  24.51: 126

John
  Gospel of: 232n55
  1.3: 234
  1.14: 115
  1.16: 231–32
  1.16–17: 231
  1.17: 231n54
  1.23: 202
  1.32: 142n37
  2.7–10: 187n43
  3.14: 126
  4.34: 137n27
  6.45: 63n40
  6.57: 169
  6.58: 172
  8.25: 192
  8.34: 81
  8.36: 237
  8.44: 171n19

# 258  INDEX OF HOLY SCRIPTURE

John *(cont.)*
  8.58: 192
  10.17: 136
  10.30: 153, 168, 192
  10.38: 153, 192
  11.39: 187n44
  12.32: 126
  12.38: 129
  13.1: 125
  13.2–11: 125n7
  13.34: 236
  14.1: 192
  14.6: 219
  14.9: 192
  14.23: 60
  14.26: 63
  17.20–21: 108
  18.4: 125
  18.6: 134
  19.10: 134
  19.30: 194, 196
  20.23: 188

Acts of the Apostles
  book of: 27
  1.3: 191n47
  1.7: 178
  1.9: 191n47
  1.9–10: 126
  2.1–4: 191n47
  3.18: 109
  4.12: 193n49
  4.32: 167
  5.38–39: 193
  8.33: 135n23
  8.38: 129n14
  10.1–8: 129n13
  10.14: 208n17–18
  11.9: 88
  11.28–30: 196n7
  15.1: 209
  15.10: 238n69
  15.10–11: 237
  15.20: 31n4
  15.28–29: 87n61
  15.29: 31n4
  16.3: 220n38
  17.3: 109n2
  18.8: 239n72
  18.18: 220n39
  21.9: 196n7
  21.26: 220n40

Romans
  Epistle to: 27, 103, 222n44, 223n46, 224n47, 236
  1.17: 237
  4.15: 222, 224, 233
  5.5: 232
  5.15–16: 68
  5.18–19: 160
  5.20: 175, 222–25
  6.3–4: 127n9
  6.14: 103
  7.6: 103
  7.7: 224
  7.12: 33
  7.23: 232
  7.24: 232
  7.25: 232
  8.2: 225n49
  8.14–16: 184n38
  8.15: 161n7
  8.27: 187n45
  8.29: 162
  8.32: 76
  9.6–8: 67
  10.4: 103, 216
  11.26–27: 111
  13.10: 234
  14.14: 88

1 Corinthians
  1.18: 128n12
  1.23: 128n12
  1.30: 160n5
  3.6: 225
  6.17: 228
  12.3: 234
  13.10: 107n86
  15.24: 185n40
  15.45: 170n17

2 Corinthians
  1.19: 33
  3.3: 63
  3.6: 107
  3.10: 105
  3.10–11: 103
  3.14: 103
  4.13: 237
  5.17: 91, 236

Galatians
  Epistle to: 11, 12, 15, 16n45, 27, 99, 103, 105, 204n12, 212, 219–21, 231, 238–39, 241
  2.11–21: 209n21
  2.12–15: 215n27
  2.19: 103
  3.7: 67
  3.10: 103
  3.11: 237n66
  3.13: 103
  3.21: 226
  3.24: 208n16
  3.24–25: 242n75
  3.26: 161n7
  3.28: 161
  3.29: 67
  4.31: 237n63
  5.3: 108n88
  5.4–6: 103
  5.6: 137n28
  5.18: 103, 239
  6.15: 103

Ephesians
  1.3–10: 171
  1.5: 161n7
  2.14: 134
  2.14–15: 103
  5.25–33: 183n36

# INDEX OF HOLY SCRIPTURE

5.29–32: 164
5.32: 163

Philippians
  2.8: 90
  2.9–11: 126
  3.20: xiv, 238n68
  4.13: 91, 243

Colossians
  1.15: 170
  1.16: 234n62
  1.24: 179n31
  2.18: 106

1 Timothy
  2.5: 237n64

Titus
  1.15: 88

Hebrews
  1.12: 94n64
  2.3: 23n74
  2.6–9: 183n34
  7.11–19: 104
  7.19: 224, 237
  8.8–9: 94n65, 100n67, 102n68
  8.10: 63n40
  10.16: 63n40
  10.38: 237n66

James
  1.14: 55

1 Peter
  2.21: 35
  2.22: 120, 136

2 Peter
  1.19: 70
  3.8: 178

1 John
  1.1–2: 115
  2.16: 57n34
  3.15: 171

Revelation
  book of: 200
  2.23: 187n45
  12.7: 23n75, 56
  21.1: 34, 176n26
  21.5: 236

www.ingramcontent.com/pod-product-compliance
Lightning Source LLC
Chambersburg PA
CBHW032031290426
44110CB00012B/751